Reviews of Information

"Information lies at the heart of biology, societies depend on it, and our ability to process information ever more efficiently is transforming our lives. By introducing the theory that enabled our information revolution, this book describes what information is, how it can be communicated efficiently, and why it underpins our understanding of biology, brains, and physical reality. Its tutorial approach develops a deep intuitive understanding using the minimum number of elementary equations. Thus, this superb introduction not only enables scientists of all persuasions to appreciate the relevance of information theory, it also equips them to start using it. The same goes for students. I have used a handout to teach elementary information theory to biologists and neuroscientists for many years. I will throw away my handout and use this book."

Simon Laughlin, Professor of Neurobiology, Fellow of the Royal Society, Department of Zoology, University of Cambridge, England.

"This is a really great book it describes a simple and beautiful idea in a way that is accessible for novices and experts alike. This "simple idea" is that information is a formal quantity that underlies nearly everything we do. In this book, Stone leads us through Shannons fundamental insights; starting with the basics of probability and ending with a range of applications including thermodynamics, telecommunications, computational neuroscience and evolution. There are some lovely anecdotes: I particularly liked the account of how Samuel Morse (inventor of the Morse code) pre-empted modern notions of efficient coding by counting how many copies of each letter were held in stock in a printer's workshop. The treatment of natural selection as "a means by which information about the environment is incorporated into DNA" is both compelling and entertaining. The substance of this book is a clear exposition of information theory, written in an intuitive fashion (true to Stone's observation that "rigour follows insight"). Indeed, I wish that this text had been available when I was learning about information theory. Stone has managed to distil all of the key ideas in information theory into a coherent story. Every idea and equation that underpins recent advances in technology and the life sciences can be found in this informative little book."

Professor Karl Friston, Fellow of the Royal Society. Scientific Director of the Wellcome Trust Centre for Neuroimaging, Institute of Neurology, University College London.

Reviews of Bayes' Rule: A Tutorial Introduction

From the Back Cover

Information Theory

A Tutorial Introduction

James V Stone

Title: Information Theory: A Tutorial Introduction
Author: James V Stone

©2015 Sebtel Press

First Edition, 2015.
Typeset in LaTeX 2_ε.
Cover design: Stefan Brazzo.
Second printing.

ISBN 978–0–9563728–5–7

The front cover depicts Claude Shannon (1916-2001).

For Nikki

Suppose that we were asked to arrange the following in two categories – *distance, mass, electric force, entropy, beauty, melody*. I think there are the strongest grounds for placing entropy alongside beauty and melody ...

Eddington A, The Nature of the Physical World, 1928.

Contents

Preface

This book is intended to provide a coherent and succinct account of information theory. In order to develop an intuitive understanding of key ideas, new topics are first presented in an informal tutorial style before being described more formally. In particular, the equations which underpin the mathematical foundations of information theory are introduced on a need-to-know basis, and the meaning of these equations is made clear by explanatory text and diagrams.

In mathematics, rigour follows insight, and not *vice versa*. Kepler, Newton, Fourier and Einstein developed their theories from deep intuitive insights about the structure of the physical world, which requires, but is fundamentally different from, the raw logic of pure mathematics. Accordingly, this book provides insights into *how* information theory works, and *why* it works in that way. This is entirely consistent with Shannon's own approach. In a famously brief book, Shannon prefaced his account of information theory for continuous variables with these words:

> We will not attempt in the continuous case to obtain our results with the greatest generality, or with the extreme rigor of pure mathematics, since this would involve a great deal of abstract measure theory and would obscure the main thread of the analysis. ... The occasional liberties taken with limiting processes in the present analysis can be justified in all cases of practical interest.
> Shannon C and Weaver W, 1949[50].

In a similar vein, Jaynes protested that:

> Nowadays, if you introduce a variable x without repeating the incantation that it is some set or 'space' X, you are accused of dealing with an undefined problem ...
> Jaynes ET and Bretthorst GL, 2003[26].

Even though this is no excuse for sloppy mathematics, it is a clear recommendation that we should not mistake a particular species of pedantry for mathematical rigour. The spirit of this liberating and somewhat cavalier approach is purposely adopted in this book, which is intended to provide insights, rather than incantations, regarding how information theory is relevant to problems of practical interest.

MatLab and Python Computer Code

It often aids understanding to be able to examine well-documented computer code which provides an example of a particular calculation or method. To support this, MatLab and Python code implementing key information-theoretic methods can be found online. The code also reproduces some of the figures in this book.

MatLab code can be downloaded from here:

http://jim-stone.staff.shef.ac.uk/BookInfoTheory/InfoTheoryMatlab.html

Python code can be downloaded from here:

http://jim-stone.staff.shef.ac.uk/BookInfoTheory/InfoTheoryPython.html

PowerPoint Slides of Figures

Most of the figures used in this book are available for teaching purposes as a pdf file and as PowerPoint slides. These can be downloaded from

http://jim-stone.staff.shef.ac.uk/BookInfoTheory/InfoTheoryFigures.html

Corrections

Please email corrections to j.v.stone@sheffield.ac.uk.

A list of corrections can be found at

http://jim-stone.staff.shef.ac.uk/BookInfoTheory/Corrections.html

Acknowledgments

Thanks to John de Pledge, John Porrill, Royston Sellman, and Steve Snow for interesting discussions on the interpretation of information theory, and to John de Pledge for writing the Python code.

For reading draft versions of this book, I am very grateful to Óscar Barquero-Pérez, Taylor Bond, David Buckley, Jeremy Dickman, Stephen Eglen, Charles Fox, Nikki Hunkin, Danielle Matthews, Guy Mikawa, Xiang Mou, John de Pledge, John Porrill, Royston Sellman, Steve Snow, Tom Stafford, Paul Warren and Stuart Wilson. Shashank Vatedka deserves a special mention for checking the mathematics in a final draft of this book. Thanks to Caroline Orr for meticulous copy-editing and proofreading.

Online code for estimating the entropy of English was adapted from code by Neal Patwari (MatLab) and Clément Pit-Claudel (Python).

For permission to use the photograph of Claude Shannon, thanks to the Massachusetts Institute of Technology.

Jim Stone.

Chapter 1

What Is Information?

> Most of the fundamental ideas of science are essentially
> simple, and may, as a rule, be expressed in a language
> comprehensible to everyone.
> Einstein A and Infeld L, 1938.

1.1. Introduction

The universe is conventionally described in terms of physical quantities
such as mass and velocity, but a quantity at least as important as
these is *information*. Whether we consider computers[30], evolution[2;19],
physics[15], artificial intelligence[9], quantum computation[46], or the
brain[17;43], we are driven inexorably to the conclusion that their
behaviours are largely determined by the way they process information.

Figure 1.1. Claude Shannon (1916-2001).

In 1948, Claude Shannon published a paper called *A Mathematical Theory of Communication*[48]. This paper heralded a transformation in our understanding of information. Before Shannon's paper, information had been viewed as a kind of poorly defined miasmic fluid. But after Shannon's paper, it became apparent that information is a well-defined and, above all, *measurable* quantity.

Shannon's paper describes a subtle theory which tells us something fundamental about the way the universe works. However, unlike other great theories such as the Darwin–Wallace theory of evolution, information theory is not simple, and it is full of caveats. But we can disregard many of these caveats provided we keep a firm eye on the physical interpretation of information theory's defining equations. This will be our guiding principle in exploring the theory of information.

1.2. Information, Eyes and Evolution

Shannon's theory of information provides a mathematical definition of information, and describes precisely how much information can be communicated between different elements of a system. This may not sound like much, but Shannon's theory underpins our understanding of how signals and noise are related, and why there are definite limits to the rate at which information can be communicated within *any* system, whether man-made or biological. It represents one of the few examples of a single theory creating an entirely new field of research. In this regard, Shannon's theory ranks alongside those of Darwin–Wallace, Newton, and Einstein.

When a question is typed into a computer search engine, the results provide useful information but it is buried in a sea of mostly useless data. In this internet age, it is easy for us to appreciate the difference between information and data, and we have learned to treat the information as a useful 'signal' and the rest as distracting 'noise'. This experience is now so commonplace that technical phrases like 'signal to noise ratio' are becoming part of everyday language. Even though most people are unaware of the precise meaning of this phrase, they have an intuitive grasp of the idea that 'data' means a combination of (useful) signals and (useless) noise.

The ability to separate signal from noise, to extract information from data, is crucial for modern telecommunications. For example, it allows a television picture to be compressed to its bare information bones and transmitted to a satellite, then to a TV, before being decompressed to reveal the original picture on the TV screen.

This type of scenario is also ubiquitous in the natural world. The ability of eyes and ears to extract useful signals from noisy sensory data, and to package those signals efficiently, is the key to survival[51]. Indeed, the *efficient coding hypothesis*[5;8;43;55] suggests that the evolution of sense organs, and of the brains that process data from those organs, is primarily driven by the need to minimise the energy expended for each bit of information acquired from the environment. More generally, a particular branch of brain science, *computational neuroscience*, relies on information theory to provide a benchmark against which the performance of neurons can be objectively measured.

On a grander biological scale, the ability to separate signal from noise is fundamental to the Darwin–Wallace theory of evolution by natural selection[12]. Evolution works by selecting the individuals best suited to a particular environment so that, over many generations, information about the environment gradually accumulates within the gene pool. Thus, natural selection is essentially a means by which information about the environment is incorporated into DNA (deoxyribonucleic acid). And it seems likely that the rate at which information is incorporated into DNA is accelerated by an age-old biological mystery, sex. These and other applications of information theory are described in Chapter 9.

1.3. Finding a Route, Bit by Bit

Information is usually measured in *bits*, and one bit of information allows you to choose between two equally probable alternatives. The word bit is derived from *bi*nary dig*it* (i.e. a zero or a one). However, as we shall see, bits and binary digits are fundamentally different types of entities.

Imagine you are standing at the fork in the road at point A in Figure 1.2, and that you want to get to the point marked D. Note that this figure represents a bird's-eye view, which you do not have; all you have is a fork in front of you, and a decision to make. If you have no prior information about which road to choose then the fork at A represents two equally probable alternatives. If I tell you to go left then you have received one bit of information. If we represent my instruction with a *binary digit* (0=left and 1=right) then this binary digit provides you with one bit of information, which tells you which road to choose.

Now imagine that you stroll on down the road and you come to another fork, at point B in Figure 1.2. Again, because you have no idea which road to choose, a binary digit (1=right) provides one bit of information, allowing you to choose the correct road, which leads to the point marked C.

Note that C is one of four possible interim destinations that you could have reached after making two decisions. The two binary digits that allow you to make the correct decisions provided two bits of information, allowing you to choose from four (equally probable) possible alternatives; 4 happens to equal $2 \times 2 = 2^2$.

A third binary digit (1=right) provides you with one more bit of information, which allows you to again choose the correct road, leading to the point marked D.

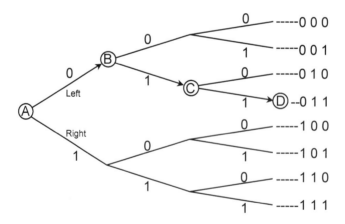

Figure 1.2. How many roads must a man walk down? For a traveller who does not know the way, each fork in the road requires one bit of information to make a correct decision. The 0s and 1s on the right-hand side summarise the instructions needed to arrive at each destination; a left turn is indicated by a 0 and a right turn by a 1.

There are now eight roads you could have chosen from when you started at A, so three binary digits (which provide you with three bits of information) allow you to choose from eight equally probable alternatives; 8 happens to equal $2 \times 2 \times 2 = 2^3 = 8$.

The decision taken at A excluded half of the eight possible destinations shown in Figure 1.2 that you could have arrived at. Similarly, the decision taken at each successive fork in the road halved the number of remaining possible destinations.

A Journey of Eight Alternatives

Let's summarise your journey in terms of the number of equally probable alternatives:

If you have 1 bit of information then you can choose between 2 equally probable alternatives (i.e. $2^1 = 2$).

If you have 2 bits of information then you can choose between 4 equally probable alternatives (i.e. $2^2 = 4$).

Finally, if you have 3 bits of information then you can choose between 8 equally probable alternatives (i.e. $2^3 = 8$).

We can restate this in more general terms if we use n to represent the number of forks, and m to represent the number of final destinations. If you have come to n forks, then you have effectively chosen from

$$m = 2^n \text{ final destinations.} \qquad (1.1)$$

Because the decision at each fork requires one bit of information, n forks require n bits of information, which allow you to choose from 2^n equally probable alternatives.

There is a saying that "a journey of a thousand miles begins with a single step". In fact, a journey of a thousand miles begins with a single decision: the direction in which to take the first step.

Key point. One bit is the amount of information required to choose between two *equally probable* alternatives.

Binary Numbers

We could label each of the eight possible destinations with a decimal number between 0 and 7, or with the equivalent *binary number*, as in Figure 1.2. These decimal numbers and their equivalent binary representations are shown in Table 1.1. Counting in binary is analogous to counting in decimal. Just as each decimal digit in a decimal number specifies how many 1s, 10s, 100s (etc) there are, each binary digit in a binary number specifies how many 1s, 2s, 4s (etc) there are. For example, the value of the decimal number 101 equals the number of 100s (i.e. 10^2), plus the number of 10s (i.e. 10^1), plus the number of 1s (i.e. 10^0):

$$(1 \times 100) + (0 \times 10) + (1 \times 1) \quad = \quad 101. \tag{1.2}$$

Similarly, the value of the binary number 101 equals the number of 4s (i.e. 2^2), plus the number of 2s (i.e. 2^1), plus the number of 1s (i.e. 2^0):

$$(1 \times 4) + (0 \times 2) + (1 \times 1) \quad = \quad 5. \tag{1.3}$$

The binary representation of numbers has many advantages. For instance, the binary number that labels each destination (e.g. 011) explicitly represents the set of left/right instructions required to reach that destination. This representation can be applied to any problem that consists of making a number of two-way (i.e. binary) decisions.

Logarithms

The complexity of any journey can be represented either as the number of possible final destinations or as the number of forks in the road which must be traversed in order to reach a given destination. We know that as the number of forks increases, so the number of possible destinations also increases. As we have already seen, if there are three forks then there are $8 = 2^3$ possible destinations.

Decimal	0	1	2	3	4	5	6	7
Binary	000	001	010	011	100	101	110	111

Table 1.1. Decimal numbers and their equivalent binary representations.

Viewed from another perspective, if there are $m = 8$ possible destinations then how many forks n does this imply? In other words, given eight destinations, what power of 2 is required in order to get 8? In this case, we know the answer is $n = 3$, which is called the *logarithm* of 8. Thus, $3 = \log_2 8$ is the number of forks implied by eight destinations.

More generally, the logarithm of m is the power to which 2 must be raised in order to obtain m; that is, $m = 2^n$. Equivalently, given a number m which we wish to express as a logarithm,

$$n = \log_2 m. \tag{1.4}$$

The subscript $_2$ indicates that we are using logs to the base 2 (all logarithms in this book use base 2 unless stated otherwise). See Appendix C for a tutorial on logarithms.

A Journey of $\log_2(8)$ Decisions

Now that we know about logarithms, we can summarise your journey from a different perspective, in terms of bits:

If you have to choose between 2 equally probable alternatives (i.e. 2^1) then you need $1(= \log_2 2^1 = \log_2 2)$ bit of information.

If you have to choose between 4 equally probable alternatives (i.e. 2^2) then you need $2(= \log_2 2^2 = \log_2 4)$ bits of information.

If you have to choose between 8 equally probable alternatives (i.e. 2^3) then you need $3(= \log_2 2^3 = \log_2 8)$ bits of information.

More generally, if you have to choose between m equally probable alternatives, then you need $n = \log_2 m$ bits of information.

Key point. If you have n bits of information, then you can choose from $m = 2^n$ equally probable alternatives. Equivalently, if you have to choose between m equally probable alternatives, then you need $n = \log_2 m$ bits of information.

1.4. A Million Answers to Twenty Questions

Navigating a series of forks in the road is, in some respects, similar to the game of '20 questions'. In this game, your opponent chooses a word (usually a noun), and you (the astute questioner) are allowed to ask 20 questions in order to discover the identity of this word. Crucially, each question must have a yes/no (i.e. binary) answer, and therefore provides you with a maximum of one bit of information.

By analogy with the navigation example, where each decision at a road fork halved the number of remaining destinations, each question should *halve* the number of remaining possible words. In doing so, each answer provides you with exactly one bit of information. A question to which you already know the answer is a poor choice of question. For example, if your question is, "Is the word in the dictionary?", then the answer is almost certainly, "Yes!", an answer which is predictable, and which therefore provides you with no information.

Conversely, a well-chosen question is one to which you have no idea whether the answer will be yes or no; in this case, the answer provides exactly one bit of information. The cut-down version of '20 questions' in Figure 1.3 shows this more clearly.

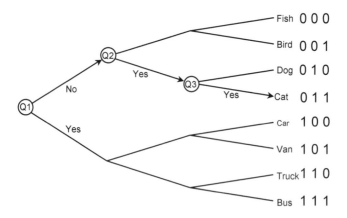

Figure 1.3. The game of '20 questions', here abbreviated to '3 questions'. Given an opponent who has one of eight words in mind, each yes/no question halves the number of remaining possible words. Each binary number on the right summarises the sequence of answers required to arrive at one word (no=0 and yes=1).

In this game, your opponent has a vocabulary of exactly eight words, and you know which words they are. Your first question (Q1) could be, "Is it inanimate?", and the answer should halve the number of possible words to four, leading you to your second question (Q2). If your second question (Q2) is, "Is it a mammal?", then the answer should again halve the number of possible words, leading to your third question (Q3). By the time you arrive at Q3, there are just two possible words left, and after you have asked the third question (e.g. "Is it 'cat'?"), your opponent's yes/no response leads you to the correct answer. In summary, you have asked three questions, and excluded all but one out of eight possible words.

More realistically, let's assume your opponent has the same vocabulary as you do (most of us have similar vocabularies, so this assumption is not entirely unreasonable). Specifically, let's assume this vocabulary contains exactly 1,048,576 words. Armed with this knowledge, each question can, in principle, be chosen to halve the number of remaining possible words. So, in an ideal world, your first question should halve the number of possible words to 524,288. Your next question should halve this to 262,144 words, and so on. By the time you get to the 19th question there should be just two words left, and after the 20th question, there should be only one word remaining.

The reason this works out so neatly is because 20 questions allow you to choose from exactly $1,048,576 = 2^{20}$ equally probable words (i.e. about one million). Thus, the 20 bits of information you have acquired with your questioning provide you with the ability to narrow down the range of possible words from about 1 million to just one. In other words, 20 questions allow you to find the correct word out of about a million possible words.

Adding one more question would not only create a new game, '21 questions', it would also double the number of possible words (to about 2 million) that you could narrow down to one. By extension, each additional question allows you to acquire up to one more bit of information, and can therefore double the initial number of words. In principle, a game of '40 questions' allows you to acquire 40 bits of information, allowing you to find one out of $2^{40} \approx 10^{12}$ words.

In terms of the navigation example, 40 bits would allow you to navigate 40 forks in the road, and would therefore permit you to choose one out of about a trillion possible routes. So the next time you arrive at your destination after a journey that involved 40 decisions, remember that you have avoided arriving at a trillion-minus-one incorrect destinations.

1.5. Information, Bits and Binary Digits

Despite the fact that the word *bit* is derived from *binary digit*, there is a subtle, but vital, difference between them. A binary digit is the value of a binary variable, where this value can be either a 0 or a 1, but a binary digit is not information *per se*. In contrast, a bit is a definite *amount of information*. Bits and binary digits are different types of entity, and to confuse one with the other is known as a *category error*.

To illustrate this point, consider the following two extreme examples. At one extreme, if you already know that you should take the left-hand road from point A in Figure 1.2 and I show you the binary digit 0 (=left), then you have been given a binary digit but you have gained no information. At the other extreme, if you have no idea about which road to choose and I show you a 0, then you have been given a binary digit and you have also gained one bit of information. Between these extremes, if someone tells you there is a 71% probability that the left-hand road represents the correct decision and I subsequently confirm this by showing you a 0, then this 0 provides you with less than one bit of information (because you already had some information about which road to choose). In fact, when you receive my 0, you gain precisely half a bit of information (see Section 5.8). Thus, even though I cannot give you a half a binary digit, I can use a binary digit to give you half a bit of information.

The distinction between binary digits and bits is often ignored, with Pierce's book[40] being a notable exception. Even some of the best textbooks use the terms 'bit' and 'binary digit' interchangeably. This does not cause problems for experienced readers as they can interpret the term 'bit' as meaning a binary digit or a bit's worth of information according to context. But for novices the failure to respect this distinction is a source of genuine confusion.

Sadly, in modern usage, the terms bit and binary digit have become synonymous, and MacKay (2003)[34] proposed that the unit of information should be called the *Shannon*.

Key point. A bit is the *amount of information* required to choose between two equally probable alternatives (e.g. left/right), whereas a binary digit is the *value of a binary variable*, which can adopt one of two possible values (i.e. 0/1).

1.6. Example 1: Telegraphy

Suppose you have just discovered that if you hold a compass next to a wire, then the compass needle changes position when you pass a current through the wire. If the wire is long enough to connect two towns like London and Manchester, then a current initiated in London can deflect a compass needle held near to the wire in Manchester.

You would like to use this new technology to send messages in the form of individual letters. Sadly, the year is 1820, so you will have to wait over 100 years for Shannon's paper to be published. Undeterred, you forge ahead. Let's say you want to send only upper-case letters, to keep matters simple. So you set up 26 electric lines, one per letter from A to Z, with the first line being A, the second line being B, and so on. Each line is set up next to a compass which is kept some distance from all the other lines, to prevent each line from deflecting more than one compass.

In London, each line is labelled with a letter, and the corresponding line is labelled with the same letter in Manchester. For example, if you want to send the letter D, you press a switch on the fourth line in London, which sends an electric current to Manchester along the wire which is next to the compass labelled with the letter D. Of course, lines fail from time to time, and it is about 200 miles from London to Manchester, so finding the location of the break in a line is difficult and expensive. Naturally, if there were fewer lines then there would be fewer failures.

With this in mind, Cooke and Wheatstone devised a complicated two-needle system, which could send only 23 different letters. Despite the complexity of their system, it famously led to the arrest of a murderer. On the first of January 1845, John Tawell poisoned his mistress, Sarah Hart, in a place called Salt Hill in the county of Berkshire, before escaping on a train to Paddington station in London. In order to ensure Tawell's arrest when he reached his destination, the following telegraph was sent to London:

> A MURDER HAS GUST BEEN COMMITTED AT SALT HILL AND THE SUSPECTED MURDERER WAS SEEN TO TAKE A FIRST CLASS TICKET TO LONDON BY THE TRAIN WHICH LEFT SLOUGH AT 742 PM HE IS IN THE GARB OF A KWAKER ...

The unusual spellings of the words JUST and QUAKER were a result of the telegrapher doing his best in the absence of the letters J, Q and Z in the array of 23 letters before him. As a result of this telegram, Tawell was arrested and subsequently hanged for murder. The role of Cooke and Wheatstone's telegraph in Tawell's arrest was widely reported in the press, and established the practicality of telegraphy.

In the 1830s, Samuel Morse and Alfred Vail developed the first version of (what came to be known as) the *Morse code*. Because this specified each letter as dots and dashes, it could be used to send messages over a single line.

An important property of Morse code is that it uses short *codewords* for the most common letters, and longer codewords for less common letters, as shown in Table 1.2. Morse adopted a simple strategy to find out which letters were most common. Reasoning that newspaper

A	• -	J	• - - -	S	• • •
B	- • • •	K	- • -	T	-
C	- • - •	L	• - • •	U	• • -
D	- • •	M	- -	V	• • -
E	•	N	- •	W	• - -
F	• • - •	O	- - -	X	- • • -
G	- - •	P	• - - •	Y	- • - -
H	• • • •	Q	- - • -	Z	- - • •
I	• •	R	• - •		

Table 1.2. Morse code. Common letters (e.g. E) have the shortest codewords, whereas rare letters (e.g. Z) have the longest codewords.

printers would have only as many copies of each letter as were required, he went to a printer's workshop and counted the copies of each letter. As a result, the most common letter E is specified as a single dot, whereas the rare J is specified as a dot followed by three dashes.

The ingenious strategy adopted by Morse is important because it enables efficient use of the communication channel (a single wire). We will return to this theme many times, and it raises a fundamental question: how can we tell if a communication channel is being used as efficiently as possible?

1.7. Example 2: Binary Images

The internal structure of most images is highly predictable. For example, most of the individual *picture elements* or *pixels* in the image of stars in Figure 1.4 are black, with an occasional white pixel, a star. Because almost all pixels are black, it follows that most pairs of adjacent pixels are also black, which makes the image's internal structure predictable. If this picture were taken by the orbiting Hubble telescope then its predictable structure would allow it to be efficiently transmitted to Earth.

Suppose you were in charge of writing the computer code which conveys the information in Figure 1.4 from the Hubble telescope to Earth. You could naively send the value of each pixel; let's call this method A. Because there are only two values in this particular image (black and white), you could choose to indicate the colour black with the binary digit 0, and the colour white with a 1. You would therefore need to send as many 0s and 1s as there are pixels in the image. For example, if the image was 100×100 pixels then you would need to send ten thousand 0s or 1s for the image to be reconstructed on Earth. Because almost all the pixels are black, you would send sequences of hundreds of 0s interrupted by the occasional 1. It is not hard to see that this is a wasteful use of the expensive satellite communication channel. How could it be made more efficient?

Another method consists of sending only the locations of the white pixels (method B). This would yield a code like $[(19, 13), (22, 30), \ldots]$, where each pair of numbers represents the row and column of a white pixel.

Figure 1.4. The night sky. Each pixel contains one of just two values.

Yet another method consists of concatenating all of the rows of the image, and then sending the number of black pixels that occur before the next white pixel (method C). If the number of black pixels that precede the first white pixel is 13 and there are 9 pixels before the next white pixel, then the first row of the image begins with 0000000000000010000000001..., and the code for communicating this would be [13, 9, ...], which is clearly more compact than the 24 binary digits which begin the first row of the image.

Notice that method A consists of sending the image itself, whereas methods B and C do not send the image, but they do send all of the *information* required to reconstruct the image on Earth. Crucially, the end results of all three methods are identical, and it is only the efficiency of the methods that differs.

In fact, whether A, B, or C is the most efficient method depends on the structure of the image. This can be seen if we take an extreme example consisting of just one white pixel in the centre of the image. For this image, method A is fairly useless, because it would require 10,000 binary values to be sent. Method B would consist of two numbers, (50, 50), and method C would consist of a single number, 5,050. If we ignore the brackets and commas then we end up with four decimal digits for both methods B and C. So these methods seem to be equivalent, at least for the example considered here.

For other images, with other structures, different *encoding methods* will be more or less efficient. For example, Figure 1.5 contains just two grey-levels, but these occur in large regions of pure black or pure

Figure 1.5. In a binary image, each pixel has 1 out of 2 possible grey-levels.

white. In this case, it seems silly to use method B to send the location of every white pixel, because so many of them occur in long runs of white pixels. This observation makes method C seem to be an obvious choice – but with a slight change. Because there are roughly equal numbers of black and white pixels which occur in regions of pure black or pure white, we could just send the number of pixels which precede the next change from black to white or from white to black. This is known as *run-length encoding.*

To illustrate this, if the distance from the first black pixel in the middle row to the first white pixel (the girl's hair) is 87 pixels, and the distance from there to the next black pixel is 31 pixels, and the distance to the next white pixel is 18 pixels, then this part of the image would be encoded as [87, 31, 18, . . .]. Provided we know the method used to encode an image, it is a relatively simple matter to reconstruct the original image from the encoded image.

1.8. Example 3: Grey-Level Images

Suppose we wanted to transmit an image of 100×100 pixels, in which each pixel has more than two possible grey-level values. A reasonable number of grey-levels turns out to be 256, as shown in Figure 1.6a. As before, there are large regions that look as if they contain only one grey-level. In fact, each such region contains grey-levels which are similar, but not identical, as shown in Figure 1.7. The similarity between nearby pixel values means that adjacent pixel values are not *independent* of

 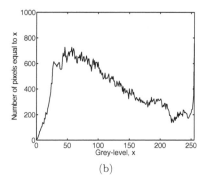

(a)   (b)

Figure 1.6. Grey-level image. (a) An image in which each pixel has one out of 256 possible grey-levels, between 0 and 255, each of which can be represented by a binary number with 8 binary digits (e.g. 255=11111111). (b) Histogram of grey-levels in the picture.

each other, and that the image has a degree of *redundancy*. How can this observation be used to encode the image?

One method consists of encoding the image in terms of the differences between the grey-levels of adjacent pixels. For brevity, we will call this *difference coding*. (More complex methods exist, but most are similar in spirit to this simple method.) In principle, pixel differences could be measured in any direction within the image, but, for simplicity, we concatenate consecutive rows to form a single row of 10,000 pixels, and then take the difference between adjacent grey-levels. We can see the result of difference coding by 'un-concatenating' the rows to reconstitute an image, as shown in Figure 1.8a, which looks like a badly printed version of Figure 1.6a. As we shall see, both images contain the same amount of information.

If adjacent pixel grey-levels in a given row are similar, then the difference between the grey-levels is close to zero. In fact, a histogram of difference values shown in Figure 1.8b shows that the most common difference values are indeed close to zero, and only rarely greater than ±63. Thus, using difference coding, we could represent almost every one of the 9,999 difference values in Figure 1.8a as a number between −63 and +63.

In those rare cases where the grey-level difference is larger than ±63, we could list these separately as each pixel's location (row and column

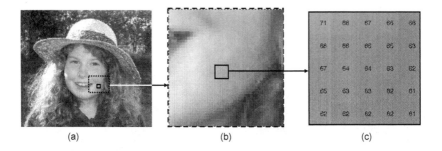

Figure 1.7. Adjacent pixels tend to have similar grey-levels, so the image has a large amount of redundancy, which can be used for efficient encoding. (a) Grey-level image.   (b) Magnified square from a.   (c) Magnified square from b, with individual pixel grey-levels indicated.

as 2×7 binary digits), and its grey-level (8 binary digits). Most coding procedures have special 'housekeeping' fragments of computer code to deal with things like this, but these account for a negligible percentage of the total storage space required. For simplicity, we will assume that this percentage is zero.

At first, it is not obvious how difference coding represents any saving over simply sending the value of each pixel's grey-level. However, because these differences are between -63 and $+63$, they span a range of 127 different values, i.e. $[-63, -62, \ldots, 0, \ldots, 62, 63]$. Any number in this range can be represented using seven binary digits, because $7 = \log 128$ (leaving one spare value).

In contrast, if we were to send each pixel's grey-level in Figure 1.6a individually, then we would need to send 10,000 grey-levels. Because each grey-level could be any value between 0 and 255, we would have to send eight binary digits ($8 = \log 256$) for each pixel.

Once we have encoded an image into 9,999 pixel grey-level differences $(d_1, d_2, \ldots, d_{9999})$, how do we use them to reconstruct the original image? If the difference d_1 between the first pixel grey-level x_1 and the second pixel grey-level x_2 is, say, $d_1 = (x_2 - x_1) = 10$ grey-levels and the grey-level of x_1 is 5, then we obtain the original grey-level of x_2 by adding 10 to x_1; that is, $x_2 = x_1 + d_1$ so $x_2 = 5 + 10 = 15$. We then continue this process for the third pixel ($x_3 = x_2 + d_2$), and so on. Thus, provided we know the grey-level of the first pixel in the original image (which can be encoded as eight binary digits), we can use the

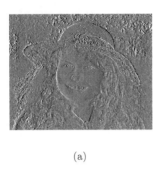

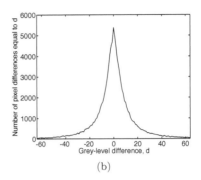

(a)   (b)

Figure 1.8. Difference coding. (a) Each pixel grey-level is the difference between adjacent horizontal grey-level values in Figure 1.6a (grey = zero difference). (b) Histogram of grey-level differences between adjacent pixel grey-levels in Figure 1.6a. Only differences between ±63 are plotted.

pixel grey-level differences to recover the grey-level of every pixel in the original image. The fact that we can reconstruct the original image (Figure 1.6a) from the grey-level differences (Figure 1.8a) proves that they both contain exactly the same amount of *information*.

Let's work out the total saving from using this difference coding method. The naive method of sending all pixel grey-levels, which vary between 0 and 255, would need eight binary digits per pixel, requiring a total of 80,000 binary digits. Using difference coding we would need seven binary digits per difference value, making a total of 70,000 binary digits. Therefore, using difference coding provides a saving of 10,000 binary digits, or 12.5%.

In practice, a form of difference coding is used to reduce the amount of data required to transmit voices over the telephone, where it is known as *differential pulse code modulation*. Using the differences between consecutive values, a voice signal which would otherwise require eight binary digits per value can be transmitted with just five binary digits.

As we shall see in subsequent chapters, a histogram of data values (e.g. image grey-levels) can be used to find an upper bound for the average amount of information each data value could convey. Accordingly, the histogram (Figure 1.6b) of the grey-levels in Figure 1.6a defines an upper bound of 7.84 bits/pixel. In contrast, the histogram (Figure 1.8b) of the grey-level differences in Figure 1.8a defines an upper bound of just 5.92 bits/pixel.

Given that the images in Figures 1.6a and 1.8a contain the same amount of information, and that Figure 1.8a contains no more than 5.92 bits/pixel, it follows that Figure 1.6a cannot contain more than 5.92 bits/pixel either. This matters because Shannon's work guarantees that if each pixel's grey-level contains an average of 5.92 bits of information, then we should be able to represent Figure 1.6a using no more than 5.92 binary digits per pixel. But this still represents an upper bound. In fact, the smallest number of binary digits required to represent each pixel is equal to the amount of information (measured in bits) implicit in each pixel. So what we really want to know is: how much information does each pixel contain?

This is a hard question, but we can get an idea of the answer by comparing the amount of computer memory required to represent the image in two different contexts (for simplicity, we assume that each pixel has eight binary digits). First, in order to display the image on a computer screen, the value of each pixel occupies eight binary digits, so the bigger the picture, the more memory it requires to be displayed. Second, a compressed version of the image can be stored on the computer's hard drive using an average of less than eight binary digits per pixel (e.g. by using the difference coding method above). Consequently, storing the (compressed) version of an image on the hard drive requires less memory than displaying that image on the screen. In practice, image files are usually stored in compressed form with the method used to compress the image indicated by the file name extension (e.g. '.jpeg').

The image in Figure 1.6a is actually 344 by 299 pixels, where each pixel grey-level is between 0 and 255, which can be represented as eight binary digits (because $2^8 = 256$), or one *byte*. This amounts to a total of 102,856 pixels, each of which is represented on a computer screen as one byte. However, when the file containing this image is inspected, it is found to contain only 45,180 bytes; the image in Figure 1.6a can be compressed by a factor of 2.28($= 102856/45180$) without any loss of information. This means that the information implicit in each pixel, which requires eight binary digits for it to be displayed on a screen, can be represented with about four binary digits on a computer's hard drive.

Thus, even though each pixel can adopt any one of 256 possible grey-levels, and is displayed using eight binary digits of computer memory, the grey-level of each pixel can be stored in about four binary digits. This is important, because it implies that each set of eight binary digits used to display each pixel in Figure 1.6a contains an average of only four bits of information, and therefore each binary digit contains only *half a bit* of information. At first sight, this seems like an odd result. But we already know from Section 1.5 that a binary digit can represent half a bit, and we shall see later (especially in Chapter 5) that a fraction of a bit is a well-defined quantity which has a reasonably intuitive interpretation.

1.9. Summary

From navigating a series of forks in the road, and playing the game of '20 questions', we have seen how making binary choices requires information in the form of simple yes/no answers. These choices can also be used to choose from a set of letters, and can therefore be used to send typed messages along telegraph wires.

We found that increasing the number of choices from two (forks in the road) to 26 (letters) to 256 (pixel grey-levels) allowed us to transmit whole images down a single wire as a sequence of binary digits. In each case, the redundancy of the data in a message allowed it to be compressed before being transmitted. This redundancy emphasises a key point: a binary digit does not necessarily provide one bit of information. More importantly, a binary digit is *not* the same type of entity as a bit of information.

So, what is information? It is what remains after every iota of natural redundancy has been squeezed out of a message, and after every aimless syllable of noise has been removed. It is the unfettered essence that passes from computer to computer, from satellite to Earth, from eye to brain, and (over many generations of natural selection) from the natural world to the collective gene pool of every species.

Chapter 2

Entropy of Discrete Variables

Information is the resolution of uncertainty.
Shannon C, 1948.

2.1. Introduction

Now that we have an idea of the key concepts of information theory, we can begin to explore its inner workings on a more formal basis. But first, we need to establish a few ground rules regarding *probability*, *discrete variables* and *random variables*. Only then can we make sense of *entropy*, which lies at the core of information theory.

2.2. Ground Rules and Terminology

Probability

We will assume a fairly informal notion of probability based on the number of times particular events occur. For example, if a bag contains 40 white balls and 60 black balls then we will assume that the probability of reaching into the bag and choosing a black ball is the same as the proportion, or *relative frequency*, of black balls in the bag (i.e. $60/100 = 0.6$). From this, it follows that the probability of an event (e.g. choosing a black ball) can adopt any value between zero and one, with zero meaning it definitely will not occur, and one meaning it definitely will occur. Finally, given a set of mutually exclusive events (such as choosing a ball, which has to be either black or white), the probabilities of those events must add up to one (e.g. $0.4 + 0.6 = 1$). See Appendix F for an overview of the rules of probability.

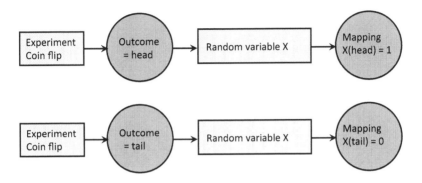

Figure 2.1. Random variables. A random variable translates the *outcome* of an experiment to an *outcome value*. Top: flipping a coin yields a head, which is mapped by the random variable X to the outcome value $X(head) = 1$, usually written as $X = 1$. Bottom: flipping a coin yields a tail, which is mapped to the outcome value $X(tail) = 0$, usually written as $X = 0$.

Discrete Variables

Elements of a set that are clearly separated from each other, like a list of integers, are called *discrete*, and the variables used to represent them are called *discrete variables*. The distribution of probability values of a discrete variable is called a *probability function*. It can be represented as a bar graph, as in Figure 2.2.

In contrast, elements which are packed together so densely that there is no space between them, like the points on a line, are represented by *continuous variables* (see Chapter 5), which have distributions called *probability density functions* (see Appendix D). We will usually refer to both probability functions and probability density functions as *probability distributions* in this text.

Random Variables

A *random variable* is used to refer to a special type of quantity; it can be either discrete or continuous. The value of a discrete random variable can be considered as a measurement made on a physical outcome of an experiment in which the number of different possible outcomes is discrete, for example as shown in Figure 2.1. In contrast, the value of a continuous random variable can be considered as a measurement made on a physical outcome of an experiment in which the values of the possible outcomes are continuous, such as temperature. The crucial point is that these outcomes are subject to a degree of randomness.

The idea of a random variable was devised for historical reasons. Although they share the name 'variable', random variables are not the same as the variables used in algebra, like the x in $3x + 2 = 5$, where the variable x has a definite, but unknown, value that we can solve for.

A random variable is represented by an upper-case letter, such as X. An experiment consisting of a coin flip has two possible physical outcomes, a head x_h and a tail x_t, which define the *alphabet*

$$A_x \;\; = \;\; \{x_h, x_t\}. \tag{2.1}$$

The *sample space* of the random variable X is the set of all possible experiment outcomes. For example, if an experiment consists of three coin flips then each time the experiment is run we obtain a sequence of three outcomes (e.g. (x_h, x_t, x_t)), which is one out of the eight possible sequences of three outcomes that comprise the sample space.

The value of the random variable is a mapping from the experiment outcome to a numerical *outcome value*. Thus, strictly speaking, a random variable is not a variable at all, but is really a *function* which maps outcomes to outcome values. In our experiment, this function maps the coin flip outcome to the number of heads observed:

$$X(x_h) \;\; = \;\; 1, \tag{2.2}$$
$$X(x_t) \;\; = \;\; 0. \tag{2.3}$$

Thus, a random variable (function) takes an *argument* (e.g. x_h or x_t), and returns an outcome value (e.g. 0 or 1). An equivalent, and more conventional, notation for defining a random variable is

$$X = \begin{cases} 0, & \text{if the outcome is a tail,} \\ 1, & \text{if the outcome is a head.} \end{cases}$$

For brevity, the different possible values of a random variable can also be written in terms of the outcomes,

$$X = x_h, \qquad (2.4)$$

$$X = x_t, \qquad (2.5)$$

or in terms of the outcome values,

$$X = 1, \qquad (2.6)$$

$$X = 0. \qquad (2.7)$$

In many experiments, different physical outcomes have different probabilities, so that different outcome values of X also have different probabilities. If the same experiment is repeated infinitely many times then the frequency with which different values of X occur defines the *probability distribution* $p(X)$ of X. There are only two possible outcomes for a coin, so $p(X)$ consists of just two probabilities,

$$p(X) = \{p(X = x_h), p(X = x_t)\}, \qquad (2.8)$$

which is usually written as

$$p(X) = \{p(x_h), p(x_t)\}. \qquad (2.9)$$

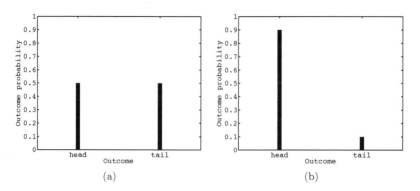

(a)   (b)

Figure 2.2. The probability distributions of two coins. (a) Probability distribution $p(X) = \{p(x_h), p(x_t)\}$ of a fair coin which lands heads up with a probability of $p(x_h) = 0.5$. (b) Probability distribution of an unfair coin which lands heads up with a probability of $p(x_h) = 0.9$.

For a fair coin both probabilities are equal to 0.5, i.e.

$$p(x_h) = 0.5, \qquad p(x_t) = 0.5, \qquad (2.10)$$

so the probability distribution is

$$
\begin{aligned}
p(X) &= \{p(x_h), p(x_t)\} & (2.11) \\
&= \{0.5, 0.5\}, & (2.12)
\end{aligned}
$$

as shown in Figure 2.2a. In contrast, if a coin is so badly bent that it lands heads up 90% of the time then

$$p(x_h) = 0.9, \qquad p(x_t) = 0.1, \qquad (2.13)$$

and the probability distribution of this coin is (see Figure 2.2b)

$$
\begin{aligned}
p(X) &= \{p(x_h), p(x_t)\} & (2.14) \\
&= \{0.9, 0.1\}. & (2.15)
\end{aligned}
$$

It is worth noting that the probabilities associated with different values of a discrete random variable like X vary continuously between zero and one, even though the values of X are discrete.

The subtle distinction between an *outcome* x and an *outcome value* $X(x)$ is sometimes vital, but in practice we only need to distinguish between them if the numbers of outcomes and outcome values are not equal (e.g. the two-dice example in Section 3.5). For example, suppose we roll a die, and we define the random variable X to be 0 when the outcome is an odd number and 1 when the outcome is an even number, so that

$$
X = \begin{cases} 0, & \text{if the outcome } x \text{ is } 1,3, \text{ or } 5, \\ 1, & \text{if the outcome } x \text{ is } 2,4, \text{ or } 6. \end{cases}
$$

In this case, the number of outcomes is six, but the number of outcome values is just two.

In the majority of cases, where we do not need to distinguish between outcomes and outcome values, we will use the lower case symbol x to represent them both. The terms outcome and outcome value are unique to this book.

All of this may seem like a lot of work just to set the value of a random variable to 0 or 1, but these definitions are key to making sense of more complicated scenarios. A brief tutorial on probability distributions is given in Appendix D.

Key point. A random variable X is a function that maps each outcome x of an experiment (e.g. a coin flip) to a number $X(x)$, which is the outcome value of x. If the outcome value of x is 1 then this may be written as $X = 1$, or as $x = 1$.

Information Theory Terminology

For historical reasons, information theory has its own special set of terms. We have encountered some of these terms before, but here, and in Figure 2.3, we give a more detailed account.

First, we have a *source* which generates *messages*. A message is an ordered sequence of k *symbols*

$$\mathbf{s} = (s_1, \ldots, s_k), \tag{2.16}$$

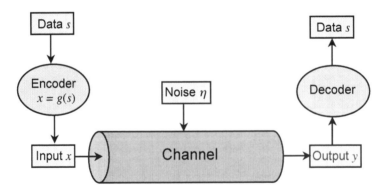

Figure 2.3. The communication channel. A message $\mathbf{s}$ is encoded as codewords $\mathbf{x}$ before being transmitted through a channel, which may corrupt the encoded message by adding noise η to produce outputs $\mathbf{y} = \mathbf{x} + \eta$. A receiver decodes the output $\mathbf{y}$ to recover inputs $\mathbf{x}$, which are then interpreted as a message $\mathbf{s}$.

where each symbol can be a number or a letter corresponding to the value of a random variable. Notice that the entire sequence **s** is represented by a letter in bold typeface, and its symbols are enclosed in round brackets.

Each symbol is an outcome value of a random variable S which can adopt any value from an alphabet of α (alpha) different symbols,

$$A_s = \{s_1, \ldots, s_\alpha\}. \tag{2.17}$$

The probability of each symbol being generated by the source is defined by the probability distribution

$$p(S) = \{p(s_1), \ldots, p(s_\alpha)\}, \tag{2.18}$$

where, by definition, the sum of $p(s)$ values must add up to one,

$$\sum_{i=1}^{\alpha} p(s_i) = 1. \tag{2.19}$$

The summation symbol $\sum$ is explained in Appendix B.

A *communication channel* is used to transmit data from its input to its output. If these data are transmitted from input to output without error then they have been successfully *communicated*. Before being transmitted, each message **s** is transformed by an *encoder*, which we can represent as a generic function g, into the *channel input* $\mathbf{x} = g(\mathbf{s})$, which is a sequence of *codewords*

$$\mathbf{x} = (x_1, \ldots, x_n), \tag{2.20}$$

where each codeword is the value of a random variable X which can adopt any one of m different values from the *codebook*

$$A_x = \{x_1, \ldots, x_m\}. \tag{2.21}$$

The probability of each codeword is defined by the probability distribution

$$p(X) = \{p(x_1), \ldots, p(x_m)\}. \tag{2.22}$$

We may choose to transmit a message as it is, so that the message and the transmitted codewords are identical (i.e. $\mathbf{x} = \mathbf{s}$). However, several symbols may be combined into a single codeword (see Section 3.4), or the message may be compressed by removing its natural redundancy. Consequently, the number of codewords in an encoded message $\mathbf{x} = g(\mathbf{s})$ may not match the number of symbols in the message $\mathbf{s}$.

If the form of compression allows the message to be decompressed perfectly then the compression is *lossless* (see Section 3.5), but if some information is discarded during compression then the message cannot be recovered exactly, and the compression is *lossy*.

A *code* is a list of symbols and their corresponding codewords. It can be envisaged as a simple look-up table (e.g. Table 2.1).

In order to ensure that the encoded message can withstand the effects of a noisy communication channel, some redundancy may be added to codewords before they are transmitted (see Section 4.7).

Transmitting a message $\mathbf{s}$ encoded as the codewords $\mathbf{x}$ produces the channel outputs

$$\mathbf{y} = (y_1, \ldots, y_n). \tag{2.23}$$

Each output is the value of a random variable Y, which can adopt any one of m different values

$$A_y = \{y_1, \ldots, y_m\}. \tag{2.24}$$

If the channel is noisy then the output y_j may be different from the codeword x_j that was transmitted.

Symbol	Codeword	Symbol	Codeword
$s_1 = 3$	$x_1 = 000$	$s_5 = 15$	$x_5 = 100$
$s_2 = 6$	$x_2 = 001$	$s_6 = 18$	$x_6 = 101$
$s_3 = 9$	$x_3 = 010$	$s_7 = 21$	$x_7 = 110$
$s_4 = 12$	$x_4 = 011$	$s_8 = 24$	$x_8 = 111$

Table 2.1. A code consists of a set of symbols (e.g. decimal numbers) or messages which are encoded as codewords (e.g. binary numbers). Here, the eight symbols are numbers which increase in steps of three, but, in principle, they could be any eight numbers or any eight entities.

The probability of each output is defined by the probability distribution

$$p(Y) \quad = \quad \{p(y_1), \ldots, p(y_m)\}. \tag{2.25}$$

Each output sequence $\mathbf{y}$ is interpreted as implying the presence of a particular input sequence $\mathbf{x}$. If this interpretation is incorrect (e.g. due to channel noise) then the result is an *error*. For a given channel, the mapping between messages and outputs, and *vice versa*, is provided by a *code*. A code consists of a message, an encoder, and a *decoder*. The decoder converts each output $\mathbf{y}$ to a (possibly incorrect) message. Channel noise induces errors in interpreting outputs; the *error rate* of a code is the number of incorrect inputs associated with that codebook divided by the number of possible inputs.

Channel capacity is the maximum amount of information which can be communicated from a channel's input to its output. Capacity can be measured in terms of the amount of information per symbol, and if a channel communicates n symbols per second then its capacity can be expressed in terms of information per second (e.g. bits/s). The capacity of a channel is somewhat like the capacity of a bucket, and the rate is like the amount of water we pour into the bucket. The amount of water (rate) we pour (transmit) into the bucket is up to us, and the bucket can hold (communicate, or transmit reliably) less than its capacity, but it cannot hold more.

In order to be totally clear on this point, we need a few more details. Consider an alphabet of α symbols, where $\alpha = 2$ if the data is binary. If a noiseless channel transmits data at a fixed rate of n symbols/s then it transmits information at a maximum *rate* or channel capacity of $n \log \alpha$ bits/s, which equals n bits/s for binary data.

However, the capacity of a channel is different from the rate at which information is actually communicated through that channel. The rate is the number of bits of information communicated per second, which depends on the code used to transmit data. The rate of a given code may be less than the capacity of a channel, but it cannot be greater; the channel capacity is the maximum rate that can be achieved when considered over all possible codes. For example, a code for binary data

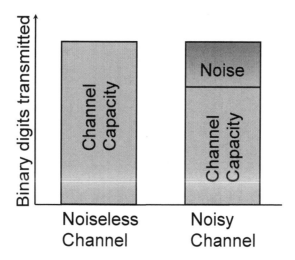

Figure 2.4. The *channel capacity* of noiseless and noisy channels is the maximum rate at which information can be communicated. If a noiseless channel communicates data at 10 binary digits/s then its capacity is $C = 10$ bits/s. The capacity of a noiseless channel is numerically equal to the rate at which it communicates binary digits, whereas the capacity of a noisy channel is less than this because it is limited by the amount of noise in the channel.

in which 0s and 1s occur equally often ensures that each binary digit (symbol) conveys one bit of information, but for any other code each binary digit conveys less than one bit (see Section 2.4). Thus, the capacity of a noiseless binary channel is numerically equal to the rate at which it transmits binary digits, whereas the capacity of a noisy binary channel is less than this, as shown in Figure 2.4.

Some of these definitions require a different interpretation for continuous variables, and we may sometimes use non-bold letters to represent messages, encoded messages and output sequences.

Key point. A message comprising symbols $\mathbf{s} = (s_1, \ldots, s_k)$ is encoded by a function $\mathbf{x} = g(\mathbf{s})$ into a sequence of codewords $\mathbf{x} = (x_1, \ldots, x_n)$, where the number of symbols and codewords are not necessarily equal. These codewords are transmitted through a communication channel to produce outputs $\mathbf{y} = (y_1, \ldots, y_n)$ which are decoded to recover the message $\mathbf{s}$.

2.3. Shannon's Desiderata

Now that we have a little experience of information, we can consider why it is defined as it is. Shannon knew that in order for a mathematical definition of information to be useful it had to have a particular minimal set of properties:

1. **Continuity**. The amount of information associated with an outcome (e.g. a coin flip) increases or decreases continuously (i.e. smoothly) as the probability of that outcome changes.
2. **Symmetry**. The amount of information associated with a sequence of outcomes does not depend on the order in which those outcomes occur.
3. **Maximal Value**. The amount of information associated with a set of outcomes cannot be increased if those outcomes are already equally probable.
4. **Additive**. The information associated with a set of outcomes is obtained by adding the information of individual outcomes.

Shannon[50] proved that the definition of information given below is the only one which possesses all of these properties.

2.4. Information, Surprise and Entropy

Suppose we are given a coin, and we are told that it lands heads up 90% of the time, as in Figure 2.2b. When this coin is flipped, we expect it to land heads up, so when it does so we are less surprised than when it lands tails up. The more improbable a particular outcome is, the more surprised we are to observe it.

One way to express this might be to define the amount of surprise of an outcome value x to be 1/(the probability of x) or $1/p(x)$, so that the amount of surprise associated with the outcome value x increases as the probability of x decreases. However, in order to satisfy the additivity condition above, Shannon showed that it is better to define surprise as the logarithm of $1/p(x)$, as shown in Figure 2.5. This is known as the *Shannon information* of x. (A reminder of the logarithmic function is provided in Appendix C.) The Shannon information of an outcome is also called *surprisal* because it reflects the amount of surprise when that outcome is observed.

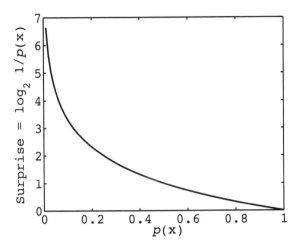

Figure 2.5. Shannon information as surprise. Values of x that are less probable have larger values of surprise, defined as $h(x) = \log_2(1/p(x))$.

If we use logarithms to the base 2 then the Shannon information of a particular outcome is measured in bits,

$$h(x) \quad = \quad \log_2 \frac{1}{p(x)} \text{ bits,} \qquad (2.26)$$

where h is standard notation for Shannon information. A general rule for logarithms states that

$$\log_2 \frac{1}{p(x)} \quad = \quad -\log_2 p(x), \qquad (2.27)$$

so that Equation 2.26 is often written as

$$h(x) \quad = \quad -\log_2 p(x) \text{ bits.} \qquad (2.28)$$

We will usually omit the $_2$ subscript from $\log_2$ unless the base of the logarithm needs to be made explicit.

Key Point. Shannon information is a measure of surprise.

How Surprised Should We Be?

In order to be surprised, we must know which outcomes are more surprising and which are less surprising. In other words, we need to know the probability of the possible outcomes which collectively define the probability distribution $p(X)$ of the random variable X. Thus, the Shannon information implicit in a given set of outcomes can only be evaluated if we know the probability of each outcome. One way to obtain this knowledge is to observe outcomes over a long period of time. Using the observed outcomes, we can estimate the probability of each outcome, and therefore build up an estimate of $p(X)$. But however it is acquired, we need the probability distribution $p(X)$ to evaluate the Shannon information of each outcome.

Entropy is Average Shannon Information

In practice, we are not usually interested in the surprise of a particular value of a random variable, but we would like to know how much surprise, on average, is associated with the entire set of possible values. That is, we would like to know the average surprise defined by the probability distribution of a random variable. The average surprise of a variable X which has a distribution $p(X)$ is called the *entropy* of $p(X)$, and is represented as $H(X)$. For convenience, we often speak of the entropy of the variable X, even though, strictly speaking, entropy refers to the distribution $p(X)$ of X.

Before we consider entropy formally, bear in mind that it is just the average Shannon information. For example, if we flip a coin n times to produce the sequence of outcomes $(x_1, \ldots, x_n)$ then the entropy of the coin is approximately

$$H(X) \approx \frac{1}{n} \sum_{i=1}^{n} \log \frac{1}{p(x_i)}. \qquad (2.29)$$

In order to explore the idea of entropy, we will consider examples using two coins: a fair coin, and a coin which lands heads up 90% of the time.

The Entropy of a Fair Coin

The average amount of surprise, unpredictability, or uncertainty about the possible outcomes of a coin flip can be found as follows. If a coin is fair or unbiased then $p(x_h) = 0.5$, as shown in Figure 2.2a, and the surprise of observing a head is

$$h(x_h) \quad = \quad \log \frac{1}{p(x_h)} \tag{2.30}$$

$$= \quad \log(1/0.5) \tag{2.31}$$

$$= \quad 1 \text{ bit.} \tag{2.32}$$

Given that $p(x_t) = 0.5$, the surprise of observing a tail is also one bit. It may seem obvious that the average surprise of this coin is also one bit, but we will make use of some seemingly tortuous reasoning to arrive at this conclusion, because we will require the same reasoning for less obvious cases.

We can find the average surprise by flipping the coin, say, 100 times, measuring the surprise of each outcome, and then taking an average over the set of 100 outcomes. Because each outcome has no effect on any other outcome, these outcomes are *independent*. If we flip a coin

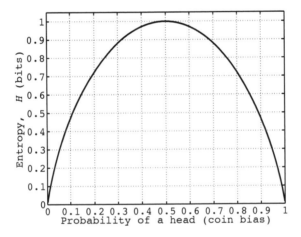

Figure 2.6. Graph of entropy $H(X)$ versus coin bias (probability $p(x_h)$ of a head). The entropy of a coin is the average amount of surprise or Shannon information in the distribution of possible outcomes (i.e. heads and tails), and has a value of one bit for a coin with a bias of $p(x_h) = 0.5$.

100 times we would expect to observe a head roughly 50 times, and a tail roughly 50 times. For the sake of argument, let's assume that we observe exactly 50 heads and 50 tails, so that the average amount of surprise is

$$H(X) \quad = \quad \frac{\left[\sum_{j=1}^{50} \log(1/p(x_h))\right] + \left[\sum_{j=1}^{50} \log(1/p(x_t))\right]}{100} \qquad (2.33)$$

$$= \quad \frac{[50 \times \log(1/p(x_h))] + [50 \times \log(1/p(x_t))]}{100}, \qquad (2.34)$$

which evaluates to

$$H(X) \quad = \quad [0.5 \times \log(1/0.5)] + [0.5 \times \log(1/0.5)] \qquad (2.35)$$

$$= \quad 1 \text{ bit per coin flip.} \qquad (2.36)$$

In summary, because the amount of surprise or Shannon information provided by observing the outcome of each flip of this fair coin is one bit, it follows that the average information $H(X)$ of each flip is also one bit.

Interpreting Entropy

There are several ways to interpret the notion of entropy, but one stands out as being particularly accessible. In general, the entropy of a variable is the logarithm of the number m of equally probable outcome values

$$H(X) \quad = \quad \log m \text{ bits.} \qquad (2.37)$$

In the above example, there are $m = 2$ equally probable outcome values, so the entropy is confirmed to be

$$H(X) \quad = \quad \log 2 \qquad (2.38)$$

$$= \quad 1 \text{ bit.} \qquad (2.39)$$

Given that we are using logarithms with a base of 2, we can raise both sides of Equation 2.37 to the power of 2 to confirm that we are dealing with

$$m = 2^{H(X)} \tag{2.40}$$

$$= 2 \text{ equally probable values.} \tag{2.41}$$

Thus, the number 2 raised to the power of the entropy $H(X)$ yields the number of equally probable outcome values which could be represented by a variable with an entropy of $H(X)$.

> **Key Point.** A variable with an entropy of $H(X)$ bits provides enough Shannon information to choose between $m = 2^{H(X)}$ equally probable alternatives.

The Entropy of an Unfair (Biased) Coin

If a coin is biased then the average amount of surprise or uncertainty is less than that of an unbiased coin, as shown in Figure 2.6. For example, if we know that the probability of a head is $p(x_h) = 0.9$ then it is quite easy to predict the result of each coin flip with a reasonable degree of accuracy (90% accuracy if we predict a head for each flip). If the outcome is a head then the amount of Shannon information is

$$h(x_h) = \log(1/0.9) \tag{2.42}$$

$$= 0.15 \text{ bits per head.} \tag{2.43}$$

On the other hand, if the outcome is a tail then the amount of Shannon information is

$$h(x_t) = \log(1/0.1) \tag{2.44}$$

$$= 3.32 \text{ bits per tail.} \tag{2.45}$$

Notice that more information is associated with the more surprising outcome (a tail, in this case).

We will follow the same line of reasoning used for Equation 2.36 to find the average amount of surprise for a coin with bias $p(x_h) = 0.9$.

If we flip this coin 100 times then we would expect to observe a head 90 times and a tail 10 times. It follows that the average amount of surprise is

$$H(X) \quad = \quad \frac{1}{100} \left[\sum_{j=1}^{90} \log \frac{1}{p(x_h)} + \sum_{j=1}^{10} \log \frac{1}{p(x_t)} \right] \qquad (2.46)$$

$$= \quad \frac{1}{100} [90 \times \log(1/p(x_h)) + 10 \times \log(1/p(x_t))]. \quad (2.47)$$

Substituting $p(x_h) = 0.9$ and $p(x_t) = 0.1$ yields

$$H(X) \quad = \quad [0.9 \times \log(1/0.9)] + [0.1 \times \log(1/0.1)] \qquad (2.48)$$

$$= \quad 0.469 \text{ bits per coin flip.} \qquad (2.49)$$

The average uncertainty of this biased coin is less than that of an unbiased coin, even though the uncertainty of one of the outcomes (a tail) is greater for a biased coin (3.32 bits) than it is for an unbiased coin (1 bit). In fact, no biased coin can have an average uncertainty greater than that of an unbiased coin (see Figure 2.6).

Because $p(x_h) = 0.9$ and $p(x_t) = 0.1$, Equation 2.48 can also be written as

$$H(X) \quad = \quad p(x_h) \log(1/p(x_h)) + p(x_t) \log(1/p(x_t)) \qquad (2.50)$$

$$= \quad 0.469 \text{ bits per coin flip.} \qquad (2.51)$$

If we define a tail as $x_1 = x_t$ and a head as $x_2 = x_h$ then we can write this more succinctly by summing over the two possible values of x_i to obtain the same answer as above:

$$H(X) \quad = \quad \sum_{i=1}^{2} p(x_i) \log \frac{1}{p(x_i)} \qquad (2.52)$$

$$= \quad 0.469 \text{ bits per coin flip.} \qquad (2.53)$$

As we will see later, an entropy of 0.469 bits implies that we could represent the information implicit in, say, 1,000 flips (which yield 1,000 outcomes) using as little as 469($= 1000 \times 0.469$) binary digits.

In this example, given that $H(X) = 0.469$ bits, the variable X could be used to represent

$$m \quad = \quad 2^{H(X)} \tag{2.54}$$

$$= \quad 2^{0.469} \tag{2.55}$$

$$= \quad 1.38 \text{ equally probable values.} \tag{2.56}$$

At first sight, this seems like an odd result. Of course, we already know that $H(X) = 0.469$ bits is the entropy of an unfair coin with a bias of 0.9. Nevertheless, translating entropy into an equivalent number of equally probable values serves as an intuitive guide for the amount of information represented by a variable. One way to think of this is that a coin with an entropy of $H(X) = 0.469$ bits has the same entropy as an imaginary die with 1.38 sides.

Entropy: A Summary

A random variable X with a probability distribution

$$p(X) \quad = \quad \{p(x_1), \ldots, p(x_m)\} \tag{2.57}$$

has an average surprise (Shannon information), which is its entropy

$$H(X) \quad = \quad \sum_{i=1}^{m} p(x_i) \log \frac{1}{p(x_i)}. \tag{2.58}$$

A succinct representation of this is

$$H(X) \quad = \quad E[\log(1/p(x))] \text{ bits,} \tag{2.59}$$

where E is standard notation for the average or *expected value* (see Appendix E).

2.5. Evaluating Entropy

Here, we show that we can either calculate the entropy of a variable X from the probability of m different outcome values defined by a probability distribution, or estimate entropy from n outcome values sampled from that probability distribution, and that we obtain approximately the same value for entropy in both cases. Specifically, as our sample size n grows infinitely large (i.e. $n \to \infty$), the value of the estimate based on the sample converges to the entropy $H(X)$ calculated from the underlying probability distribution. Given that entropy is the average Shannon information of a variable, readers unfamiliar with such matters should read the brief tutorial in Appendix E on how to obtain an average (e.g. entropy) from a distribution.

Calculating Entropy From a Probability Distribution

If we have a die with eight sides, as in Figure 2.7a, then there are $m = 8$ possible outcomes,

$$A_x = \{1, 2, 3, 4, 5, 6, 7, 8\}. \tag{2.60}$$

Because this is a fair die, all eight outcomes occur with the same probability of $p(x) = 1/8$, which defines the uniform probability distribution

$$p(X) = \{1/8, 1/8, 1/8, 1/8, 1/8, 1/8, 1/8, 1/8\} \tag{2.61}$$

shown in Figure 2.7b. The entropy of this distribution can be evaluated using the definition in Equation 2.58, i.e.

$$H(X) = \sum_{i=1}^{m=8} 1/8 \times \log \frac{1}{1/8} \tag{2.62}$$

$$= \log 8 \tag{2.63}$$

$$= 3 \text{ bits.} \tag{2.64}$$

Because the information associated with each outcome is exactly three bits, the average is also three bits and is therefore the entropy of X.

Given that X has an entropy of $H(X) = 3$ bits, it can represent

$$m = 2^{H(X)} \tag{2.65}$$

$$= 2^3 \tag{2.66}$$

$$= 8 \text{ equally probable values.} \tag{2.67}$$

More generally, given a die with m sides, the probability of each outcome is $p(x_i) = 1/m$, so, according to Equation 2.58, the entropy of an m-sided die is

$$H(X) \quad = \quad \sum_{i=1}^{m} 1/m \times \log \frac{1}{1/m} \tag{2.68}$$

$$= \quad \log m \text{ bits,} \tag{2.69}$$

which confirms that entropy is the logarithm of the number of equally probable outcomes.

We can also work back from the entropy $H(X)$ to the value of $p(x_i)$. Substituting $p(x_i) = 1/m$ in 2.65 yields

$$2^{H(X)} \quad = \quad 1/p(x_i), \tag{2.70}$$

so if a die has an entropy of $H(X)$ bits then the probability of each outcome is given by

$$p(x_i) \quad = \quad 2^{-H(X)}. \tag{2.71}$$

Estimating Entropy From a Sample

If we throw a die $n = 1,000$ times then we have a sample of n outcomes $\mathbf{x} = (x_1, x_2, \ldots, x_n)$, where each outcome is chosen from m different possible outcomes. Given that the Shannon information of one outcome x_j is

$$h(x_j) \quad = \quad \log 1/p(x_j), \tag{2.72}$$

we can denote the average Shannon information of the finite sample $\mathbf{x}$ as $\overline{h}(\mathbf{x})$, which is calculated as

$$\overline{h}(\mathbf{x}) \quad = \quad \frac{1}{n} \sum_{j=1}^{n} h(x_j) \text{ bits} \tag{2.73}$$

$$= \quad \frac{1}{n} \sum_{j=1}^{n} \log \frac{1}{p(x_j)} \text{ bits.} \tag{2.74}$$

If the sample size n is large then the entropy of the sample is approximately the same as the entropy of the random variable X, i.e.

$$\overline{h}(\mathbf{x}) \approx H(X). \tag{2.75}$$

Equation 2.74 is defined over n *instances* of x in a given sample, in which two instances (outcomes) may have the same value, whereas Equation 2.58 is defined over the m *unique outcomes* in X. Usually $n \gg m$ (i.e. n is much greater than m).

The definition of entropy in Equation 2.58 looks very different from Equation 2.74, which is more obviously the average Shannon information of a sample of outcome values. This is because Equation 2.58 is used to calculate entropy from a probability distribution of m different outcome values, whereas Equation 2.74 is used to estimate entropy from a sample of n outcome values chosen independently from that distribution.

Whether we calculate entropy from the known probability of each value as in Equation 2.58, or from the average of a sample of values as in Equation 2.74, it is important to note that entropy is the average amount of Shannon information provided by a single value of a variable.

2.6. Properties of Entropy

In essence, entropy is a measure of *uncertainty*. When our uncertainty is reduced, we gain information, so information and entropy are two sides of the same coin. However, information as conceived by Shannon

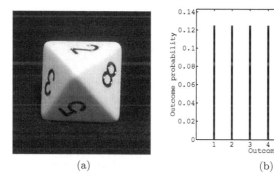

(a)   (b)

Figure 2.7. (a) An 8-sided die.   (b) The uniform normalised histogram (probability distribution) of outcomes has an entropy of $\log 8 = 3$ bits.

has a rather subtle interpretation, which can easily lead to confusion. Accordingly, it is worth a moment's thought to consider the meaning of information and entropy.

Average information actually shares the same definition as entropy, but whether we call a given quantity information or entropy usually depends on whether it is being given to us or taken away. For example, a variable may have high entropy, so our initial uncertainty about the value of that variable is large and is, by definition, exactly equal to its entropy. If we are then told the value of that variable then, on average, we have been given an amount of information equal to the uncertainty (entropy) we initially had about its value. Thus, receiving an amount of information is equivalent to having exactly the same amount of entropy taken away.

> **Key point.** The average uncertainty of a variable X is summarised by its entropy $H(X)$. If we are told the value of X then the amount of information we have been given is, on average, exactly equal to its entropy.

Doubling the Number of Sides

If we double the number of sides on the die from eight to 16 then we double the number of possible outcomes. Following the same line of reasoning as in Equations 2.62–2.64, the entropy of outcome values is $H(X) = \log 16 = 4$ bits. Doubling the number of sides from eight to 16 increases the entropy from three to four bits, and therefore adds exactly one bit (i.e. $\log 2$) to the entropy of the distribution of outcome values.

> **Key point.** Doubling the number of possible values of a variable adds one bit to its entropy.

Doubling the Number on Each Side

As we have just seen, the entropy of a discrete random variable X depends on the *number* of different outcome values and on the probability of each outcome value. But it does not depend on the particular outcome values that X can adopt. For example, we could double all the outcome values on an 8-sided die to define the alphabet $A_x = \{2, 4, 6, 8, 10, 12, 14, 16\}$. However, each of these values would still occur with the probability $(1/8)$ defined in Equation 2.61, so the entropy would still be $H(X) = 3$ bits. In contrast, doubling the values of a continuous variable does change its entropy (see Section 5.5).

Key point. The entropy of a discrete variable depends only on the probability distribution of its values. Changing the values of a discrete variable does not change its entropy provided the *number* of values stays the same.

2.7. Independent and Identically Distributed Values

When a die is thrown, each outcome value is chosen from the same uniform distribution of values. Additionally, it does not depend on any other outcome, so values are said to be *independent*. Outcome values that are chosen independently from the same uniform distribution are said to be *independent and identically distributed*, which is usually abbreviated to *iid*.

These considerations imply that the entropy of a sequence is given by Equation 2.58 only if its values are chosen independently from the same distribution (i.e. if they are iid). However, if consecutive values are related (e.g. as in an English sentence) then they do not provide independent information. In this case, the elements of the sequence are not iid, and the sequence has less entropy than the summed (over-estimated) entropies of its individual elements calculated using Equation 2.58.

If a source generates values chosen from an underlying distribution which remains constant over time then the source is said to be *stationary*. Unless stated otherwise, all sources in this text are assumed to be stationary.

2.8. Bits, Shannons, and Bans

The maximum amount of information associated with a discrete variable is the logarithm of the number m of equally probable values it can adopt. Thus, because a binary variable can adopt $m = 2$ states, it conveys up to $n = 1$ bit of information.

However, the translation from m possible values to an amount of information depends on the base of the logarithm used to do the translation (see Appendix C). If we used base 10 instead of base 2 then we would obtain a different answer, even though the underlying amount of information would remain the same. By analogy, consider an amount of water that can be expressed either as two pints or about 1.14 litres; the amount of water is the same in both cases, but the units in which it is measured are different.

If we measure information using logarithms with the base $e = 2.72$ (as used in natural logarithms) then the units are called *nats*. In contrast, if we measure information using logarithms with base 10 then the units are called *bans*, named after the English town of Banbury. The ban was named during World War II by the British code-breakers of Bletchley Park (including Alan Turing), where the German code had to be broken on a daily basis. Data were tabulated using special cards or *banburies* printed in Banbury, and the code-breaking method was called *Banbarismus*[34]. Finally, because the word bit is often mistakenly used to refer to a binary digit (see Section 1.5), a less ambiguous name is the *Shannon*[34], for which an appropriate abbreviation would be *Sh*.

2.9. Summary

Entropy is a core concept in information theory. But it is also quite subtle and demands a sound grasp of probability, random variables and probability distributions, which were introduced in this chapter. After defining key technical terms, we considered entropy as the average amount of surprise of a particular variable, like the flipping of a coin or the throw of a die. Both of these were used as examples for calculating entropy.

Chapter 3

The Source Coding Theorem

Gratiano speaks an infinite deal of nothing.
Shakespeare W, 1598.

3.1. Introduction

Most natural signals, like sounds and images, convey information in a relatively dilute form, so that a large amount of data contains a small amount of information. There are two reasons why information is so dilute in natural signals.

First, values that are close to each other tend to have similar values (e.g. in images), or to be related to each other (e.g. in English), so that different signal values partially duplicate the information they carry.

A second, more subtle, reason involves the distribution of values in a signal. The optimal distribution for a given communication channel depends on the constraints that apply. For example, if a channel has fixed lower and upper bounds then recoding an iid signal so that all of its values occur equally often (i.e. a uniform distribution) guarantees that each binary digit carries as much information as possible (i.e. one bit). Thus, for a channel with fixed bounds, the optimal distribution is uniform.

Together, these considerations suggest that a signal can be conveyed through a communication channel most efficiently if (1) it is first transformed to a signal with independent values, and (2) the values of this transformed signal have a distribution which has been optimised for that particular channel.

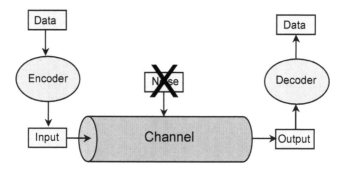

Figure 3.1. The discrete noiseless channel. Data in the form of symbols from a source are encoded as codewords (e.g. binary numbers) before being transmitted as inputs through a communication channel. At the other end, a receiver decodes these codewords to recover the original message.

The source coding theorem is so called because it is really about the coding of messages before they are transmitted through a communication channel, as in Figure 3.1. It states that messages can be recoded as described above, but it does not state *how* such recoding can be achieved. However, once the theorem had been proved, researchers began to search for, and soon found, coding schemes that were close to the theoretical limits defined by Shannon.

Shannon's theorem is remarkable because it not only applies to all sequences in which elements are independent, but also to structured sequences like English text; that is, sequences which contain short-range and long-range dependencies between their elements. But before we can appreciate Shannon's source coding theorem, we need to know more about channel capacity, which was introduced in Chapter 2.

3.2. Capacity of a Discrete Noiseless Channel

The capacity C of a discrete noiseless channel is the maximum number of bits it can communicate, usually expressed in units of bits per second or bits per symbol. Given that a binary digit can convey a maximum of one bit, a channel which communicates at the rate of R binary digits per second can communicate information at the rate of $C = R$ bits/s, its *channel capacity*. Thus, channel capacity is numerically equal to the number of binary digits communicated per second. Of course, if each binary digit carries less than one bit then the channel communicates information at a lower rate $R < C$ bits/s. In practice, to achieve a rate R close to the channel capacity C the transmitted codewords (e.g. binary digits) must be used wisely.

Consider a source which generates a stream of data in the form of symbols $s_1, s_2, \ldots$, with an entropy of $H(S)$ bits per symbol, and a channel which transmits the corresponding encoded inputs $x_1, x_2, \ldots$, where each input consists of C binary digits. Each symbol could, for example, consist of eight binary digits, where each binary digit carries only half a bit of information (as in the final part of Section 1.8); in the absence of any encoding (i.e. $x_i = s_i$), each input would carry only $C/2$ bits of information. To pre-empt the next section, *Shannon's source coding theorem guarantees that for any message there exists an encoding of symbols such that each channel input of C binary digits can convey, on average, close to C bits of information.*

This encoding process yields inputs with a specific distribution $p(X)$. The shape of this distribution determines its entropy $H(X)$ and therefore how much information each input carries. Thus, the capacity of a channel is defined in terms of the particular distribution $p(X)$ which maximises the amount of information per input, i.e.

$$C = \max_{p(X)} H(X) \text{ bits per input.} \qquad (3.1)$$

This states that channel capacity C is achieved by the distribution $p(X)$ which makes $H(X)$ as large as possible. If the channel transmits one input per second (for example) then we can state this in terms of the number of bits per second,

$$C = \max_{p(X)} H(X) \text{ bits/s,} \qquad (3.2)$$

so that the maximum number of symbols communicated per second is

$$C/H(X) \text{ symbols/s.} \qquad (3.3)$$

It can be shown that a uniform distribution $p(X)$ maximises $H(X)$.

An equivalent definition of capacity was given by Shannon[48]. He defined the channel capacity of a noiseless channel as the logarithm of the number $N(t)$ of inputs (encoded messages) that can be communicated through the channel in a time interval t, given by

$$C = \lim_{t \to \infty} \frac{\log N(t)}{t} \text{ bits/s.} \tag{3.4}$$

So as t approaches infinity, the logarithm of the number of encoded messages that can be conveyed per second approaches the channel capacity. The reason for including the proviso "as t approaches infinity" is because some messages are encoded using extremely long codewords which are averaged out when measuring over long time periods. If we omit this nicety then the channel capacity is simply the logarithm of the number of distinguishable encoded messages that could be communicated each second.

Note that this definition does not refer to the number of encoded messages actually communicated per second, but to the number of different encoded messages that *could be communicated* per second.

For example, you may be able to say one word per second, but you choose each word from a vocabulary of about $m = 1,000$ words. If we assume you are a channel then you could generate information at a maximum rate of $\log 1000 = 9.96$ bits/s which is, by definition, your channel capacity.

However, this capacity can only be achieved if (1) you generate all words equally often, and (2) you generate words in random order (i.e. the words are iid, see Section 2.7). If you do not generate all words equally often then some words will be more frequent, making them less surprising, so that they convey less Shannon information than others. Similarly, if you do not generate words in random order then some words will be fairly predictable; in a common phrase like *thank you*, the word *you* is very predictable. By definition, predictable words are unsurprising, and such words convey less Shannon information than unpredictable words. Thus, any form of inequality in the frequency of your words, or any form of redundancy in your words, means that you would generate information at a rate which is less than your channel capacity.

We can check that the definition in Equation 3.4 accords with our intuitions by using an example channel. Consider a channel that can convey nine binary digits per second. Each set of nine binary digits can adopt one out of a total of $N = 2^9$ binary numbers, so the message that is actually sent in one second is chosen from $N = 2^9$ different possible messages that could have been sent. Similarly, in t seconds, a total of $9t$ binary digits can be sent, where this message is one out of 2^{9t} different messages that could have been sent. According to Equation 3.4, the capacity of a channel which communicates nine binary digits per second is

$$C = \frac{\log 2^{9t}}{t} = 9t/t = 9 \text{ bits/s.} \tag{3.5}$$

In other words, if a channel conveys nine binary digits per second then the maximum amount of information it can convey (i.e. its capacity) is an average of nine bits per second.

We have not done anything new in this section, except to define what we mean by channel capacity, and to check that it makes sense intuitively. Next, we examine Shannon's source coding theorem.

Key Point. The capacity C of a noiseless channel is the maximum number of bits it can communicate per second, and is numerically equal to the number of binary digits it communicates per second.

3.3. Shannon's Source Coding Theorem

Now that we are familiar with the core concepts of information theory, we can quote Shannon's source coding theorem in full. This is also known as Shannon's *fundamental theorem for a discrete noiseless channel*, and as the *first fundamental coding theorem*.

> Let a source have entropy H (bits per symbol) and a channel have a capacity C (bits per second). Then it is possible to encode the output of the source in such a way as to transmit at the average rate $C/H - \epsilon$ symbols per second over the channel where ϵ is arbitrarily small. It is not possible to transmit at an average rate greater than C/H [symbols/s]. Shannon and Weaver, 1949[50].
>
> [Text in square brackets has been added by the author.]

Note that the Greek letter ϵ (epsilon) is traditionally used to denote a very small quantity. In essence, Shannon's source coding theorem states that the messages from a source which generates information at the rate of H bits/s can be encoded so that they can be transmitted at a rate arbitrarily close to the capacity C of a channel, provided $H < C$. To modern eyes, familiar with computers, this may seem to be a circular argument. However, in Shannon's day it was a revelation.

3.4. Calculating Information Rates

The channel capacity C is usually expressed in bits/s, and if the channel is binary then this means that it communicates C binary digits/s. The full capacity of the channel is utilised only if the outcome values generated by the source are encoded such that each transmitted binary digit represents an average of one bit of information. In order to reinforce our intuitions about channel capacity, we consider two examples below. For the present these examples involve rolling a die because this avoids the problems associated with encoding variables which are not iid.

Coding for an 8-Sided Die

Why would you want to construct a code for a variable with eight possible values? For example, you might have a telephone voice signal in which the amplitude of the signal at each millisecond is represented as a decimal value between 1 and 8. This coarse amplitude *quantisation* would be less than ideal, and (unlike die outcomes) the similarity between consecutive values mean the signal is not iid, but we shall ignore such niceties here.

As described in Section 2.5, if each outcome value generated by a source is a number that results from rolling an 8-sided die then each outcome value or symbol is between 1 and 8. Each of these symbols can be encoded with exactly three binary digits (because $3 = \log 8$). Each of the eight possible symbols $A_s = \{s_1, \ldots, s_8\}$ is equally probable, and each outcome does not depend on any other outcome, so the outcome variable is iid and has a uniform probability distribution. Given these very particular conditions, each outcome s_i conveys exactly three bits,

Symbol	Codeword
$s_1 = 1$	$x_1 = 000$
$s_2 = 2$	$x_2 = 001$
$s_3 = 3$	$x_3 = 010$
$s_4 = 4$	$x_4 = 011$
$s_5 = 5$	$x_5 = 100$
$s_6 = 6$	$x_6 = 101$
$s_7 = 7$	$x_7 = 110$
$s_8 = 8$	$x_8 = 111$

Table 3.1. Each outcome s from an 8-sided die has a value which can be represented as a 3-digit binary codeword x.

and therefore conveys an *average* of $H = 3$ bits/symbol, which is (by definition) its entropy.

If the channel capacity C is 3 bits/s then to communicate information at the rate of 3 bits/s the source symbols must be encoded such that each binary digit in each codeword x provides one bit of information. In this case, simply converting decimal to binary (minus one) provides the necessary encoding, as shown in Table 3.1, where each symbol s_i is encoded as a codeword x_i in the form of a binary number.

Using this simple code, each outcome value s_i from the roll of the die is transmitted as a codeword x_i which is decoded at the other end of the communication channel. For example, if the die shows $s_4 = 4$ then this is coded as the codeword $x_4 = 011$, which is decoded as 4 when it is received at the other end of the communication channel. According to Shannon's source coding theorem, the maximum rate R at which these symbols can be transmitted as codewords is

$$R = C/H \tag{3.6}$$
$$= \frac{3\ \text{bits/s}}{3\ \text{bits/symbol}} \tag{3.7}$$
$$= 1\ \text{symbol/s,} \tag{3.8}$$

and, because we know that each symbol (die outcome value) represents three bits, this amounts to a communication rate of $R = 3$ bits/s.

In this case, encoding each decimal number into a binary number allows information to be communicated at a rate equal to the channel capacity, so this is called an *efficient code*.

More generally, we can work out the efficiency of a code by comparing the average number of binary digits per codeword with the entropy $H(S)$ of the symbol alphabet. If the average number of binary digits in each codeword is $L(X)$ then the *coding efficiency* of this simple code is

$$\frac{H(S)}{L(X)} = \frac{3 \text{ bits/symbol}}{3 \text{ binary digits/symbol}} \quad (3.9)$$

$$= 1 \text{ bit/binary digit}. \quad (3.10)$$

The coding efficiency has a range between zero and one, so the code above is maximally efficient.

Coding for a 6-Sided Die

Now consider a more subtle example, in which the numbers $s_1 = 1$ and $s_6 = 6$ are obtained from throwing a 6-sided die, defining the alphabet

$$A_s = \{1, 2, 3, 4, 5, 6\} \quad (3.11)$$

$$= \{s_1, s_2, s_3, s_4, s_5, s_6\}. \quad (3.12)$$

According to Equation 2.69, each symbol from a die of $m = 6$ sides provides an average of

$$H = \log 6 \quad (3.13)$$

$$= 2.58 \text{ bits/symbol}, \quad (3.14)$$

so Shannon's source coding theorem guarantees that each symbol can be encoded with an average of 2.58 binary digits, in principle.

If the channel communicates one binary digit per second then in this example the channel capacity is $C = 1$ bit per second. Shannon's source coding theorem states that it should be possible to find an encoding which allows us to communicate information at a maximum rate of one bit per second, or, equivalently,

$$R = C/H \quad (3.15)$$

$$= \frac{1 \text{ bit/s}}{2.58 \text{ bits/symbol}} \quad (3.16)$$

$$\approx 0.387 \text{ symbols/s}. \quad (3.17)$$

How can this be achieved in practice? As a first attempt, we could encode each symbol using a simple binary code. This consists of coding each symbol as a codeword of three binary digits, by using the first six rows in Table 3.1. However, because our encoding uses three binary digits per symbol (where each symbol carries 2.58 bits), this code has a coding efficiency of only

$$\frac{H(S)}{L(X)} = \frac{2.58 \text{ bits/symbol}}{3 \text{ binary digits/symbol}} \qquad (3.18)$$

$$= 0.86 \text{ bits/binary digit.} \qquad (3.19)$$

Because the channel allows us to transmit exactly one binary digit each second, we end up with a communication rate of

$$R = C/H \qquad (3.20)$$

$$= \frac{0.86 \text{ bits/s}}{2.58 \text{ bits/symbol}} \qquad (3.21)$$

$$\approx 0.333 \text{ symbols/s,} \qquad (3.22)$$

which is less than the maximum rate of $R = 0.387$ symbols/s in Equation 3.17. This is well below the channel capacity (one bit or 0.387 symbols), so it is an inefficient code. Can we improve on this?

We can do better if we encode more than one symbol in each codeword. Specifically, if we send the outcome values of three throws at a time then there are a total of $6 \times 6 \times 6 \times = 216$ possible combinations of outcome values, and we can label each of these 216 combinations with a number between 1 and 216.

Now, for any observed outcome value resulting from three die throws, we can encode its label as a binary number. In order to represent 216 numbers, we need eight binary digits. This is because eight binary digits provide 256 $(= 2^8)$ labels. Because we use eight binary digits for each triplet of symbols (i.e. three die outcome values), we are using $8/3 \approx 2.66$ binary digits per symbol. We know that, on average, there

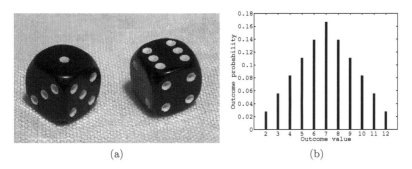

(a)   (b)

Figure 3.2. (a) A pair of dice.   (b) Normalised histogram of dice outcome values shown in Table 3.2 has an entropy of 3.27 bits per outcome value.

are 2.58 bits/symbol (Equation 3.14), so the coding efficiency is

$$\frac{H(S)}{L(X)} = \frac{2.58 \text{ bits/symbol}}{2.66 \text{ binary digits/symbol}} \qquad (3.23)$$

$$= 0.970 \text{ bits/binary digit}, \qquad (3.24)$$

which is a substantial improvement on 0.86 bits/binary digit. Because the channel allows us to transmit exactly one binary digit each second, we end up with a communication rate of

$$R = \frac{0.970 \text{ bits/s}}{2.58 \text{ bits/symbol}} \qquad (3.25)$$

$$\approx 0.376 \text{ symbols/s}, \qquad (3.26)$$

which is closer to the maximum rate of $C/H = 0.387$ symbols/s in Equation 3.17 than was achieved from the simple binary code of 0.333 symbols/s in Equation 3.22.

> **Key Point.** If each independently chosen value of a variable represents a non-integer number of bits then an efficient encoding can be obtained by combining several symbols in a single binary codeword.

3.5. Data Compression

So far, we have been dealing mostly with variables that have uniform distributions, but the importance of the ideas developed above only becomes apparent for non-uniform distributions.

The outcome of throwing a pair of 6-sided dice is a pair of decimal numbers, shown in Table 3.2. If we define the outcome value as the sum of this pair of numbers then each outcome value is a number between 2 and 12. This defines an alphabet of $m = 11$ possible outcome values

$$A_s = \{2, 3, 4, 5, 6, 7, 8, 9, 10, 11, 12\} \tag{3.27}$$

$$= \{s_1, s_2, s_3, s_4, s_5, s_6, s_7, s_8, s_9, s_{10}, s_{11}\}, \tag{3.28}$$

represented by the symbols $s_1, \ldots, s_{11}$, which occur with the frequencies shown in Table 3.2. There are a total of 36 possible ordered pairs of die outcomes, each occurring with equal probability (i.e. 1/36). By dividing each outcome frequency by 36 we obtain an outcome probability, shown in Figure 3.2b. Using Equation 2.59, we can then use these probabilities to find the entropy

$$H(S) = \sum_{i=1}^{m=11} p(s_i) \log \frac{1}{p(s_i)} \tag{3.29}$$

$$= 3.27 \text{ bits/symbol.} \tag{3.30}$$

Symbol	Sum	Dice	Freq	p	h	Code x
s_1	2	1:1	1	0.03	5.17	10000
s_2	3	1:2, 2:1	2	0.06	4.17	0110
s_3	4	1:3, 3:1, 2:2	3	0.08	3.59	1001
s_4	5	2:3, 3:2, 1:4, 4:1	4	0.11	3.17	001
s_5	6	2:4, 4:2, 1:5, 5:1, 3:3	5	0.14	2.85	101
s_6	7	3:4, 4:3, 2:5, 5:2, 1:6, 6:1	6	0.17	2.59	111
s_7	8	3:5, 5:3, 2:6, 6:2, 4:4	5	0.14	2.85	110
s_8	9	3:6, 6:3, 4:5, 5:4	4	0.11	3.17	010
s_9	10	4:6, 6:4, 5:5	3	0.08	3.59	000
s_{10}	11	5:6, 6:5	2	0.06	4.17	0111
s_{11}	12	6:6	1	0.03	5.17	10001

Table 3.2. A pair of dice have 36 possible outcomes, with outcome values between 2 and 12, which can be encoded as 11 codewords.
Symb: symbol used to represent sum of dice values.
Sum: outcome value, total number of dots for a given throw of the dice.
Dice: pair of dice outcomes that could generate each symbol.
Freq: number of different outcome pairs that could generate each symbol.
p: the probability that the pair of dice generate a given symbol (freq/36).
h: surprisal of outcome value, $h = p \log(1/p)$ bits.
Code: Huffman codeword for each symbol (see Section 3.6).

Even though some values are less frequent (and therefore more surprising) than others, the average amount of information associated with the throw of two dice is 3.27 bits. So according to Shannon's source coding theorem, we should be able to transmit each symbol (value) using an average of no more than 3.27 binary digits/symbol.

Suppose we simply coded each of the 11 values as a binary codeword. If we used three binary digits per outcome value then we could code for $8 = 2^3$ different outcome values (which is not enough), but if we used four binary digits per outcome value then we could code for up to $16 = 2^4$ different outcome values (which is too many). Thus, using this coding, we need at least four binary digits per symbol in order to code for 11 different outcome values. However, because the codewords for five of the outcome values would never be used, this is clearly not an efficient code.

As before, we can work out exactly how efficient this code is by comparing the average number of binary digits per codeword, $L(X)$, with the entropy of Equation 3.30. If we use four binary digits per codeword for each symbol then the average codeword length is $L(X) = 4$, and the coding efficiency is

$$\frac{H(S)}{L(X)} = \frac{3.27 \text{ bits/symbol}}{4.00 \text{ binary digits/symbol}} \tag{3.31}$$

$$= 0.818 \text{ bits/binary digit.} \tag{3.32}$$

As an aside, if the 11 outcomes were equally probable (as if we had an 11-sided die) then the distribution of values would be uniform, and the entropy would be

$$\log 11 = 3.46 \text{ bits.} \tag{3.33}$$

In contrast, the distribution of the 11 outcomes from two dice is not uniform, see Figure 3.2. Indeed, in order for a single die to have the same entropy as two 6-sided dice (i.e. 3.27 bits), it would have to have

9.65 sides, because such a die would yield

$$m = 2^{H(S)} \tag{3.34}$$
$$= 2^{3.27} \tag{3.35}$$
$$= 9.65 \text{ equally probable values.} \tag{3.36}$$

Even though it is not physically possible to make such a die, it is an intriguing idea.

To return to the topic of coding efficiency, can we get closer to the lower limit of 3.27 binary digits/symbol defined in Equation 3.30? The answer is yes, and one of the most well-known compression methods for doing so is called *Huffman coding*.

3.6. Huffman Coding

Huffman coding, invented by David Huffman in 1952, is one of many methods for efficiently encoding the symbols in a message into a corresponding set of codewords. A key property of a Huffman code is that frequent symbols have short codewords, whereas rare symbols have long codewords. The length of the codeword used to represent each symbol matters because long codewords require the transmission of more binary digits than short codewords. Consequently, for messages which consist of independent symbols, the lossless compression achieved by Huffman coding is close to the entropy of those messages, and if messages are encoded in binary then 0s and 1s occur with about the same frequency.

Indeed, a reassuring property of Huffman codes (which is a type of *symbol code*) is the *source coding theorem for symbol codes*[34]:

> Given a discrete variable X with entropy $H(X)$, there exists a symbol code in which the expected codeword length $L(X)$ of each codeword is greater than or equal to $H(X)$ and is less than $H(X) + 1$; that is,

$$H(X) \le L(X) < H(X) + 1. \tag{3.37}$$

Huffman coding is a lossless compression method, so an encoded message can be decoded without any loss of information.

The details of Huffman coding are explained using the small example in Figure 3.3. In essence, Huffman coding consists of finding the two least probable symbols, and then combining them to make an imaginary composite symbol. The two least probable symbols are then replaced with the composite symbol, whose probability is the sum of the probabilities of its components. This process is repeated (including composite symbols) until there is just one symbol left. Each time two symbols are combined, the two paths between those symbols and the new composite symbol are each labelled with a 1 (for each upper path) or a 0 (for each lower path), forming a tree that spreads from left to right. When the tree is complete, the code for each symbol is obtained by concatenating the binary numbers that lead to that symbol, reading from right to left.

In a Huffman code, not every codeword is short for every symbol, but the average codeword length is short, as shown by the Huffman code for the dice outputs shown in Table 3.2. As before, we can work out the efficiency of a Huffman code by comparing the average number of binary digits per codeword $L(X)$ with the entropy, which defines a lower limit for $L(X)$. If the number of binary digits in the codeword x_i is $L(x_i)$ then the average codeword length for a pair of dice is

$$L(X) \quad = \quad \sum_{i=1}^{m=11} p(x_i)\, L(x_i) \qquad (3.38)$$

$$= \quad 3.31 \text{ binary digits/symbol.} \qquad (3.39)$$

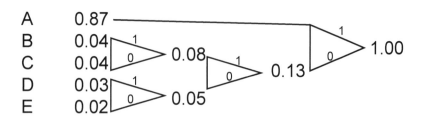

Figure 3.3. Simple example of a Huffman code for five symbols (A-E), which occur with the probabilities shown on the left. Reading from right to left, the final code is $A = 1, B = 011, C = 010, D = 001, E = 000$.

Here, $L(X)$ is close to the theoretical minimum (3.27 bits) defined by the entropy of the original message in Equation 3.30, and the coding efficiency of this Huffman code is

$$\frac{H(S)}{L(X)} = \frac{3.27 \text{ bits/symbol}}{3.31 \text{ binary digits/symbol}} \tag{3.40}$$
$$= 0.99 \text{ bits/binary digit.} \tag{3.41}$$

Note that the difference between the average number of binary digits in the Huffman code and the entropy of the original message is less than one binary digit. Thus, the Huffman code not only satisfies the optimality condition in Equation 3.37, but (in this case) it also comes close to the theoretical limit of one bit per binary digit.

A useful feature of Huffman codes is that they are *prefix codes*, which means that the border between any two consecutive codewords is easy to detect. This is because the n binary digits in each codeword are always different from the first n binary digits in any other codeword, so that no codeword is the *prefix* of any other codeword.

Huffman Coding of Images

In Chapter 1, the grey-level differences shown in Figure 1.8a are derived from the grey-levels in Figure 1.6a. A naive coding of the 127 heights in the histogram of difference values shown in Figure 1.8b would require $7(\approx \log 127)$ binary digits per histogram height. If we give the set of 127 histogram heights to the Huffman coding method then the resultant codewords have an average length of $L = 5.97$ binary digits, which is just larger than the measured entropy $H = 5.94$ of the histogram of grey-level differences. The coding efficiency of this Huffman code is therefore

$$\frac{H(S)}{L(X)} = \frac{5.94 \text{ bits/difference}}{5.97 \text{ binary digits/difference}}$$
$$= 0.99 \text{ bits/binary digit.} \tag{3.42}$$

However, recall that the figure of 5.94 bits/difference is itself an overestimate because it takes no account of the fact that nearby pixels have similar grey-levels. So even though Huffman coding does a good job of encoding pixel differences, it takes no account of, and does not attempt to remove, dependencies between nearby symbols in a message. This is important when considering messages in which symbols are not independent, such as images and English text.

Huffman Coding of English Letters

Using the relative frequencies of letters in English shown in Table 3.3, we can work out that English has an entropy no greater than $H = 4.11$ bits/letter. Note that this estimate includes a space character, which we treat as an extra letter, making a total of 27 letters. For now, we will ignore the non-independence of letters, so we know that 4.11 bits is an over-estimate. Applying Huffman coding to these relative frequencies, we find that they can be encoded using an average of 4.15 binary digits/letter, which gives a coding efficiency of $4.11/4.15 = 0.990$ bits per binary digit.

Because 4.15 binary digits allow us to discriminate between about 18 equally probable alternatives ($2^{4.15} = 17.8$), the 27 observed unequal probabilities have about the same entropy as 18 equally probable letters. This suggests that we could replace the 26 letters

Letter	Freq (%)	Letter	Freq (%)
a	5.75	n	5.96
b	1.28	o	6.89
c	2.63	p	1.92
d	2.85	q	0.08
e	9.13	r	5.08
f	1.73	s	5.67
g	1.33	t	7.06
h	3.13	u	3.34
i	5.99	v	0.69
j	0.06	w	1.19
k	0.84	x	0.73
l	3.35	y	1.64
m	2.35	z	0.07
-	-	SP	19.28

Table 3.3. The frequency of each letter in English. These percentages imply that if all letters were equiprobable and independent then each letter would provide an average of 4.11 bits of information. However, the non-uniform distribution of letters and the correlations between nearby letters in English means that each letter conveys only about 1.3 bits. SP=space character, treated as an extra letter. Data from MacKay (2003)[34].

of the alphabet (plus a space character) with 18 letters which occur independently and with equal probability.

Naturally, Shannon was aware of the problem of producing efficient encodings, but his own method, *Shannon–Fano coding*, was largely superseded by Huffman coding. However, both Shannon–Fano and Huffman coding are based on the assumption that the symbols in a message are mutually independent. But letters (symbols) in English are not independent, so the entropy of English must be less than the estimate of 4.11 bits/letter given above.

Using a method based on our ability to predict the next letter in a sequence of English text, Shannon[49] estimated the entropy of English to be about 1.3 bits/letter. Using the same logic as above, the fact that $2^{1.3} = 2.46$ implies that we could replace the conventional alphabet with just three independent, equally probable letters. Using purely statistical methods like those in the next section, it has been estimated that there is an upper bound of 1.75 bits/letter[10].

3.7. The Entropy of English Letters

How can we estimate the entropy of a Shakespeare play? More precisely, given any sequence of letters where consecutive letters are not independent, how can we estimate its entropy?

The short answer is that we express the probabilities of the letters in terms of the probabilities of mutually independent blocks of letters, and then use these in the standard definition of entropy (Equation 2.58). The long answer below is a summary of Shannon's proof for estimating the entropy of messages in which symbols are not independent.

English Entropy: Informal Account

In order to calculate the entropy of English, we need to know the probability of each letter. However, the probability of each letter depends on the letter that precedes it, and the letter before that, and so on, and on the letter that follows it, and the letter after that, and so on. The probability of a letter is a *conditional probability*, because its occurrence depends on (i.e. is conditional on) the identity of nearby letters. In short, we need to take account of the context of each letter in order to estimate its conditional probability. Obtaining accurate estimates of these conditional probabilities is extremely difficult.

In contrast, the relative frequency of each letter shown in Table 3.3 and Figure 3.4 is an *unconditional probability*. For clarity, we will use the term relative frequency to refer to unconditional probabilities. The entropy of a letter x is determined by its average Shannon information, where this average is taken over the set of conditional probabilities implied by letters in the vicinity of x, and it can be shown that the average Shannon information of a letter based on its conditional probability is less than (or equal to) the average Shannon information based on its relative frequency. So if the entropy of a letter is estimated based on letter frequencies alone then that estimate will be too large.

The Shannon information of a letter is related to how predictable it is from its context. Clearly, predicting the identity of a letter becomes easier as the number of surrounding letters taken into account increases, as shown in Figure 3.5. By implication, the uncertainty of a hidden letter's identity decreases as the number of surrounding letters taken into account increases. When averaged over all letters, the degree of uncertainty stops decreasing beyond some 'uncertainty horizon', as in Figure 3.6. At this point, the average uncertainty of each letter is equal to the entropy of English.

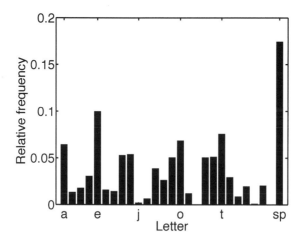

Figure 3.4. Relative frequency of letters in Shakespeare's Romeo and Juliet. This distribution has an entropy of $G_1 = 4.12$ bits/letter.

Some mathematicians would complain that, strictly speaking, the concept of entropy applies to an *ensemble* of English letter sequences, rather than to any particular sequence. For example, the structure of a particular sequence of letters depends on the first letter in the sequence, which therefore affects the estimated entropy of that sequence. In order to preclude such problems, the entropy of English is defined as the entropy of an ensemble, which consists of infinite number of sequences. In practice, however, the entropy of any variable must be estimated from a finite number of observations.

English Entropy: A More Formal Account

We are going to consider what happens to the dependence between blocks of consecutive letters as we increase the number N of letters in each block, and how this affects the uncertainty of letters in blocks of different lengths. Shannon's analysis included all possible blocks, but for convenience we will assume that blocks consist of consecutive and non-overlapping segments of text, as shown in Figure 3.7. This simplification does not alter the results obtained.

If $N = 1$ then the probability of each letter in each 1-letter block B is estimated as its relative frequency. If these relative frequencies are used to estimate the entropy of English H then the resultant approximation is called G_1.

If $N = 2$ then the identity of each letter in a block depends more on the other letter in that block than on the letters in most other

Figure 3.5. The predictability of letters should increase with increasing context. By Randall Munroe, reproduced with permission from xkcd.com.

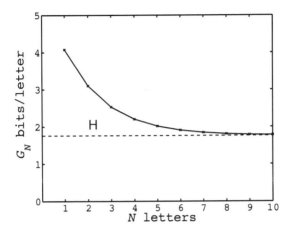

Figure 3.6. How the amount of entropy per letter G_N decreases as the number N of letters taken into account increases, using a corpus of 70 million characters[45]. G_N approaches the entropy H of English letters (dashed line) as N increases.

blocks, because most other blocks are taken from unrelated parts of the original text. As can be seen from Figure 3.8, 2-letter blocks are not all equally probable. But if they were then each letter would be as unpredictable with its partner as it is on its own. So the fact that 2-letter blocks are not all equally probable implies that each letter is *more* predictable with its partner than it is on its own, which means that the average uncertainty G_2 of each letter in a 2-letter block is less than the uncertainty of each letter considered on its own (i.e. from its frequency). Similarly, the uncertainty G_3 of each letter's identity in a 3-letter block is less than the uncertainty G_2 of each letter's identity in a 2-letter block.

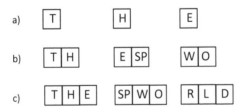

Figure 3.7. As block size increases from (a) $N = 1$ to (c) $N = 3$, the ability to predict each letter from other letters in the same block increases. Consequently, the mean surprisal per letter decreases as block size increases.

In other words, it is easier to guess the identity of a hidden letter if we know the identity of its immediate neighbours, and the more neighbours we know, the easier it is to guess. So, as the block length N increases, the identity of each letter in a block depends less and less on the letters in other blocks, which implies that blocks become increasingly independent as the length of blocks is allowed to increase.

Now, supposing the identity of each letter in English does not depend on any letter that is more than 10 letters away. In practice, the dependency between nearby letters diminishes rapidly as inter-letter distances increase, as shown in Figure 3.6. Once the block length has grown to $N = 10$, the identity of every letter in a given block B_k depends on other letters in that block and exactly two other blocks: the previous block B_{k-1}, and the next block B_{k+1}. All other blocks contain letters which are more than 10 letters away from, and therefore independent of, every letter in block B_k.

If the original text is sufficiently long, and if there are a large number of blocks, then the dependency between adjacent blocks just described accounts for a tiny proportion of the overall dependency between all blocks. Thus, the more blocks there are, and the longer each block is, the smaller the dependency between blocks. By analogy, it is as if each block is one of a large number of independent super-symbols, and if the

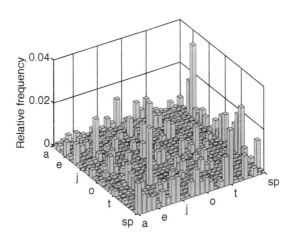

Figure 3.8. Relative frequency of pairs of letters in Romeo and Juliet. Each column represents the relative frequency of one ordered pair of letters.

blocks are independent then finding their entropy is relatively simple. The only question is, how long do those blocks have to be to ensure that they are independent?

The block length beyond which inter-letter dependence falls to zero is called the *correlation length* N_C. Once the block length exceeds the correlation length, it is as if all blocks are effectively independent, so increasing the block length N beyond N_C has a negligible effect on the estimated entropy G_N. At this point, G_N equals the entropy of English; that is, $G_N = H$. This matters because Shannon's theorems are expressed in terms of infinite block lengths, but in practice these theorems apply to any block length which exceeds the correlation length of the sequence under consideration.

Key point. As the number of letters in each block increases, the average uncertainty of each letter decreases.

English Entropy: Formal Account

If we take account of the relative frequency of each letter x then we effectively have a block length of $N = 1$. In this case, our *first order* estimate of the entropy of English H is

$$G_1 \quad = \quad \sum_{i=1}^{m=27} p(x_i) \log \frac{1}{p(x_i)} \tag{3.43}$$

$$= \quad 4.08 \text{ bits/letter}, \tag{3.44}$$

where we have included the space character as the 27th letter. The estimates reported here are based on 70 million characters[45]; the value of G_1 is based on slightly different frequency estimates from those listed in Table 3.3.

Using a block length of $N = 2$ effectively takes account of the dependencies between adjacent letters. Because there are $729(= 27^2)$ distinct pairs of letters, we can consider these to be 729 distinct blocks $B_k = [x_i, y_j]$, where k has a range from 1 to 729, and $p(B_k)$ is the relative frequency of a particular ordered pair of letters. For example, if we take $i = 3$ and $j = 5$ then the 2-letter block is $B = [x_3, y_5] = [ce]$, and $p([ce])$ is the relative frequency of the block $[ce]$. These relative frequencies can be used to obtain a *second order* estimate G_2 of H,

$$G_2 = \frac{1}{2} \sum_{i=1}^{27} \sum_{j=1}^{27} p([x_i, y_j]) \log \frac{1}{p([x_i, y_j])} \qquad (3.45)$$

$$= \frac{1}{2} \sum_{k=1}^{m=729} p(B_k) \log \frac{1}{p(B_k)} \qquad (3.46)$$

$$= 3.32 \text{ bits/letter}, \qquad (3.47)$$

where we have divided by two to take account of the fact that each block contains two letters (remember that G_2 is the average Shannon information per letter).

This is fine, as far as it goes, but what we really want to know is the entropy of a letter x_i given *all* of the letters which affect the probability of x_i. Thus, the figure of 3.32 bits/letter for the entropy of English letters is still an over-estimate because it ignores any dependencies which extend beyond two letters.

Such long-range dependencies can be taken into account if we use blocks of $N = 3$ letters. In order to evaluate G_3, the calculation is based on $19,683(= 27^3)$ distinct letter triplets:

$$G_3 = \frac{1}{3} \sum_{i} \sum_{j} \sum_{k} p([x_i, y_j, z_k]) \log \frac{1}{p([x_i, y_j, z_k])} \qquad (3.48)$$

$$= \frac{1}{3} \sum_{k=1}^{m=19,683} p(B_k) \log \frac{1}{p(B_k)} \qquad (3.49)$$

$$= 2.73 \text{ bits/letter}. \qquad (3.50)$$

Of course, some letter triplets are very common (e.g. *and, the*), and these will dominate the weighted average of surprisal values implicit in G_3. In contrast, other letter triplets are rare (e.g. *nud*) in English, and these contribute little to the estimate of entropy. More generally, the key to understanding Shannon's source coding theorem is the fact that a small proportion of possible letter sub-sequences are common, whereas most other sub-sequences are practically non-existent.

For any given block length N, the Nth order estimate of entropy is

$$G_N = \frac{1}{N} \sum_{k=1}^{27^N} p(B_k) \log \frac{1}{p(B_k)} \text{ bits/letter.} \qquad (3.51)$$

In principle, the process of calculating G_N for larger values of N can be repeated indefinitely. Once we have taken account of dependencies over all letter ranges up to the correlation length N_C, each probability $p(B_k)$ entered into the calculation is independent of almost all other probabilities. If all block probabilities are independent then G_{N_C} is the entropy per letter as measured in blocks of N_C letters; therefore, because G does not increase for blocks containing more than N_C letters, G_{N_C} is equivalent to the entropy of English, so $G_{N_C} = H$ bits/letter. In practice, as N increases, the estimated entropy of English converges to a value of about $G_{N_C} = 1.8$ bits/letter.

If the entropy of English is $H = 1.8$ bits/letter then Shannon's source coding theorem guarantees that we should be able to communicate letters using just over 1.8 binary digits per letter. Next, we consider one simple method for achieving this.

Efficient Transmission of English

The correlation length of English text is almost certainly not greater than $N_C = 10$ letters, and we will assume that $N_C = 10$. The number of possible 10-letter sub-sequences is about 200 million million,

$$m_C = 27^{10} \qquad (3.52)$$
$$\approx 206 \times 10^{12}, \qquad (3.53)$$

and if all of these sub-sequences were equally probable then they could be represented with

$$\log 206 \times 10^{12} = 47.5 \text{ binary digits.} \qquad (3.54)$$

At this point it is worth noting that, as part of the source coding theorem, Shannon proved that (see Section 3.8):

1. the most common sub-sequences comprise a tiny proportion of the possible sub-sequences;

2. these common sub-sequences occur with a collective probability of about one;

3. each of these sub-sequences occurs with about the same probability.

Specifically, the source coding theorem implies that the number of (equally probable) 10-letter sub-sequences observed in practice is

$$m_H = 2^{1.8 \times 10} \tag{3.55}$$

$$= 262,144 \tag{3.56}$$

so each 10-letter sub-sequence can be represented with only

$$\log_2 2^{1.8 \times 10} = 18 \text{ binary digits.} \tag{3.57}$$

In the case of English text, this implies that:

1. the most common 10-letter sub-sequences comprise a tiny proportion of all possible sub-sequences;

2. these 262,144 most common 10-letter sub-sequences occur with a collective probability of about one;

3. each of these 262,144 sub-sequences occurs with about the same probability.

Finally, if 262,144 sub-sequences occur with about the same probability, and if these are the only sub-sequences that occur, then it follows that each sub-sequence occurs with a probability of about 1/262,144. As for the remainder, of which there are more than 205 million million, Shannon's theorem implies that these sub-sequences occur with a collective probability of about zero. Notice that, because each of the 262,144 10-letter sub-sequences (symbols) occurs with the same probability, Huffman coding would provide no additional savings in terms of the number of binary digits required to represent them.

A correlation length of 10 letters implies that all 10-letter sub-sequences are mutually independent. This implies that we could transmit English text using the following simple strategy. First, use a large corpus of text to rank each 10-letter sub-sequence according to its frequency. Next, identify the 262,144 most common 10-letter sub-sequences, and allocate one codeword to each sub-sequence, where each codeword is represented as 18 binary digits. In doing this, we have effectively constructed a look-up table (a codebook) with entries numbered from 1 to 262,144. If we want to transmit a message across the world then the receiver must have a copy of this look-up table, but if we are going to use this table often then the cost of transmitting it to the receiver is relatively small. Next, we take the message to be transmitted, break it up into consecutive 10-letter sub-sequences, and use the look-up table to find the associated codewords. Finally we send the codeword in the form of 18 binary digits. When this codeword is received, the receiver simply finds the codeword on their copy of the look-up table to recover the original 10-letter sub-sequence.

We have thus sent a message which looks as if it might require 47.5 binary digits for each 10-letter sub-sequence (see Equation 3.54), but using only 18 binary digits per sub-sequence. Equivalently, we have sent a message which looks as if it might require 4.75 binary digits for each letter, but using only 1.8 binary digits per letter.

Ironically, before Morse made use of the letter-by-letter code described in Section 1.6, he had devised a system conceptually similar to the one outlined above. Specifically, he made a list of commonly used phrases and assigned a number to each one. For example, the third phrase might be *The 9pm train will be late*. When he wanted to transmit this message, he simply transmitted the number 3 as the binary number 11 (sent as two dashes, for example). It is almost as if Morse had recognised, long before Shannon's formal proofs existed, that the number of possible messages far exceeds the number of messages actually used, and that this is the key to efficient communication.

As Shakespeare noted in Romeo and Juliet:

> What's in a name? That which we call a rose
> By any other name would smell as sweet.
> Shakespeare W, 1597.

Indeed, for the purposes of communication, it is not the name itself that matters, but the number of different possible words from which the name was chosen.

Just as English consists of sequences of non-independent letters which can be efficiently encoded as blocks of independent sub-sequences, so images consist of sequences of non-independent grey-levels which can be efficiently encoded as (square) blocks of independent sub-sequences. Thus, the line of reasoning applied to English text also applies to images, and to most other natural sequences (e.g. music, movies, DNA).

3.8. Why the Theorem is True

In essence, Shannon's source coding theorem is based on the observation that most events that could occur almost certainly do not, and those that do, occur with about the same probability as each other. The truth of Shannon's source coding theorem can be glimpsed from a type of mathematical logic called a *counting argument*, which is used here to give a rough idea of Shannon's proof.

Consider a source which generates messages, where each message consists of n binary digits $\mathbf{s} = (s_1, \ldots, s_n)$. Crucially, we assume that the source statistics are iid, so the probability P that each binary digit equals 1 remains stable over time. This is not an unreasonable assumption, because many practical examples of sources have a nice stable probability profile (e.g. the probability of each letter in English text does not change from year to year). In principle, the number of different *possible* messages of length n that could be generated by this source is huge, specifically, $m_{max} = 2^n$. But, as we shall see, the number m of different messages actually generated will almost certainly be much, much smaller than m_{max} (i.e. $m << m_{max}$). So, in practice, if we want to communicate information about the source messages then we only have to worry about m of them. This is the key to Shannon's source coding theorem.

If n is large (i.e. messages are long) then all of the roughly m different messages $\mathbf{s}_1, \ldots, \mathbf{s}_m$ generated by the source will contain about nP binary digits equal to 1. For example, if $P = 1/8 = 0.125$ and $n = 8,000$ then the most common messages generated will contain about 1,000 1s. More importantly, as the messages are allowed to get longer, the *law of large numbers* guarantees that almost all messages generated will contain nP 1s.

In fact, Shannon's proof relies on the assumption that messages are very long, but for the purposes of illustration we shall use a short message. What is plausibly true for large values of n is less plausibly true for small n, but the spirit of the Shannon's proof applies to both cases.

If $n = 8$ then each message looks like

$$\mathbf{s} \;=\; (s_1, s_2, s_3, s_4, s_5, s_6, s_7, s_8), \tag{3.58}$$

with examples shown in Table 3.4. In principle, the number of different possible messages is $m_{max} = 2^8 = 256$. However, if $P = 0.125$ then $nP = 1$, so the most common messages generated contain one 1, and there are exactly $m = 8$ such messages. We can work out the probability that a message contains one 1 and seven 0s as follows. The probability of a 1 in the first binary digit of a message is $P_1 = 0.125$, and the probability of a 0 in the second binary digit is $P_2 = (1 - 0.125) = 0.875$, $P_3 = 0.875$, and so on. Because these probabilities are independent, the probability that a message contains one 1 and seven 0s is not affected by the order in which they occur (see

	Message								Codeword		
$\mathbf{s}_1$	1	0	0	0	0	0	0	0	$\mathbf{x}_1$	0	0	0
$\mathbf{s}_2$	0	1	0	0	0	0	0	0	$\mathbf{x}_2$	0	0	1
$\mathbf{s}_3$	0	0	1	0	0	0	0	0	$\mathbf{x}_3$	0	1	0
$\mathbf{s}_4$	0	0	0	1	0	0	0	0	$\mathbf{x}_4$	1	1	1
$\mathbf{s}_5$	0	0	0	0	1	0	0	0	$\mathbf{x}_5$	1	0	0
$\mathbf{s}_6$	0	0	0	0	0	1	0	0	$\mathbf{x}_6$	1	0	1
$\mathbf{s}_7$	0	0	0	0	0	0	1	0	$\mathbf{x}_7$	1	1	0
$\mathbf{s}_8$	0	0	0	0	0	0	0	1	$\mathbf{x}_8$	1	1	1
...				...					Not needed		
$\mathbf{s}_{256}$	1	1	1	1	1	1	1	1	Not needed		

Table 3.4. Why Shannon's source coding theorem is true. Each message (row) from a source contains $n = 8$ binary digits, so up to 256 different messages can be generated. If the probability that each binary digit equals 1 is $P = 1/8$ then most messages contain one 1, so there are effectively only eight different messages, $\mathbf{s}_1, \dots, \mathbf{s}_8$, which can be represented by eight codewords $\mathbf{x}_1, \dots, \mathbf{x}_8$, each of which contains three binary digits.

Appendix F), and is therefore

$$P_1 \times P_2 \times \ldots \times P_8 \quad = \quad 0.125 \times 0.875^7 \tag{3.59}$$

$$= \quad 0.049. \tag{3.60}$$

The actual value of this probability is less important than the fact that its value is the same irrespective of where the 1 occurs in each message. It follows that all of the $m = 8$ different messages $\mathbf{s}_1, \ldots, \mathbf{s}_8$ (with one 1 in each message) are generated with the same probability, and therefore they all have the same relative frequency p in the distribution of messages; we do not yet know the value of this relative frequency, but we do know it is the same for all eight messages. So far, we have established two facts. Given $n = 8$ and $P = 0.125$:

1. each of the $m = 8$ messages $\mathbf{s}_1, \ldots, \mathbf{s}_m$ generated contains one 1;
2. these messages have the same relative frequency p.

As noted above, these 'facts' are really only true for large values of n, but we will continue to pretend they are also exactly true for the small value of n used in this example.

We already know that the total number of possible messages is $m_{max} = 256$, and this includes messages with every possible number of 1s. However, if we assume that only $m = 8$ different messages are actually generated, and that each of these contains exactly one 1, then the number of different messages generated is much smaller than the number of possible messages.

In order to clinch the source coding argument, we need to review a crucial observation. We know that if we have $m = 8$ equally probable outcome values, such as the integers $1, \ldots, 8$, then we can encode each message as one of eight binary codewords $\mathbf{x}_1, \ldots, \mathbf{x}_8$. And because we only need eight such codewords, this means we only need

$$n_w \quad = \quad \log 8 \tag{3.61}$$

$$= \quad 3 \tag{3.62}$$

binary digits per codeword, i.e.

$$\mathbf{x} = (x_1, \ldots, x_3). \tag{3.63}$$

In other words, we can send $m = 8$ equally probable integers using exactly $n_w = 3$ binary digits per codeword. Of course, each outcome value does not have to be an integer; it could just as easily be represented as a message of eight binary digits, as shown in Table 3.4. This means that we can encode each of the messages $\mathbf{s}_1, \ldots, \mathbf{s}_8$ with a codeword of just three binary digits.

Because the $m = 8$ messages are generated with equal probability, and because we assume that they comprise all of the messages that get generated in practice, it follows that the probability (measured as relative frequency) of each message must be

$$p \quad = \quad 1/m \tag{3.64}$$

$$= \quad 0.125. \tag{3.65}$$

This should not be confused with Equation 3.60, which is the probability that a message contains one 1.

If we have $m = 8$ messages, each of which is generated with the same probability p, then we know (from Equation 2.69) that the entropy is

$$H \quad = \quad \mathrm{E}[\log(1/p)] \tag{3.66}$$

$$= \quad \log m \tag{3.67}$$

$$= \quad 3 \text{ bits per message.} \tag{3.68}$$

Thus, even though the source could generate 256 different messages, the 8-binary-digit messages generated have, in practice, an entropy of only $H = 3$ bits per message, and can be encoded with $n_w = H = 3$ binary digits per codeword.

At this point, we should note two caveats. First, if $P = 0.5$ exactly then $m = m_{max}$, and therefore $m = 2^n$ and $H = n$ bits. However, even tiny deviations from $P = 0.5$ ensure that $m \ll m_{max}$.

Second, the example above used $nP = 1$, but even if $nP > 1$ then $m < 2^n$ (unless $P = 0.5$). These caveats are more apparent from a careful reading of the next section, which is for readers who wish for more technical details.

Why Does the Source Generate Only m Distinct Messages?

The general reason that a source, which *could* generate $m_{max} = 2^n$ distinct messages, generates only $m = 2^H$ messages, is as follows. The number of distinct messages of length n which contain n_1 1s and n_0 0s is just the number of different ways of distributing n_1 1s and n_0 0s over n positions (binary digits). This can be calculated as a *binomial coefficient*, which is defined as

$$C_{n,n_1} = \frac{n!}{n_1! n_0!}, \tag{3.69}$$

where $n! = n \times (n-1) \times \cdots \times 1$. When considered over all values between $n_1 = 0$ and $n_1 = n$, the total number of possible distinct messages is

$$\sum_{n_1=0}^{n} C_{n,n_1} = 2^n, \tag{3.70}$$

which is reassuring, given that we know there are 2^n possible messages.

For long messages, we can safely assume that almost all m messages generated by the source contain nP 1s. It follows that the value of the binomial coefficient is about zero ($C_{n,n_1} \approx 0$) unless n_1 is equal to nP. So the number of distinct messages generated is approximately equal to the number of messages that contain nP 1s,

$$\sum_{n_1=0}^{n} C_{n,n_1} \approx C_{n,nP} \tag{3.71}$$

$$= m, \tag{3.72}$$

where comparison with Equation 3.70 implies that $m < 2^n$.

Next, we will find the logarithm of the number m, and, in so doing, we will confirm that it is indeed the entropy of the source. This can be achieved with the aid of *Stirling's approximation*, which states that if n is large then $\ln n! \approx n[(\ln n) - 1]$. This is defined in terms of natural logarithms, so we begin with the natural logarithm of Equation 3.69:

$$\ln C_{n,n_1} = \ln n! - \ln n_1! - \ln n_0!. \tag{3.73}$$

From Equation 3.72, we can assume that $n_1 = nP$, so that Stirling's approximation yields

$$\ln m \approx n[(\ln n) - 1] - n_1[(\ln n)_1 - 1] - n_0[(\ln n_0) - 1] \quad (3.74)$$
$$= n \ln n - n_1 \ln n_1 - n_0 \ln n_0 - (n - (n_1 + n_0)). \quad (3.75)$$

Given that $n = n_0 + n_1$, this can be rewritten as

$$\ln m = (n_0 + n_1) \ln n - n_1 \ln n_1 - n_0 \ln n_0 \quad (3.76)$$
$$= n_1(\ln n - \ln n_1) + n_0(\ln n - \ln n_0) \quad (3.77)$$
$$= n \left(\left[\frac{n_1}{n} \ln \frac{n}{n_1} \right] + \left[\frac{n_0}{n} \ln \frac{n}{n_0} \right] \right) \quad (3.78)$$
$$= n(p_1 \ln 1/p_1 + p_0 \ln 1/p_0). \quad (3.79)$$

The final step involves the substitutions $p_1 = n_1/n$ and $p_0 = n_0/n$, where p_1 is the probability that each binary digit is equal to 1, and p_0 is the probability that it is equal to 0. We can recognise Equation 3.79 as the entropy of a message containing n binary digits, expressed in units of nats (because we used natural logarithms). If we use logarithms of base 2 then we can translate this into bits, and we find that the source generates messages with an average of

$$\log_2 m = n(p_1 \log_2(1/p_1) + p_0 \log_2(1/p_0))$$
$$= n \sum_{i=0}^{1} p_i \log_2 \frac{1}{p_i} \text{ bits per message}, \quad (3.80)$$

which is the equation for the entropy of a binary number containing n binary digits.

The preceding account is not a rigorous proof of Shannon's source coding theorem, but it conveys the key ideas which underpin the proofs presented by Shannon and others.

3.9. Kolmogorov Complexity

As mentioned in Section 3.3, we can interpret Shannon's source coding theorem in terms of data compression. This interpretation was developed independently by the Russian mathematician Andrey Kolmogorov(1933)[28]. He defined *algorithmic complexity* to be the length of the shortest computer program capable of describing a given object (e.g. a message). Algorithmic complexity is now known as *Kolmogorov complexity*.

For example, the first million digits of the number π, which begins

$$\pi \quad = \quad 3.14159265358979323846264338327950288419716939937510\dots$$

can be generated by a computer program containing many fewer than one million binary digits. In fact, π can be obtained using one of several methods, such as the *Leibniz formula*

$$\pi \quad = \quad 4 \times \left(1 - \frac{1}{3} + \frac{1}{5} - \frac{1}{7} + \frac{1}{9} \dots \right), \quad\quad (3.81)$$

which can be written more succinctly as

$$\pi \quad = \quad 4 \times \sum_{k=0}^{\infty} \frac{(-1)^k}{2k+1}. \quad\quad (3.82)$$

Using a computer program, this can be written as a simple 'for' loop, which would generate the infinite digits of π. However, the shortest

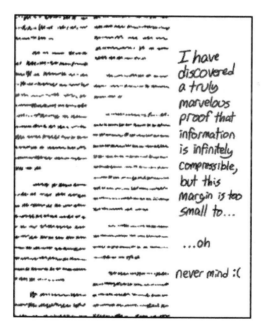

Figure 3.9. What if the Kolmogorov complexity of every object were zero? By Randall Munroe, reproduced with permission from xkcd.com.

program capable of generating π contains a small, finite, but *unknown* number n_π of binary digits. If the shortest program contains n_π binary digits then it must also contain n_π bits because, if it contains more than n_π binary digits then each binary digit would convey less than 1 bit, which means that a shorter program must exist. Thus, the infinite number of digits in π would have been compressed to n_π bits. This implies that the apparently random, infinitely long sequence of digits in π can be represented with just n_π binary digits. And, because the Kolmogorov complexity of the number π is the length of the shortest program that can generate π, it follows that the Kolmogorov complexity of π is n_π bits. The link to Shannon's definition of information is that the Kolmogorov complexity of a random sequence of digits is approximately equal to the entropy of that sequence.

However, Kolmogorov complexity is *non-computable*. This means that there is no definite method or *algorithm* for finding the Kolmogorov complexity of a given object or number, except by exhaustive search (i.e. trying out all possible computer programs). For the example of π considered above, this means that, irrespective of the brevity of the program we devise in order to generate π, we can never be certain that a shorter program does not exist.

3.10. Summary

Shannon's source coding theorem is essentially about encoding messages into codewords efficiently, which is really a form of data compression. In order to understand this theorem, we first examined the idea of channel capacity, the maximum rate at which information can be communicated through a communication channel. After quoting Shannon's source coding theorem, we explored its relevance to coding theory, and we found that some codes are not very efficient, in the sense that each binary digit in an encoded message represents much less than the theoretical upper limit of one bit of information. Finally, we considered the transmission of data in which symbols are not independent, and found that they can be encoded to obtain independent blocks of symbols. A key implication of this is that Shannon's source coding theorem applies to natural sequences (e.g. English, images) with non-independent symbols.

Chapter 4

The Noisy Channel Coding Theorem

> Uncertainty which arises by virtue of freedom of choice on the part of the sender is desirable uncertainty. Uncertainty which arises because of errors or because of the influence of noise is undesirable.
>
> Weaver W, 1949.

4.1. Introduction

Shannon's noisy channel coding theorem cannot be understood without a firm grasp of mutual information, so we will spend a substantial portion of this chapter exploring this topic.

Mutual information is a general measure of association between two variables, like the input and output of a communication channel (Figure 4.1). It has many properties that apply to both discrete and continuous variables. So, by way of introduction, we begin with a general account that applies to both types of variables.

Given two variables X and Y, the *mutual information* $I(X, Y)$ between them is the average information that we gain about Y after we have observed a single value of X. Because mutual information is a symmetric quantity, it is also the average information that we gain about X after we have observed a single value of Y. Equivalently, mutual information is the average reduction in uncertainty about X that results from knowing the value of Y, and *vice versa*.

To give a less terse definition, the uncertainty we have about the value of Y is initially summarised by its entropy $H(Y)$. If X and Y are related then after observing a single value of X we have more

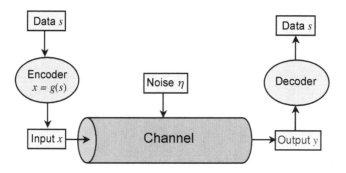

Figure 4.1. A noisy communication channel.

information about Y, and so our uncertainty about Y is reduced to some value less than $H(Y)$. If we average across all possible values of X and Y then after observing X our uncertainty about Y is reduced by an amount which is the mutual information $I(X, Y)$ between X and Y. The amount of residual uncertainty we have about the value of Y after observing a single value of X is the *conditional entropy* $H(Y|X)$. Because we usually consider noise η as being added to the input as it passes through the channel, this particular conditional entropy $H(Y|X)$ is also called the *noise entropy*, $H(\eta) = H(Y|X)$. And, because the mutual information between two variables is symmetric, all of this remains true if the roles of X and Y are swapped.

In order to appreciate the formal definition of mutual information, we first need to consider the entropy of joint distributions in the context of a communication channel. The remainder of this chapter concerns discrete variables.

4.2. Joint Distributions

Consider a source which generates messages for transmission over a noisy communication channel, as shown in Figure 4.1. At any point in time, this source generates one of four different messages, each of which consists of a single symbol. Each message could be an integer (0–3), an English word, or even an entire book, but, for simplicity, we assume that each message is an integer (i.e. $s_1 = 0, s_2 = 1, s_3 = 2, s_4 = 3$).

If we wish to send one instance of each message through a noisy communication channel, how many binary digits do we need? Well, we know that if there is no noise, and if the messages are equally probable, then we could simply encode each message as a different binary number and send that, requiring a maximum of $2 = \log 4$ binary digits per message. But the channel is noisy, which increases the number of binary digits required to represent each message.

We are going to estimate mutual information from a sample of 128 input and output message pairs. For simplicity, we assume that our sampling process is perfect, inasmuch as the quantities we measure from our relatively small sample accurately reflect the underlying statistics of the channel.

The four distinct messages are represented by the alphabet

$$A_s = \{0, 1, 2, 3\} \tag{4.1}$$
$$= \{s_1, s_2, s_3, s_4\}, \tag{4.2}$$

and they are generated by the source in unequal proportions as defined by the probability distribution

$$p(S) = \{p(s_1), p(s_2), p(s_3), p(s_4)\}. \tag{4.3}$$

In this example, no special encoding of each message occurs before transmission, so each symbol is represented as a binary codeword. Each codeword can adopt one of $m_y = 4$ values

$$A_x = \{00, 01, 10, 11\} \tag{4.4}$$
$$= \{x_1, x_2, x_3, x_4\}, \tag{4.5}$$

which occur with probabilities defined by the probability distribution

$$p(X) = \{p(x_1), p(x_2), p(x_3), p(x_4)\}. \tag{4.6}$$

We are using a trivial encoding here, so $p(X) = p(S)$.

$Y \downarrow \ X \rightarrow$	x_1	x_2	x_3	x_4	Sum
y_1	12	15	2	0	29
y_2	4	21	10	0	35
y_3	0	10	21	4	35
y_4	0	2	15	12	29
Sum	16	48	48	16	128

Table 4.1. Counts of input values X and corresponding output values Y.

After being transmitted, each input emerges as a (possibly different) output, which can adopt any one of $m_y = 4$ values,

$$A_y \ = \ \{00, 01, 10, 11\} \qquad (4.7)$$
$$= \ \{y_1, y_2, y_3, y_4\}, \qquad (4.8)$$

which occur with probabilities defined by the probability distribution

$$p(Y) \ = \ \{p(y_1), p(y_2), p(y_3), p(y_4)\}. \qquad (4.9)$$

Given that each codeword can adopt one of four possible values, and that each output adopts one of four possible values (e.g. the integers 1–4), there are 16 possible input/output pairs. The set of 16 input/output pairs can be represented as a set of four input or source values X together with four corresponding channel output values Y, as in Table 4.1.

$Y \downarrow \ X \rightarrow$	x_1	x_2	x_3	x_4	$p(Y)$
y_1	0.094	0.117	0.016	0.00	0.227
y_2	0.031	0.164	0.078	0.00	0.273
y_3	0.00	0.078	0.164	0.031	0.273
y_4	0.00	0.016	0.117	0.094	0.227
$p(X)$	0.125	0.375	0.375	0.125	1

Table 4.2. Joint probability distribution $p(X, Y)$. The numbers in the table margins are the marginal distributions $p(X)$ and $p(Y)$. The probability $p(x_i, y_j)$ in each cell is obtained by dividing the corresponding number in Table 4.1 by 128.

We can gain a visual impression of how accurately the communication channel communicates information by recording a sample of, say, 128 encoded messages $x_1, \ldots, x_{128}$, and their corresponding output values $y_1, \ldots, y_{128}$, in a 4×4 grid, as in Table 4.1. If we divide the frequency of each pair (x_i, y_j) by the total number of pairs (i.e. 128) then we obtain an estimate of the probability that $X = x_i$ and $Y = y_i$, as shown in Table 4.2. Note that we have used the same subscript notation for the elements in an alphabet and the elements in a message.

The probability that $X = x_i$ and $Y = y_j$ is called the *joint probability* $p(x_i, y_j)$. Each joint probability $p(x_i, y_j)$ can be visualised as the ith column and jth row of an $n \times n$ array, the *joint probability distribution*

$$p(X, Y) = \begin{pmatrix} p(x_1, y_1) & p(x_2, y_1) & p(x_3, y_1) & p(x_4, y_1) \\ p(x_1, y_2) & p(x_2, y_2) & p(x_3, y_2) & p(x_4, y_2) \\ p(x_1, y_3) & p(x_2, y_3) & p(x_3, y_3) & p(x_4, y_3) \\ p(x_1, y_4) & p(x_2, y_4) & p(x_3, y_4) & p(x_4, y_4) \end{pmatrix}.$$

The entire joint probability distribution can be visualised as a three-dimensional histogram of vertical columns, where the height of each column reflects the value $p(X, Y)$ of the probability assigned to each input/output pair of values, as in Figure 4.2. For convenience, we assume that the input/output statistics of our sample given in Table 4.1 perfectly represent the underlying joint distribution, even though this would not usually be the case in practice.

There are two things worth noting here. First, as stated in the Ground Rules (Section 2.2), the probabilities must sum to one. This is because probabilities behave like proportions and just as we would expect all 16 proportions to sum to one, so we would expect all 16 probabilities to sum to one. This is a defining feature of a probability distribution, as shown in Table 4.2. Second, even though the joint distribution function $p(X, Y)$ is a discrete distribution because the random variables X and Y are discrete, each of the 16 probability values it defines is represented by a continuous variable with a value between zero and one.

Entropy of the Joint Probability Distribution

The entropy of a joint distribution is a straightforward generalisation of the entropy of a single variable,

$$H(X,Y) \;=\; \sum_{i=1}^{m_x}\sum_{j=1}^{m_y} p(x_i, y_j) \log \frac{1}{p(x_i, y_j)} \qquad (4.10)$$

$$=\; \mathrm{E}\left[\log \frac{1}{p(x,y)}\right] \text{ bits per pair,} \qquad (4.11)$$

where m_x is the number of different values of X and m_y is the number of different values of Y (as in Table 4.2). The term *bits per pair* is used to emphasise the fact that the joint entropy $H(X,Y)$ is the average amount of Shannon information of each pair of values, where this average is taken over all possible pairs.

Just as the entropy of a single variable (with finite bounds) can be considered to be a measure of its uniformity, so the entropy of a joint distribution is also a measure of its uniformity (provided X and Y lie within a fixed range). If all possible pairs of values are equally probable then this defines a uniform joint distribution, known as a *maximum entropy* joint distribution. In contrast, if some pairs of values occur

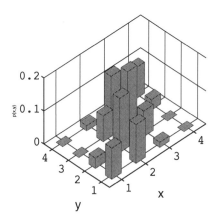

Figure 4.2. The discrete joint probability distribution $p(X,Y)$. The probability that an input/output pair has the particular combination of values x_i and y_j is obtained by dividing the ijth cell in Table 4.1 by the total number of pairs, 128.

with a high probability and others occur with low probability then this defines a joint distribution with lower entropy.

Marginalisation

In order to evaluate the mutual information between X and Y, we need to consider the distributions of X and Y. The distribution of X can be obtained by summing each value of $p(X, Y)$ over all possible values of Y. For example, if we want the value of the distribution $p(X)$ at $X = x_i$ then this is obtained by summing over all values of Y for the fixed value of $X = x_i$:

$$p(x_i) \quad = \quad \sum_{j=1}^{m_y} p(x_i, y_j). \tag{4.12}$$

This is equivalent to summing the values in the ith column of Table 4.2 over all rows. If we consider the value of $p(x_i)$ for all m_x values of X

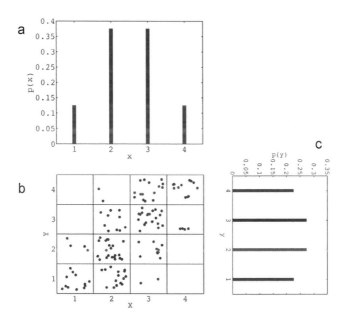

Figure 4.3. Visualising the joint probability distribution. (a) Distribution of input values is one of the marginal distributions $p(X)$ of $p(X, Y)$.   (b) Joint distribution $p(X, Y)$ of 128 input/output pairs.   (c) The output distribution is the other marginal distribution $p(Y)$ of $p(X, Y)$. Positions of points in (b) have integer values, which have been jittered to make them visible.

then we obtain the *marginal distribution*,

$$p(X) = \sum_{j=1}^{m_y} p(X, y_j) \tag{4.13}$$

$$= \{0.125, 0.375, 0.375, 0.125\}, \tag{4.14}$$

as shown in Table 4.2. Similarly, the marginal distribution $p(Y)$ is obtained by summing over values of X,

$$p(Y) = \sum_{i=1}^{m_x} p(x_i, Y) \tag{4.15}$$

$$= \{0.227, 0.273, 0.273, 0.227\}, \tag{4.16}$$

as shown in Table 4.2. If we want the value of the distribution $p(Y)$ at a particular value $Y = y_j$ then this is obtained by summing over all values of X for the fixed value of $Y = y_j$,

$$p(y_j) = \sum_{i=1}^{m_x} p(x_i, y_j). \tag{4.17}$$

This is equivalent to summing the values in the jth row of Table 4.2 over all columns.

Statistical Independence

If X and Y are *statistically independent* then knowing the value of X provides absolutely no information about the corresponding value of Y, and *vice versa*. This implies that the probability of any two values (e.g. x_i and y_j) of X and Y occurring together is the same as the probability of x_i multiplied by the probability of y_j:

$$p(x_i, y_j) = p(x_i)p(y_j) \quad \text{if } X \text{ and } Y \text{ are independent.} \tag{4.18}$$

When considered over all values of X and Y this implies that if two variables are independent then the joint distribution is given by the product of its two marginal distributions:

$$p(X,Y) \quad = \quad p(X)p(Y). \tag{4.19}$$

Here, the product $p(X)p(Y)$ is interpreted as an *outer product*, which means that the ith column and jth row of the joint distribution $p(X,Y)$ is the product $p(x_i)p(y_j)$.

Given this definition, if two variables are independent then the entropy of their joint probability distribution $p(X,Y)$ can be rewritten as the sum of their individual entropies,

$$H(X,Y) \quad = \quad E\left[\log \frac{1}{p(x,y)}\right] \tag{4.20}$$

$$= \quad E\left[\log \frac{1}{p(x)p(y)}\right] \tag{4.21}$$

$$= \quad E\left[\log \frac{1}{p(x)}\right] + E\left[\log \frac{1}{p(y)}\right], \tag{4.22}$$

which can be rewritten as two summations,

$$H(X,Y) \quad = \quad \sum_{i=1}^{m_x} p(x_i)\log \frac{1}{p(x_i)} + \sum_{j=1}^{m_y} p(y_j)\log \frac{1}{p(y_j)} \tag{4.23}$$

$$= \quad H(X) + H(Y) \text{ bits per outcome pair.} \tag{4.24}$$

Thus, if X and Y are independent then

$$H(X) + H(Y) - H(X,Y) = 0 \text{ bits per outcome pair.} \tag{4.25}$$

For example, if two dice are thrown then the value of each die does not depend on the value of the other die, so they are independent (see Section 3.5). Over many throws, the pairs X and Y of values could be recorded in a 6×6 table representing the joint distribution of values. Because all 36 pairs are equally probable, this joint distribution $p(X,Y)$ is uniform and has an entropy of

$$H(X,Y) \quad = \quad \log 36$$

$$= \quad 5.17 \text{ bits per outcome pair.} \tag{4.26}$$

The distribution of values for one die X yields the uniform marginal distribution

$$p(X) \quad = \quad \{1/6, 1/6, 1/6, 1/6, 1/6, 1/6\}, \tag{4.27}$$

which has an entropy of

$$H(X) \quad = \quad \log 6 \tag{4.28}$$
$$= \quad 2.59 \text{ bits per outcome.} \tag{4.29}$$

Similarly, the distribution of values for the other die yields the uniform marginal distribution $p(Y) = p(X)$, which also has an entropy of $H(Y) = 2.59$ bits per outcome. Because these marginal distributions represent independent variables, the joint entropy $H(X, Y)$ is the sum of the entropies of the marginal distributions:

$$H(X, Y) \quad = \quad H(X) + H(Y)$$
$$= \quad 5.17 \text{ bits per outcome pair.} \tag{4.30}$$

The use of the terms *bits per outcome pair* and *bits per outcome* are not conventional, but are used here to stress precisely what the entropy is referring to. We shall use the more conventional term *bits* for the remainder of this chapter.

Key point. If X and Y are independent then the entropy of the joint distribution $p(X, Y)$ is equal to the summed entropies of its marginal distributions, $H(X, Y) = H(X) + H(Y)$.

4.3. Mutual Information

Given a communication channel, the key question is this: what proportion of the entropy in the output reflects information in the input? In other words, how much of the entropy in the output is telling us about the input, and how much is just noise? This question leads naturally to the notion of mutual information.

For a channel with inputs represented by the random variable X and outputs represented by Y, the rate at which information is communicated is the mutual information between X and Y, which depends on three entities:

1. the entropy $H(X)$ of the input X;
2. the entropy $H(Y)$ of the output Y;
3. the relationship between X and Y.

If the output distribution has high entropy then it has the potential to provide a lot of information about input values. However, there is no point in having high output entropy and low input entropy, because then the large variability in the output values would have little to do with the corresponding small variations in input values.

Similarly, there is no point in having high input entropy and low output entropy, because then some of the variability in the input values is effectively 'input noise', inasmuch as it induces no corresponding variability in the output.

Finally, there is no point in having high input and high output entropy if the inputs and outputs are mutually independent. In this case, all of the output entropy, which could be providing information about the input, is just output noise.

In summary, to communicate as much information as possible through a noisy channel:

1. the input entropy should be high;
2. the output entropy should be high;
3. the noise entropy should be low.

The relationships between input entropy, output entropy and mutual information can be visualised from several equivalent perspectives, as shown in Figures 4.4–4.7.

The mutual information between X and Y is defined as

$$I(X,Y) \;=\; \sum_{i=1}^{m_x} \sum_{j=1}^{m_y} p(x_i, y_j) \log \frac{p(x_i, y_j)}{p(x_i)p(y_j)}, \qquad (4.31)$$

which is more easily understood as the mean or expected value (see Appendix E) of the ratio

$$I(X,Y) \;=\; \mathrm{E}\left[\log \frac{p(x,y)}{p(x)p(y)}\right] \text{ bits.} \qquad (4.32)$$

We can separate the numerator and denominator of this ratio,

$$I(X,Y) \quad = \quad \mathrm{E}[\log p(x,y) - \log(p(x)p(y))] \quad\quad (4.33)$$
$$= \quad \mathrm{E}[\log p(x,y)] - \mathrm{E}[\log(p(x)p(y))], \quad\quad (4.34)$$

where the final term can be rewritten as

$$\mathrm{E}[\log(p(x)p(y))] = \mathrm{E}[\log p(x)] + \mathrm{E}[\log p(y)], \quad\quad (4.35)$$

so that

$$I(X,Y) \quad = \quad \mathrm{E}[\log p(x,y)] - \mathrm{E}[\log p(x)] - \mathrm{E}[\log p(y)] \quad\quad (4.36)$$
$$= \quad \mathrm{E}[\log(1/p(x))] + \mathrm{E}[\log(1/p(y))] - \mathrm{E}[\log(1/p(x,y))] \quad (4.37)$$
$$= \quad H(X) + H(Y) - H(X,Y) \text{ bits.} \quad\quad (4.38)$$

Finally, if we rearrange Equation 4.38 then we can see that the joint entropy acts a kind of 'container' for the various entropy components, including mutual information

$$H(X,Y) \quad = \quad H(X) + H(Y) - I(X,Y). \quad\quad (4.39)$$

> **Key point.** The mutual information between two variables X and Y is the average reduction in uncertainty about the value of X provided by the value of Y, and *vice versa*.

Calculating Mutual Information

In order to reinforce our intuitive understanding of the ideas introduced so far, we will work out the entropies associated with the distribution defined in Table 4.2.

The entropy of the marginal distribution $p(X)$ can be calculated from Table 4.2 as

$$H(X) \quad = \quad \sum p(x_i) \log \frac{1}{p(x_i)} \quad\quad (4.40)$$
$$= \quad 0.125 \log(1/0.125) + 0.375 \log(1/0.375) +$$
$$0.375 \log(1/0.375) + 0.125 \log(1/0.125) \quad (4.41)$$
$$= \quad 1.81 \text{ bits.} \quad\quad (4.42)$$

Similarly, the entropy of the marginal distribution $p(Y)$ can be calculated from Table 4.2 as

$$
\begin{aligned}
H(Y) &= \sum p(y_j) \log \frac{1}{p(y_j)} &\text{(4.43)}\\
&= 0.227 \log(1/0.227) + 0.273 \log(1/0.273) + \\
&\quad\ 0.273 \log(1/0.273) + 0.227 \log(1/0.227) &\text{(4.44)}\\
&= 1.99 \text{ bits.} &\text{(4.45)}
\end{aligned}
$$

The entropy of the joint distribution defined in Table 4.2 can be calculated by substituting the 16 probabilities into Equation 4.11 to give

$$
H(X,Y) = 3.30 \text{ bits.} \qquad\qquad \text{(4.46)}
$$

However, some of the entries in Table 4.2 are zero, so $p(x_i, y_j) = 0$, which implies a surprise value of infinity. To deal with such cases, we define the product $p(x_i, y_j) \log(1/p(x_i, y_j))$ to be zero if $p(x_i, y_j) = 0$.

We can immediately tell that X and Y are not independent because the total entropy of the marginal distributions is larger than the entropy of the joint distribution,

$$
\begin{aligned}
H(X) + H(Y) &= 1.811 + 1.99 &\text{(4.47)}\\
&= 3.80 \text{ bits.} &\text{(4.48)}
\end{aligned}
$$

Finally, these results can be used to calculate the mutual information,

$$
\begin{aligned}
I(X,Y) &= H(X) + H(Y) - H(X,Y) &\text{(4.49)}\\
&= 1.81 + 1.99 - 3.30 \text{ bits} &\text{(4.50)}\\
&= 0.509 \text{ bits.} &\text{(4.51)}
\end{aligned}
$$

Thus, on average, each value of X reduces our uncertainty about the corresponding value of Y by about half of a bit, and *vice versa*.

When considered in terms of output entropy, this implies that only 0.256 (i.e. $I(X,Y)/H(Y) = 0.509/1.99$) of the output entropy is information about the input, and the remainder is just channel noise.

4.4. Conditional Entropy

An alternative way of viewing mutual information can be obtained by considering the entropy of the output in relation to channel noise. If we do not know the value of the input X then our uncertainty about the output Y is given by its entropy $H(Y)$. But if we do know the value of X then our uncertainty about Y is reduced from $H(Y)$ to a quantity called the *conditional entropy* $H(Y|X)$, which is the average uncertainty in the value of Y after X is observed. The vertical bar in $H(Y|X)$ is read as 'given', so that $H(Y|X)$ is the entropy of Y given X. In other words, the reduction in uncertainty regarding X induced by knowing Y is the difference between $H(Y)$ and $H(Y|X)$,

$$I(X,Y) \;=\; H(Y) - H(Y|X). \tag{4.52}$$

Key point. The conditional entropy $H(Y|X)$ is the average uncertainty in Y after X is observed, and is therefore the average uncertainty in Y that cannot be attributed to X.

We can prove Equation 4.52 as follows. From Section 4.3 we have

$$I(X,Y) \;=\; \sum_{i=1}^{m_x}\sum_{j=1}^{m_y} p(x_i,y_j)\log\frac{p(x_i,y_j)}{p(x_i)p(y_j)}. \tag{4.53}$$

According to the product rule (see Appendix F), $p(x,y) = p(y|x)p(x)$, where $p(y|x)$ is the *conditional probability* that $Y = y$ given that $X = x$. We can use this to rewrite Equation 4.53 as

$$I(X,Y) \;=\; \sum_{i=1}^{m_x}\sum_{j=1}^{m_y} p(x_i,y_j)\log\frac{p(y_j|x_i)}{p(y_j)}, \tag{4.54}$$

which in turn can be rewritten as the difference

$$I(X,Y) \;=\; \sum_{i=1}^{m_x}\sum_{j=1}^{m_y} p(x_i,y_j)\log\frac{1}{p(y_j)} - \sum_{i=1}^{m_x}\sum_{j=1}^{m_y} p(x_i,y_j)\log\frac{1}{p(y_j|x_i)},$$

where the first term on the right is the entropy $H(Y)$ and the final term is the conditional entropy $H(Y|X)$, yielding Equation 4.52.

By symmetry, Equation 4.52 implies that

$$I(X,Y) \;=\; H(X) - H(X|Y), \tag{4.55}$$

where $H(X|Y)$ is the average uncertainty we have about the value of X after Y is observed. The conditional entropy $H(X|Y)$ is the average uncertainty in X after Y is observed, and is therefore the average uncertainty in X that cannot be attributed to Y.

Conditional Entropy and Noise

Given that the output Y is equal to the input X plus some channel noise η, we can find an expression for the entropy of the channel noise as follows. We begin by substituting

$$Y \;=\; X + \eta, \tag{4.56}$$

in Equation 4.52, which yields

$$I(X,Y) \;=\; H(Y) - H([X + \eta]|X). \tag{4.57}$$

If the value of X is known then the uncertainty in X is zero, so it makes no contribution to the conditional entropy $H([X+\eta]|X)$, and therefore

$$I(X,Y) \;=\; H(Y) - H(\eta|X). \tag{4.58}$$

However, the value of the noise η is independent of the value of X, so $H(\eta|X) = H(\eta)$, which allows us to rewrite Equation 4.58 as

$$I(X,Y) \;=\; H(Y) - H(\eta). \tag{4.59}$$

Comparing this to Equation 4.52 implies that

$$H(Y|X) \;=\; H(\eta), \tag{4.60}$$

so the entropy of the noise is the conditional entropy $H(Y|X)$.

Notice that we use the Greek letter η to represent a single value, and an enlarged version η to represent the random variable.

For the example given in Table 4.2, we can rearrange Equation 4.59 to calculate the entropy of channel noise as

$$
\begin{aligned}
H(\eta) &= H(Y) - I(X,Y) & (4.61) \\
&= 1.99 - 0.509 & (4.62) \\
&= 1.481 \text{ bits.} & (4.63)
\end{aligned}
$$

> **Key point.** In a communication channel with input X and output $Y = X + \eta$, the conditional entropy $H(Y|X)$ is the entropy of the channel noise $H(\eta)$ added to X by the channel.

Schematic Representations of Mutual Information

Historically, mutual information has been represented using Venn diagrams, as shown in Figures 4.4a and 4.4b. The channels represented in these two figures have identical input and output entropies, but they differ in the amount of overlap. In both cases, the input entropy is smaller than the output entropy because the channel adds some noise to each input before it emerges as a corrupted output.

The noisy channel implicit in Figure 4.4a has outputs which have little to do with the corresponding inputs, so this channel does not communicate data accurately. This can be seen from the relatively large proportion $H(Y|X)$ of output entropy $H(Y)$ which is just noise,

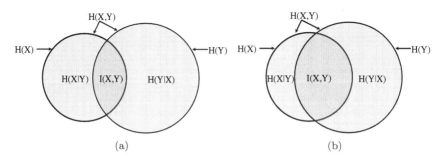

Figure 4.4. Venn diagrams of mutual information $I(X, Y)$ between input X and output Y. Each circle represents the entropy of one variable, and the total area of the three labelled regions represents the joint entropy $H(X, Y) = I(X, Y) + H(X|Y) + H(Y|X)$. The input entropy and output entropy is the same in (a) and (b), but the mutual information in (a) is smaller.

and also from the relatively small proportion of output entropy which is shared with the input entropy $H(X)$. This shared input/output entropy is the mutual information $I(X, Y)$.

In contrast, the less noisy channel implicit in Figure 4.4b has outputs which are largely determined by the corresponding inputs, so this channel does communicate data fairly accurately. This can be seen from the relatively small proportion $H(Y|X)$ of output entropy $H(Y)$ which is just noise, and also from the relatively large proportion of output entropy which is shared with the input entropy $H(X)$, giving the mutual information $I(X, Y)$.

MacKay (2003) [34] showed that some areas in these Venn diagrams can become negative under certain circumstances. A representation which overcomes this problem is shown in Figure 4.5 (used in Jessop (1995) [27] and MacKay (2003) [34]). This representation stresses the fact that the joint entropy acts as a container for all of the other constituent entropies. So, for a given amount of joint entropy, the amount of mutual information depends on the amount of overlap between the input and output entropies.

4.5. Noise and Cross-Talk

In Chapter 2, we interpreted entropy in terms of the number of equally probable input or output values. Shannon also used this interpretation to give an intuitive understanding of the conditional entropies $H(X|Y)$ and $H(Y|X)$. In his proofs, Shannon showed that the inputs (encoded messages) are all equally probable, provided they are sufficiently long.

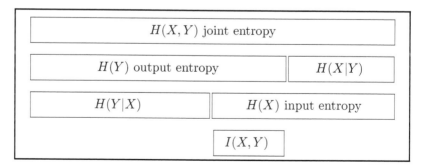

Figure 4.5. The relationship between the input entropy $H(X)$, output entropy $H(Y)$, joint entropy $H(X, Y)$, mutual information $I(X, Y)$, and the conditional entropies $H(X|Y)$ and $H(Y|X)$.

If a communication channel is noisy then there is inevitably a degree of *cross-talk* between input and output. Specifically, each input x_i could result in many different outputs $(y_1, \ldots, y_{m_{y|x}})$, and each output y_j could be the result of many different inputs $(x_1, \ldots, x_{m_{x|y}})$, as shown in the *fan diagram* of Figure 4.6. Shannon showed that the number $m_{y|x}$ of different outputs which could be generated by each input is limited by the channel noise

$$m_{y|x} = 2^{H(\eta)} = 2^{H(Y|X)}. \tag{4.64}$$

Of course, noise can also affect the number $m_{x|y}$ of different inputs that could yield each output:

$$m_{x|y} = 2^{H(X|Y)}. \tag{4.65}$$

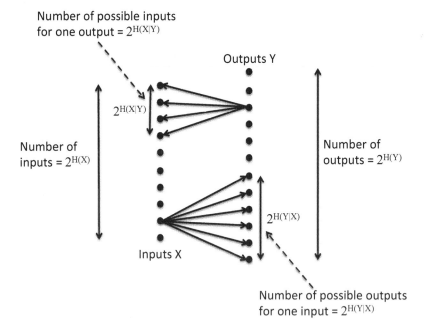

Figure 4.6. A fan diagram shows how channel noise affects the number of possible outputs given a single input, and *vice versa*. If the noise η in the channel output has entropy $H(\eta) = H(Y|X)$ then each input value could yield one of $2^{H(Y|X)}$ equally probable output values. Similarly, if the noise in the channel input has entropy $H(X|Y)$ then each output value could have been caused by one of $2^{H(X|Y)}$ equally probable input values.

We refer to $H(Y|X)$ as the entropy of the channel noise because we are usually interested in estimating the input from an observed output, and the noise η added to the input by the channel has a direct effect on our ability to estimate the input. However, noise can also affect our ability to estimate the output from an observed input. The extent to which noise affects each of these estimates is captured by the two complementary conditional entropies $H(X|Y)$ and $H(Y|X)$.

An alternative, but equivalent, interpretation of this is depicted in Figure 4.7. Because the channel adds noise, the output entropy is usually larger than the input entropy, and this is reflected in the areas of the shaded (outermost) discs in Figures 4.7a and 4.7b. The mutual information represented by the cross-hatched discs appears as part of the input and output entropy (these discs have the same area in both (a) and (b)). However, even though the amount of mutual information within the input and output entropy is the same, the *proportion* of input entropy occupied by the mutual information is relatively large, whereas the proportion of output entropy occupied by the mutual information is relatively small. Consequently, the amount of input noise $H(X|Y)$ is small compared to the output noise $H(Y|X)$.

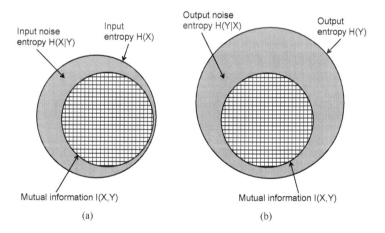

Figure 4.7. Visualising mutual information. The cross-hatched discs represent the mutual information of the same channel. They are the same size in (a) and (b), because they represent the same amount of mutual information.

> **Key point.** The conditional entropy $H(Y|X)$ is the uncertainty of Y after X is observed, and the conditional entropy $H(X|Y)$ is the uncertainty of X after Y is observed.

4.6. Noisy Pictures and Coding Efficiency

In order to make these quantities more tangible, we will assume that the input or source is represented by the binary image X shown in Figure 4.8a, and the output Y is represented by the noisy version of this image, shown in Figure 4.8b.

Because the channel is noisy, each pixel value has some probability of being corrupted. In this example, the channel is a *binary symmetric channel*, in which there is a 10% probability that each source pixel will be changed (either from 0 to 1, or *vice versa*) by the time it reaches the output. The joint probabilities for the four possible input/output pairs are shown in Table 4.3.

In the input image in Figure 4.8a, a proportion 0.724 of the pixels are black (0), and 0.276 of them are white (1), so its entropy is

$$
\begin{aligned}
H(X) &= p(0)\log(1/p(0)) + p(1)\log(1/p(1)) & (4.66) \\
&= 0.724 \times \log(1/0.724) + 0.276 \times \log(1/0.276) & (4.67) \\
&= 0.851 \text{ bits/pixel.} & (4.68)
\end{aligned}
$$

(a) (b)

Figure 4.8. (a) Binary image, in which each pixel is either black or white. This is the input X to a communication channel. (b) Output Y of a noisy communication channel, in which each pixel has had a 10% probability of being changed.

In fact, because adjacent pixels tend to have similar values, this is an over-estimate. So the estimate of 0.851 bits/pixels is really the maximum entropy that these data could possess if data values were independent.

Similarly, in the output image in Figure 4.8b, a proportion 0.679 of the pixels are black, and 0.322 of them are white. If we again ignore the correlations between neighbouring pixel values, its entropy is

$$
\begin{aligned}
H(Y) &= p(0)\log(1/p(0)) + p(1)\log(1/p(1)) & (4.69) \\
&= 0.679 \times \log(1/0.679) + 0.322 \times \log(1/0.322) & (4.70) \\
&= 0.906 \text{ bits/pixel.} & (4.71)
\end{aligned}
$$

Because we know the state of each input pixel and the corresponding output pixel, we can work out the joint probability of each of the four possible input/output pairs of pixel values (i.e. 00, 01, 10, 11), listed in Table 4.3. These joint probabilities can then be used to estimate the joint entropy of the pair of input/output images (i.e. the average Shannon information per pair of input/output pixels),

$$
\begin{aligned}
H(X,Y) &= \sum_{i=1}^{2}\sum_{j=1}^{2} p(x_i, y_j) \log \frac{1}{p(x_i, y_j)} & (4.72) \\
&= p(0,0)\log(1/p(0,0)) + p(0,1)\log(1/p(0,1)) + \\
&\quad p(1,0)\log(1/p(1,0)) + p(1,1)\log(1/p(1,1)), & (4.73)
\end{aligned}
$$

which evaluates to

$$
\begin{aligned}
H(X,Y) &= 0.651 \times \log(1/0.651) + 0.073 \times \log(1/0.073) + \\
&\quad 0.028 \times \log(1/0.028) + 0.249 \times \log(1/0.249) & (4.74) \\
&= 1.32 \text{ bits.} & (4.75)
\end{aligned}
$$

State	Input=0	Input=1
Output=0	$p(0,0) = 0.651$	$p(0,1) = 0.028$
Output=1	$p(1,0) = 0.073$	$p(1,1) = 0.249$

Table 4.3. Joint probabilities for corresponding pixels in input image X and output image Y in Figure 4.8. Each cell represents $p(input, output)$.

We can now work out the mutual information of the input and output images in Figure 4.8:

$$\begin{aligned} I(X,Y) &= H(X) + H(Y) - H(X,Y) & (4.76)\\ &= 0.851 + 0.906 - 1.321 & (4.77)\\ &= 0.436 \text{ bits.} & (4.78) \end{aligned}$$

Thus, each value of the output Y reduces our uncertainty about the corresponding value of the input X by about half of a bit.

Calculating Conditional Entropy

We can use the values calculated above to find the conditional entropy $H(X|Y)$. Before we observe an output y_j, our average uncertainty about the value of the input X is $H(X) = 0.851$ bits. Rearranging Equation 4.55 yields

$$\begin{aligned} H(X|Y) &= H(X) - I(X,Y) & (4.79)\\ &= 0.851 - 0.436 & (4.80)\\ &= 0.415 \text{ bits.} & (4.81) \end{aligned}$$

Thus, after we have observed y_j, our average uncertainty about the value of X is reduced by $I(X,Y)$ bits, to 0.415 bits.

Rearranging Equation 4.52 yields an equation for the conditional entropy $H(Y|X)$ based on output entropy and mutual information, which can be used with estimates based on our data:

$$\begin{aligned} H(Y|X) &= H(Y) - I(X,Y) & (4.82)\\ &= 0.906 - 0.436 & (4.83)\\ &= 0.470 \text{ bits.} & (4.84) \end{aligned}$$

As a check on our informal reasoning in Section 4.4, where we concluded that $H(Y|X) = H(\eta)$, we can also calculate the entropy of the noise added by the channel, and then compare it to the conditional entropy $H(Y|X)$. Given that each pixel's state is flipped with a probability $p = 0.1$ (or, equivalently, that 10% of pixel states are flipped), this amounts to channel noise η with an entropy of

$$
\begin{aligned}
H(\eta) &= p\log(1/p) + (1-p)\log(1/(1-p)) & (4.85)\\
&= 0.1\log(1/0.1) + 0.9\log(1/0.9) & (4.86)\\
&= 0.332 + 0.137 & (4.87)\\
&= 0.469 \text{ bits.} & (4.88)
\end{aligned}
$$

The small difference between Equations 4.84 and 4.88 is due to the fact that the figure of 0.469 bits is based on the known probability that a pixel's value will get flipped, whereas the figure of 0.470 is estimated from data which resulted from flipping pixel values. Just as we would not expect two coin flips to always yield a head and a tail, so we should not expect estimates based on data to be an exact match to estimates based on the known underlying probabilities.

Transmission Efficiency

Given that the output entropy is $H(Y) = 0.906$ bits and that the mutual information is $I(X, Y) = 0.436$ bits, the proportion of output entropy that is also shared by the input is (see Figure 4.7b)

$$
\begin{aligned}
\frac{I(X, Y)}{H(Y)} &= \frac{0.436}{0.906} & (4.89)\\
&= 0.481. & (4.90)
\end{aligned}
$$

This is one measure of how efficiently information is communicated from input to output, and is defined here as the *transmission efficiency*. A transmission efficiency of 0.481 means that almost half of the entropy of the output depends on the input, and the remainder is due to noise within the channel.

4.7. Error Correcting Codes

The examples considered in Chapter 3 showed how it is possible to remove redundancy from a message in order to find a compact (efficient) coding. This is desirable for the noiseless channel assumed for Shannon's source coding theorem. However, for Shannon's noisy channel coding theorem, removing redundancy makes the encoded message vulnerable to the aimless effects of noise. For this reason, it makes sense to add redundancy to the encoded message before it is transmitted, and the particular form of redundancy added allows errors introduced during transmission to be detected and/or corrected. We now consider a basic form of *error correcting code*.

The simplest forms of error correcting codes are called *block codes*. As an example (from Pierce (1961)[40]) of a block code, if we want to communicate a message of 16 binary digits,

$$\mathbf{s} = [1\,1\,0\,1\,0\,0\,1\,1\,0\,1\,0\,1\,1\,0\,0\,0], \tag{4.91}$$

then we can add redundancy as follows. First, we arrange the digits into a 4 × 4 grid,

$$\mathbf{s} = \begin{array}{|c|c|c|c|}
\hline
1 & 1 & 0 & 1 \\
\hline
0 & 0 & 1 & 1 \\
\hline
0 & 1 & 0 & 1 \\
\hline
1 & 0 & 0 & 0 \\
\hline
\end{array}$$

then we check the *parity* within each row and column, and finally, we add an extra *parity binary digit* to obtain the encoded message

$$\mathbf{x} = \begin{array}{|c|c|c|c||c|}
\hline
1 & 1 & 0 & 1 & 1 \\
\hline
0 & 0 & 1 & 1 & 0 \\
\hline
0 & 1 & 0 & 1 & 0 \\
\hline
1 & 0 & 0 & 0 & 1 \\
\hline
\hline
0 & 0 & 1 & 1 & - \\
\hline
\end{array}$$

Notice that if a row/column has an even number of 1s then we add a parity digit of 0, otherwise we add a parity digit of 1. This adds an extra row on the right-hand side and an extra column at the bottom. In this augmented 5 × 5 array, there are an even number of 1s in every row and in every column. If the communication channel only accepts one binary digit at a time then we have to concatenate successive rows, so the encoded message now has 24 binary digits,

$$\mathbf{x} = [1\,1\,0\,1\,1\,0\,0\,1\,1\,0\,0\,1\,0\,1\,0\,1\,0\,0\,0\,1\,0\,0\,1\,1]. \tag{4.92}$$

But how does the addition of parity binary digits help to correct transmission errors?

Suppose the first binary digit of the original encoded message is changed during transmission, so that the message received (with the erroneous zero marked with an asterisk) is

$$
\mathbf{y} =
\begin{array}{|c|c|c|c||c|}
\hline
0^* & 1 & 0 & 1 & 1 \\
\hline
0 & 0 & 1 & 1 & 0 \\
\hline
0 & 1 & 0 & 1 & 0 \\
\hline
1 & 0 & 0 & 0 & 1 \\
\hline\hline
0 & 0 & 1 & 1 & - \\
\hline
\end{array}
$$

In this corrupted message, the parity binary digits in the first row and column no longer tally with the number of 1s. This error can be detected easily because there is no longer an even number of 1s in every row and column. Note that this is true only for the first row and column, whereas all other parity binary digits do tally. In other words, the parity binary digits tell us there is an error, and they also tell us where that error is, making it easy to correct the error.

The parity binary digit is often called a *parity bit*. However, because the value of each parity binary digit is completely determined by the values of the binary digits in the 4×4 grid, each parity binary digit provides zero bits of information in the encoded message. However, if the message is corrupted within a communication channel then each parity digit in the channel output can provide information about the correct state of each binary digit in the message.

In this example, the number of extra parity binary digits was eight, for an original message of 16 binary digits, so we have increased the number of binary digits communicated by a factor of $24/16 = 1.5$. More generally, if we have a message of $m = n \times n$ binary digits which is encoded in this way then the total number of binary digits transmitted would be $(n \times n) + 2n$, which increases the number of binary digits transmitted by a factor of $(n^2 + 2n)/n^2 = 1 + 2/n$. So the parity overhead associated with this strategy shrinks fairly rapidly as the length of the block code increases.

However, we need to remember that a 4×4 block code allows us to correct one error in every 24 (i.e. $4 \times 4 + 8$) binary digits transmitted, whereas an $n \times n$ block code allows us to correct only one error in every $n^2 + 2n$ binary digits transmitted. For example, if the block code length is defined by $n = 20$ then adding parity digits increases the number of binary digits transmitted in each block from $n \times n = 400$ to 440, which is a factor of $440/400 = 1.1$, and allows us to correct only one error in every 440 binary digits transmitted. So, once again, there is a trade-off between the robustness of the encoded message and the number of extra binary digits required to make the message robust.

Redundancy is Good, and Bad

As we have seen from the examples above, data that contains redundant values can be compressed by removing the redundancy. Additionally, if some values occur more often than others then this implies that further compression can be achieved by recoding data so that all recoded values occur equally often. This reduces the amount of data to be transmitted, but it also makes the data more prone to the effects of noise. Images and language are both highly redundant. This is good because it means that most data values are implicit in the rest of the data, which makes each data value robust with respect to the effects of noise. But it is also bad, because we have to process relatively large amounts of data to recover the relatively small amounts of information they contain.

4.8. Capacity of a Noisy Channel

The most general definition of channel capacity for any channel is

$$C = \max_{p(X)} I(X, Y) \text{ bits.} \tag{4.93}$$

This states that channel capacity C is achieved by the distribution $p(X)$ which makes the mutual information $I(X, Y)$ between input and output as large as possible. Using Equation 4.55, we can rewrite Equation 4.93:

$$C = \max_{p(X)} H(X) - H(X|Y) \text{ bits.} \tag{4.94}$$

If there is no noise then $H(X|Y) = 0$, so this reduces to the definition of channel capacity for noiseless channels (Equation 3.2).

4.9. Shannon's Noisy Channel Coding Theorem

As discussed at the end of Chapter 1, all practical communication channels are noisy. To take a trivial example, the voice signal coming out of a telephone is not a perfect copy of the speaker's voice signal, because various electrical components introduce spurious bits of noise into the telephone system.

As we have seen, the effects of noise can be reduced by using error correcting codes. These codes reduce errors, but they also reduce the rate at which information is communicated. More generally, any method which reduces the effects of noise also reduces the rate at which information can be communicated.

Taking this line of reasoning to its logical conclusion seems to imply that the only way to communicate information with zero error is to reduce the effective rate of information transmission to zero, and in Shannon's day this was widely believed to be true. Then Shannon proved that information can be communicated, with vanishingly small error, at a rate which is limited only by the channel capacity.

Before quoting Shannon's theorem, we should note that he used the word 'equivocation' to mean the average uncertainty that remains regarding the value of the input after the output is observed, i.e. the conditional entropy $H(X|Y)$.

Now we give Shannon's *fundamental theorem for a discrete channel with noise*, also known as the *second fundamental coding theorem*, and as *Shannon's noisy channel coding theorem*[50]:

> Let a discrete channel have the capacity C and a discrete source the entropy per second H. If $H \leq C$ there exists a coding system such that the output of the source can be transmitted over the channel with an arbitrarily small frequency of errors (or an arbitrarily small equivocation). If $H \geq C$ it is possible to encode the source so that the equivocation is less than $H - C + \epsilon$ where ϵ is arbitrarily small. There is no method of encoding which gives an equivocation less than $H - C$.

In essence, Shannon's theorem states that it is possible to use a communication channel to communicate information with a low error rate ϵ (epsilon), at a rate arbitrarily close to the channel capacity of C bits/s, but it is not possible to communicate information at a rate greater than C bits/s.

The Noisy Typewriter

As an example of Shannon's theorem in action, we can make use of the noisy typewriter, shown in Figure 4.9. As its name suggests, the noisy typewriter produces letters (outputs) that are unreliably related to the (input) letter typed. Specifically, each typed letter produces one of three letters that are near (alphabetically) to the typed letter. For example, if the letter B is typed then the output could be A, B or C, and each of these outputs occurs with a probability of 1/3. Similarly, if C is typed then the output could be B, C or D, and if D is typed then the output could be C, D or E, and so on (for reasons that will become apparent, we use the space character as the 26th letter, and Z as the 27th letter). The problem is that any output (e.g. C) could have been produced by any one of three inputs (e.g. B, C, or D), so the inputs are *confusable* given any particular output.

However, we can make this particular noisy communication channel communicate information without any error (i.e. with $\epsilon = 0$). If we restrict the inputs to every third letter in the alphabet, starting at B, then each input yields an output which is one of three letters. But because each output triplet contains three unique letters (i.e. the triplets are disjoint), each input message gives rise to a non-confusable set of output letters. The decoding method consists of a look-up table

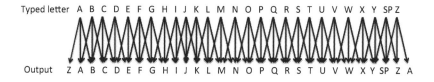

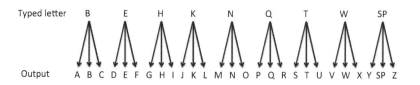

Figure 4.9. The noisy typewriter. Top: Each typed letter yields one of three possible letters. For example, output C could have been produced by typing B, C or D. Bottom: To ensure that outputs are not confusable, we use only every third letter in the alphabet. SP = space, which is treated as the 26th letter here.

which maps each disjoint output triplet (e.g. [A, B, C]) to a unique input (e.g. B). For example, if the channel output is

XFZAEYXDU

then by using the look-up table we can recover the original message:

WE BE WET.

Note that we have rearranged the final triplet in our table to form [Y SPACE Z], so that we have access to the space character.

Using this code, there are nine possible inputs. If all inputs are used equally often, and if we type at a rate of one letter per second, then the entropy of the channel input is

$$H(X) = \log 9 \tag{4.95}$$
$$= 3.17 \text{ bits/s}. \tag{4.96}$$

Again, if all nine inputs are used equally often then all 27 outputs will also occur equally often, so the output entropy is

$$H(Y) = \log 27 \tag{4.97}$$
$$= 4.76 \text{ bits/s}. \tag{4.98}$$

For each typed letter, there are three equally probable outputs, so the average uncertainty in Y given X is

$$H(Y|X) = \log 3 \tag{4.99}$$
$$= 1.59 \text{ bits/s}, \tag{4.100}$$

which we can recognise as the entropy of the channel noise η. From these entropies, we can work out that the mutual information is

$$I(X,Y) = H(Y) - H(Y|X) \tag{4.101}$$
$$= 4.76 - 1.59 \tag{4.102}$$
$$= 3.17 \text{ bits/s}. \tag{4.103}$$

We can confirm this as follows. Using this code, transmission is free of errors, so the average uncertainty $H(X|Y)$ in the input given an output is zero. This allows us to calculate the mutual information as

$$I(X,Y) \quad = \quad H(X) - H(X|Y) \tag{4.104}$$

$$= \quad 3.17 - 0.00 \tag{4.105}$$

$$= \quad 3.17 \, \text{bits/s.} \tag{4.106}$$

Also, we know that the mutual information cannot be larger than the input entropy, so if the mutual information is the same as the input entropy then it follows that the channel capacity equals the input entropy. In other words, of all the possible input distributions, the uniform distribution of inputs used here is guaranteed to maximise the mutual information of this particular channel, which (according to Equation 4.93) is the channel capacity $C = 3.17 \, \text{bits/s}$. In general, provided the entropy of the noise distribution is fixed (e.g. a binary symmetric channel), a uniform input distribution is guaranteed to maximise the mutual information of a discrete noisy channel.

We could object that this typewriter is not much use, because it has only 9 letters. But, by using the code described above, we have turned a noisy device into a reliable communication channel. Additionally, if we treat this noisy typewriter as a communication channel then we can encode any message we choose, and then transmit it through this channel with 100% reliability. For example, if our message uses 27 equally probable letters then we need $\log 27 = 4.75$ binary digits to represent each letter. Thus, given that each typed letter represents 3.17 bits, we could use two typed letters to transmit each letter in our message. In this way, we have effectively transformed a noisy typewriter into a fully functional error-free communication channel.

In this example, the error rate is zero. However, what makes the noisy coding theorem remarkable is that Shannon proved the error rate can be reduced to an arbitrarily small value for *any* data set.

4.10. Why the Theorem is True

Describing Shannon's proof in detail would require more mathematical tools than we have available here, so this is a brief summary which gives a flavour of his proof.

Consider a discrete or continuous channel with a fixed amount of channel noise and capacity C. We have a set of N messages $\mathbf{s}_1, \ldots, \mathbf{s}_N$ which have been encoded to produce inputs $\mathbf{x}_1, \ldots, \mathbf{x}_N$ such that the entropy H of these inputs is less than the channel capacity C. Now imagine that we construct a bizarre codebook in which each randomly chosen input $\mathbf{x}_i$ gets interpreted as a fixed, but randomly chosen, output $\mathbf{y}_i$. By chance, some outputs will get assigned the same, or very similar, inputs, and *vice versa*, leading to a degree of cross-talk. Consequently, when we use this codebook to decode outputs, we are bound to misclassify a proportion of them. This proportion is the error rate of the codebook. We then repeat this madness until we have recorded the error rate of all possible codebooks.

Shannon proved that, provided $H \leq C$, when averaged over all possible codebooks, the average error approaches zero as the length of the inputs $\mathbf{x}$ increases. Consequently, if we make use of long inputs, so that the *average* error rate ϵ is small, then *there must exist at least one codebook which produces an error as small as* ϵ. Notice that if all codebooks produce the same error rate ϵ then the average error rate is also ϵ, but if just one codebook has an error greater than ϵ then at least one codebook has an error rate smaller than ϵ.

As Pierce (1961)[40] notes, some people regard the logic which underpins Shannon's proof as weird, but such an outrageous proof also gives some insight into the distinctive mind which created it.

Key point. When averaged over all possible codebooks, if the average error rate is ϵ then there must exist at least one codebook which produces an error as small as ϵ.

4.11. Summary

Mutual information is a subtle concept, so it is important to understand it properly. One way to think of it is as the average amount of uncertainty in the value of one variable that is eliminated when the value of another variable is known. When considered in terms of communication channels, it is the amount of uncertainty in the value of the input that is eliminated when the value of the output is known.

After an informal account of mutual information, we considered the inputs and outputs of a noisy channel for the case of a binary image and represented its joint probability distribution in a 2×2 table. This was used to calculate the entropies of the input, output, and joint distribution, which were then used to calculate the mutual information of the noisy channel.

We also explored a simple form of error correcting code, which works by adding redundancy to encoded messages. However, we found that such error correcting codes always require an increase in the total number of binary digits, which reduces the amount of information per binary digit transmitted.

We then examined Shannon's noisy channel coding theorem. An example of this theorem 'in action' was provided in the form of a noisy typewriter. Finally, we considered why Shannon's noisy channel coding theorem is true.

Chapter 5

Entropy of Continuous Variables

All things physical are information-theoretic in origin.
Wheeler J, 1990.

5.1. Introduction

So far, we have considered entropy and mutual information in the context of discrete random variables (e.g. coin flipping). However, we also need a definition of entropy for continuous random variables (e.g. temperature). In many cases, results obtained with discrete variables can easily be extended to continuous variables, but information theory is not one of those cases.

Even though Shannon derived a measure of entropy for continuous variables from the definition used for discrete variables, MacKay (2003)[34] simply notes that the equation which defines continuous entropy is illegal. Others effectively ignore the problem by considering entropy only in the context of discrete variables. None of these are very helpful if our data consist of samples from a continuous variable, such as daily temperature or the heights of 5,000 people, where we wish to estimate the entropy of these data (as in Figure 5.1). Fortunately, there are ways to generalise the discrete definition of entropy to obtain sensible measures of entropy for continuous variables[26;36;39;41;53].

In this chapter we will follow the historical development of entropy for continuous variables. Thus, we begin with a seemingly innocuous definition (which leads to infinities), before considering definitions which allow entropy to be calculated.

5.2. The Trouble With Entropy

To estimate the entropy of any variable, it is necessary to know the probability associated with each of its possible values. For continuous variables this amounts to knowing its *probability density function* or *pdf*, which we refer to here as its distribution (see Appendices D and E). We can use a pdf as a starting point for estimating the entropy of a continuous variable by making a histogram of a large number of measured values. However, this reveals a fundamental problem, as we shall see below.

In order to make a histogram of any continuous quantity X, such as human height, we need to define the width Δx of bins in the histogram. We then categorise each measured value of X into one histogram bin, as in Figure 5.1. Then the probability that a randomly chosen value of X is in a given bin is simply the proportion of values of X in that bin (see Appendix D). The entropy of this histogram is then given by the average surprisal of its bins (here indexed with i),

$$H(X^\Delta) = \sum_i (\text{prob } X \text{ is in } i\text{th bin}) \times \log \frac{1}{\text{prob } X \text{ is in } i\text{th bin}}, \quad (5.1)$$

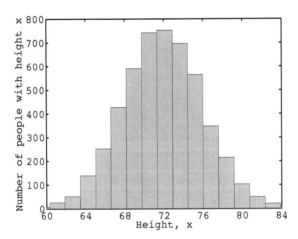

Figure 5.1. A histogram of $n = 5,000$ hypothetical values of human height X, measured in inches. This histogram was constructed by dividing values of X into a number of intervals or bins, where each bin has width Δx, and then counting how many values are in each bin.

where X^Δ indicates that we are dealing with a continuous variable which has been discretised using a histogram in which each bin has a width equal to Δx. We have purposely not specified the number of bins; in principle, it can be infinite. In practice, it suffices to simply use enough bins to include all of the values in our data set, as in Figure 5.1.

The probability that a randomly chosen value of X is in the ith bin is given by the area a_i of the ith bin, expressed as a proportion of the total area A of all bins. A bin which contains n_i values has an area equal to its height n_i times its width Δx,

$$a_i \;=\; n_i \times \Delta x, \tag{5.2}$$

so that

$$\text{the probability that } X \text{ is in the } i\text{th bin} = a_i/A, \tag{5.3}$$

where

$$A \;=\; \sum_i a_i. \tag{5.4}$$

In effect, the ith bin area in this *normalised histogram* is the proportion

$$P_i \;=\; a_i/A \tag{5.5}$$

of the total histogram area. It will prove useful later to note that the sum of these proportions (i.e. total area) of this normalised histogram is necessarily equal to 1:

$$\sum_i P_i \;=\; 1. \tag{5.6}$$

If the ith bin in this normalised histogram has height $p(x_i)$ and width Δx then its area (height times width) can be obtained from

$$P_i \;=\; p(x_i)\,\Delta x, \tag{5.7}$$

which allows us to rewrite Equation 5.1 more succinctly as

$$H(X^{\Delta}) = \sum_i P_i \log \frac{1}{P_i}. \tag{5.8}$$

Given that the probability P_i corresponds to the area of the ith column, we can interpret the height $p(x_i) = P_i/\Delta x$ of the ith column as a *probability density*. Substituting Equation 5.7 in Equation 5.8 yields

$$H(X^{\Delta}) = \sum_i p(x_i)\Delta x \times \log \frac{1}{p(x_i)\Delta x}. \tag{5.9}$$

However, given that the final term can be written as

$$\log \frac{1}{p(x_i)\,\Delta x} = \log \frac{1}{p(x_i)} + \log \frac{1}{\Delta x}, \tag{5.10}$$

we can rewrite Equation 5.9 as

$$H(X^{\Delta}) = \left[\sum_i p(x_i)\,\Delta x \log \frac{1}{p(x_i)}\right] + \left[\log \frac{1}{\Delta x}\sum_i P_i\right],$$

where, according to Equation 5.6, the sum $\sum P_i = 1$, so that

$$H(X^{\Delta}) = \left[\sum_i p(x_i)\,\Delta x \log \frac{1}{p(x_i)}\right] + \log \frac{1}{\Delta x}. \tag{5.11}$$

Thus, as the bin width approaches zero, the first term on the right becomes an integral, but the second term diverges to infinity:

$$H(X) = \left[\int_{x=-\infty}^{\infty} p(x)\log \frac{1}{p(x)}\,dx\right] + \infty. \tag{5.12}$$

And there's the rub. For a continuous variable, as the bin width Δx approaches zero, so $1/\Delta x$, and therefore $\log(1/\Delta x)$, and therefore entropy of X, diverges to infinity.

One consequence of this is that the entropy of a continuous variable increases with the precision of our measurements (which determines the bin width), as shown in Figure 5.2. This makes sense if we bear in mind that increasing the precision of the measurements ought to increase the information associated with each measurement. For example, being told that a table is measured as five feet wide and that the device used to measure its width had a precision of ± 0.1 inch provides more information than being told that the measurement device had a precision of ± 1 inch. In practice, it means that we must always take account of the bin width when comparing the entropies of two different continuous variables.

As we shall see in Section 6.4, the problem of infinities disappears for quantities which involve the difference between two entropies, such as mutual information.

Key point. The estimated entropy $H(X^\triangle)$ of a (discretised) continuous variable increases as the width of bins in that variable's histogram decreases.

5.3. Differential Entropy

Equation 5.12 states that the entropy of a continuous variable is infinite, which is true, but not very helpful. If all continuous variables have infinite entropy then distributions that are obviously different have the same (infinite) entropy.

A measure of entropy called the *differential entropy* of a continuous variable ignores this infinity; it is defined as

$$H_{dif}(X) \;=\; \int_{x=-\infty}^{\infty} p(x) \log \frac{1}{p(x)} \, dx, \tag{5.13}$$

where the subscript dif denotes differential entropy (although this is not used where the intended meaning is unambiguous). Thus, the differential entropy is that part of the entropy which includes only the 'interesting' part of Equation 5.12.

Key point. The entropy of a continuous variable is infinite because it includes a constant term which is infinite. If we ignore this term then we obtain the *differential entropy* $H_{dif}(X) = \mathrm{E}[\log(1/p(x))]$, the mean value of $\log(1/p(X))$.

Calculating Differential Entropy

In practical terms, given a large sample of values from an unknown distribution $p(X)$, how can we estimate the differential entropy of these data? Our first step is to construct a histogram, on the assumption that this is an approximation to an underlying continuous distribution $p(X)$. Using this histogram, the differential entropy $H_{dif}(X)$ can then be estimated from a discrete approximation to Equation 5.13:

$$H_{dif}(X^\triangle) \approx \sum_i p(x_i) \, \Delta x \log \frac{1}{p(x_i)}. \tag{5.14}$$

From Equation 5.7, we can substitute $P_i = p(x_i) \, \Delta x$ to obtain

$$H_{dif}(X^\triangle) \approx \sum_i P_i \log \frac{\Delta x}{P_i} \tag{5.15}$$

$$= \sum_i P_i \log \frac{1}{P_i} + \sum_i P_i \log \Delta x \tag{5.16}$$

$$= \left[\sum_i P_i \log \frac{1}{P_i} \right] - \log \frac{1}{\Delta x}. \tag{5.17}$$

From Equation 5.8, we can recognise the first term on the right as $H(X^\triangle)$, so that the differential entropy in Equation 5.13 can be approximated as

$$H_{dif}(X) \approx H(X^\triangle) - \log \frac{1}{\Delta x}. \tag{5.18}$$

Estimates of differential entropy $H_{dif}(X^\triangle)$ (calculated using Equation 5.17) are shown in Figure 5.2 together with estimates of entropy $H(X^\triangle)$ (calculated using Equation 5.8), for comparison.

Note that these data are drawn from a *Gaussian distribution* (see Section 5.6 and Appendix G). This particular Gaussian distribution has a standard deviation equal to one, which implies a differential entropy of $H_{dif}(X) = 2.05$ bits (see Equation 5.47). Thus, for the large data set (of 1 million values) and the 'reasonable' bin widths in Figures 5.2b and 5.2c, Equation 5.17 provides a good approximation to the known value of differential entropy[11].

Substituting Equation 5.14 in Equation 5.11, the discretised version of X has a predicted entropy of

$$H(X^\Delta) \approx H_{dif}(X) + \log \frac{1}{\Delta x}, \qquad (5.19)$$

which is in good agreement with the values in in Figure 5.2.

An alternative approach consists of fitting a parametric function (e.g. Gaussian) to the data and then using an analytic expression to find the differential entropy of the fitted function (e.g. Equation 5.47). This parametric method is related to the more general *kernel estimation methods*. For more recent advances, see Nemenman *et al* (2002)[36].

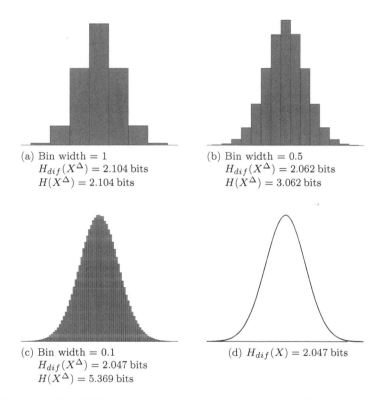

(a) Bin width = 1
$H_{dif}(X^\Delta) = 2.104$ bits
$H(X^\Delta) = 2.104$ bits

(b) Bin width = 0.5
$H_{dif}(X^\Delta) = 2.062$ bits
$H(X^\Delta) = 3.062$ bits

(c) Bin width = 0.1
$H_{dif}(X^\Delta) = 2.047$ bits
$H(X^\Delta) = 5.369$ bits

(d) $H_{dif}(X) = 2.047$ bits

Figure 5.2. (a-c) Effect of histogram bin width Δx on the differential entropy $H_{dif}(X^\Delta)$ and entropy $H(X^\Delta)$ of 1 million samples from the Gaussian distribution shown in (d), which has a variance of one and a differential entropy $H_{dif}(X) = 2.05$ bits (see Equation 5.47). $H_{dif}(X^\Delta)$ values were estimated using Equation 5.17, and $H(X^\Delta)$ values were estimated using Equation 5.8.

5.4. Under-Estimating Entropy

This section can be skipped by readers unfamiliar with Bayes' rule[52] (see Appendix F). Whether a variable X is continuous or discrete, using the relative frequency (i.e. proportion) of observed values to estimate the probability of that value yields biased estimates of entropy. For clarity, we will assume X is discrete and has m possible values, but the analysis here applies to both discrete and continuous variables.

In this section only, we will use P_i to represent the probability of the ith value of X, and $\hat{P}_i$ to represent the estimated value (i.e. relative frequency) of P_i. For reasons we will not discuss, $\hat{P}_i$ is called the *maximum likelihood estimate* (MLE) of P_i. We will make a distinction between the true entropy based on P_i values

$$H(X) \quad = \quad \sum_{i=1}^{m} P_i \log \frac{1}{P_i} \tag{5.20}$$

and the (maximum likelihood) estimate of entropy based on $\hat{P}_i$ values

$$H_{MLE}(X) \quad = \quad \sum_{i=1}^{m} \hat{P}_i \log \frac{1}{\hat{P}_i}. \tag{5.21}$$

Each estimate $\hat{P}_i$ implicitly assumes a uniform prior probability distribution for P_i values (i.e. all values of P_i are *a priori* equally probable). However, because entropy is a logarithmic function of P_i, this uniform prior imposes a non-uniform prior on entropy. In other words, by assuming a uniform prior for P_i, we implicitly assume that some values of entropy are more probable than others, which is an unwarranted assumption in this case.

It can be shown that the resultant biased estimate of entropy H_{MLE} based on $\hat{P}_i$ values tends to be smaller than the true entropy, and that this bias is reduced by using a uniform prior distribution for entropy[39].

Key point. If a variable X has entropy H, and if each value of the probability distribution $p(X)$ is estimated as a relative frequency then the resultant estimated entropy H_{MLE} tends to be smaller than H.

5.5. Properties of Differential Entropy

Here, we explore what happens to the entropy of a continuous variable X when it is transformed to another variable Y. In subsequent sections, we shall see how this can be used to transform a variable X so that each value of Y provides as much information as possible.

Entropy of Transformed Variables

Consider two continuous variables X and Y which are related by a function g:

$$y = g(x). \tag{5.22}$$

If the function g is *monotonic* then each value of X gets mapped to a unique value of Y, and it can be shown that the entropies of X and Y are related by

$$H_{dif}(Y) = H_{dif}(X) + \mathrm{E}[\log |dY/dX|], \tag{5.23}$$

where the vertical bars indicate absolute value.

Multiplying by a Constant

The entropy of a discrete variable does not depend on the values of that variable but only on the number of values and the probability that each value occurs. For example, doubling all values of a die increases the range of values (from 1–6 to 2–12), but it does not alter the entropy of the resultant histogram of observed values (see Section 2.5). However, unlike a discrete variable, the entropy of a continuous variable does depend on the range of values.

For example, if X is multiplied by a constant c so that $Y = cX$ then the derivative

$$dY/dX = c, \tag{5.24}$$

is constant, and therefore

$$\mathrm{E}[\log |dY/dX|] = \log |c|. \tag{5.25}$$

119

Substituting this into Equation 5.23,

$$H_{dif}(Y) \quad = \quad H_{dif}(X) + \log|c| \text{ bits.} \tag{5.26}$$

For example, if $Y = 2X$ then

$$dY/dX \quad = \quad 2, \tag{5.27}$$

and therefore

$$E[\log|dY/dX|] \quad = \quad 1, \tag{5.28}$$

so that

$$H_{dif}(Y) \quad = \quad H_{dif}(X) + 1 \text{ bit.} \tag{5.29}$$

Thus, even though Y is completely determined by X, Y contains one more bit of information than X. How can this be? This apparent paradox is related to the difficulty in defining continuous entropy. If we take a pragmatic approach and simply assume that finite measurement precision translates to a fixed width of measurement 'bins' then, by doubling the range of X, we have doubled the number of bins in the measured range, giving one more bit of information.

> **Key point.** Multiplying a continuous variable X by a constant c changes the range of values, which changes the entropy of X by an amount $\log|c|$.

Adding a Constant

If $Y = X + c$ then the distribution $p(Y)$ of Y values is the same as the distribution $p(X)$ of X values, but it is shifted along the x-axis by a distance c so that $p(Y) = p(X + c)$. As in the previous examples, we evaluate the derivative

$$dY/dX \quad = \quad (dX + c)/dX \tag{5.30}$$

$$= \quad 1, \tag{5.31}$$

and therefore

$$\text{E}[\log |dY/dX|] \quad = \quad 0. \tag{5.32}$$

Substituting this into Equation 5.23 implies that if $Y = X + c$ then

$$H_{dif}(Y) \quad = \quad H_{dif}(X) \text{ bits.} \tag{5.33}$$

Thus, adding a constant to X has no effect on its entropy.

Key point. Adding a constant c to a continuous variable X has no effect on its entropy.

5.6. Maximum Entropy Distributions

The reason we are interested in maximum entropy distributions is because entropy equates to information, so a maximum entropy distribution is also a *maximum information distribution*. In other words, the amount of information conveyed by each value from a maximum entropy distribution is as large as it can possibly be. This matters because if we have some quantity S with a particular distribution $p(S)$ and we wish to transmit S through a communication channel, then we had better transform (encode) it into another variable X with a maximum entropy distribution $p(X)$ before transmitting it. An example of how the fly's eye does just this is given in Section 7.7.

Specifically, given a variable S, which we wish to transmit along a communication channel by encoding S as another variable X, what distribution should X have to ensure each transmitted value of X conveys as much information as possible? For example, if S is the outcome of throwing a pair of dice then the distribution of S is shown in Figure 3.2b, which is clearly not uniform. More importantly, if we simply encode the outcome values S between 2 and 12 as their corresponding binary numbers X, then the distribution of 0s and 1s in the resultant set of codewords is far from uniform. However, if S is encoded as a binary variable X using Huffman coding then the distribution of 0s and 1s in the resultant set of codewords is almost uniform (i.e. the proportion of 0s and 1s is about the same). Of all the possible distributions of 0s and 1s, the uniform distribution has maximum entropy, and is therefore a *maximum entropy distribution.* Thus, Huffman coding implicitly encodes iid data as a maximum entropy distribution, which is consistent with the fact that it provides almost one bit per binary digit (i.e. it provides a fairly efficient code).

In contrast, for continuous variables, the distribution with maximum entropy is not necessarily the uniform distribution. We consider three types of continuous variable, each of which has a different particular constraint but is free to vary in every other respect. These constraints are:

1. fixed upper and lower bounds;

2. fixed mean, with all values greater than or equal to zero;

3. fixed variance (e.g. power).

Each of these constraints is associated with a different maximum entropy distribution. For the constraints above, the maximum entropy distributions are (1) uniform, (2) exponential, and (3) Gaussian.

Entropy of a Uniform Distribution

Consider a random variable X with fixed upper and lower bounds, distributed uniformly between zero and a so that the probability density

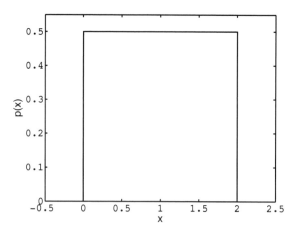

Figure 5.3. A uniform distribution with a range between zero and two has an area of one $(= 2 \times 0.5)$, and an entropy of $\log 2 = 1$ bit.

$p(x)$ has the same value for all values of X, for example as in Figure 5.3. The width times the height of $p(X)$ must be one, so $p(x) \times a = 1$, and so the probability density function of a variable with a uniform distribution is

$$p(x) = 1/a. \tag{5.34}$$

The probability density $p(x)$ of x is therefore equal to $1/a$ between zero and a, and equal to zero elsewhere. By convention, a random variable X with a uniform distribution which is non-zero between zero and a is written as

$$X \sim U(0, a). \tag{5.35}$$

The entropy of this uniform distribution is therefore

$$H_{dif}(X) \quad = \quad \int_{x=0}^{a} p(x) \log a \, dx \tag{5.36}$$

$$= \quad \log a \text{ bits.} \tag{5.37}$$

This result is intuitively consistent with the entropy of discrete variables. For example, in the case of a discrete variable, we know from Equation 2.69 that doubling the number of possible outcome values increases the entropy of that variable by one bit (i.e. by $\log 2$ bits). Similarly, for a continuous variable, doubling the range of continuous values effectively doubles the number of possible outcome values (provided we are content to accept that this number is infinitely large for a continuous variable) and also increases the entropy of that continuous variable by one bit. Thus, if the range of X values is increased from a to $b = 2a$ then the entropy of $Y = 2X$ should increase by exactly one bit in relation to the entropy of X, i.e.

$$H_{dif}(Y) \quad = \quad \log b \tag{5.38}$$

$$= \quad \log 2a \tag{5.39}$$

$$= \quad \log a + 1 \text{ bits,} \tag{5.40}$$

which is the expected result.

More importantly, it can be shown[41] that if a variable has a fixed lower and upper bound (e.g. zero and a) then *no probability distribution can have a larger entropy than the uniform distribution.*

> **Key point.** Given a continuous variable X with a fixed range (e.g. between zero and two), the distribution with maximum entropy is the uniform distribution.

An odd feature of the entropy of continuous distributions is that they can have zero or *negative entropy*. For example, if X has a range of $a = 1$ then $H_{dif}(X) = 0$, and if $a = 0.5$ then $H_{dif}(X) = -1$. One way to think about this is to interpret the entropy of a uniform distribution relative to the entropy of a distribution with an entropy of $H_{dif}(X) = 0$ (i.e. with a range of $a = 1$). If $a = 2$ then this distribution has an entropy which is $H_{dif}(X) = 1$ bit larger than the entropy of a distribution with $a = 1$. And if $a = 0.5$ then the distribution has an entropy which is one bit smaller than that of a distribution with $a = 1$. Similar remarks apply to the entropy of any continuous distribution.

Entropy of an Exponential Distribution

An exponential distribution is defined by one parameter, which is its *mean, μ*. The probability density function of a variable with an

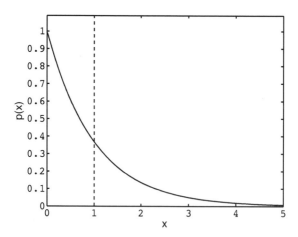

Figure 5.4. An exponential distribution with a mean of $\mu = 1$ (indicated by the vertical dashed line) has an entropy of $H_{dif}(X) = 1.44$ bits.

exponential distribution is

$$p(x) = \begin{cases} \frac{1}{\mu} e^{-\frac{x}{\mu}} & x \geq 0 \\ 0 & x < 0, \end{cases} \qquad (5.41)$$

as shown in Figure 5.4 for $\mu = 1$. By convention, a random variable X with an exponential distribution which has a mean of μ is written as

$$X \sim \exp(\mu). \qquad (5.42)$$

It can be shown[41] that the entropy of an exponential distribution with mean μ is

$$H_{dif}(X) = \log e\mu \text{ bits.} \qquad (5.43)$$

More importantly, if we know nothing about a variable except that it is positive and that its mean value is μ then the distribution of X which has maximum entropy is the exponential distribution.

Key point. Given a continuous positive variable X which has a mean μ, but is otherwise unconstrained, the distribution with maximum entropy is the exponential distribution.

Entropy of a Gaussian Distribution

A Gaussian distribution is defined by two parameters, its *mean* μ and its *variance* v, which is the square of its *standard deviation* σ, so $v = \sigma^2$. (See Figure 5.5 and Appendix G.) The probability density function of a variable with a Gaussian distribution is

$$p(x) = \frac{1}{\sigma\sqrt{2\pi}} e^{-\frac{(x-\mu)^2}{2\sigma^2}}, \qquad (5.44)$$

where the mean determines the location of the peak of the probability distribution, and the variance, which is the average squared difference between x and the mean,

$$v = \mathrm{E}[(x - \mu)^2], \qquad (5.45)$$

determines how spread out the Gaussian distribution is. By convention, a random variable X with a Gaussian distribution which has mean μ and variance v is written as

$$X \ \sim \ N(\mu, v). \tag{5.46}$$

It can be shown[41] that the entropy of a Gaussian variable is

$$
\begin{aligned}
H_{dif}(X) \ &= \ 1/2 \log 2\pi e \sigma^2 & (5.47) \\
&= \ 1/2 \log 2\pi e + \log \sigma & (5.48) \\
&= \ 2.05 + \log \sigma \text{ bits.} & (5.49)
\end{aligned}
$$

Given that $\log 1 = 0$, a Gaussian distribution with a standard deviation of $\sigma = 1$ has an entropy of 2.05 bits. If X is constrained to have a fixed variance σ^2 (which equates to power in terms of physics) then it can be shown[41] that *no probability distribution has larger entropy than the Gaussian distribution*.

Key point. Given a continuous variable X which has a variance σ^2, but is otherwise unconstrained, the distribution with maximum entropy is the Gaussian distribution.

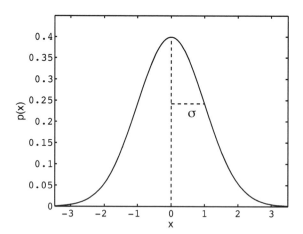

Figure 5.5. A Gaussian distribution with a mean of $\mu = 0$ and a standard deviation of $\sigma = 1$ (indicated by the horizontal dashed line), has an entropy of $H_{dif} = 2.05$ bits.

Why Information Looks Like Pure Noise

One particularly intriguing consequence of the final result above is that in order for a signal to carry as much information as possible, it should be indistinguishable from pure noise.

Most physical systems that generate a signal have limits defined by the amount of available energy per second, which amounts to a power limitation, and this, in turn, corresponds exactly to a limit on the variance of a signal. We already know that a signal with a fixed variance carries as much information as possible only if it is Gaussian, which is why it is desirable to make power-limited signals have a Gaussian distribution. Thus, when we measure some power-limited quantity, like the voice on a telephone, we should recode it into a signal with a Gaussian distribution in order to convey as much information as possible for each watt of power expended. But what about the noise that inevitably gets added to that signal?

Noise usually consists of a mixture of unwanted signals from other sources, and the *central limit theorem* guarantees that such mixtures tend to be Gaussian (see Appendix G). Consequently, when our recoded Gaussian signal gets corrupted by Gaussian noise, it yields a (signal plus noise) measurement with a Gaussian distribution of values.

So, when a neurophysiologist measures the output of brain cells, he does not complain if his recordings look like pure Gaussian noise, because that is precisely what Shannon would predict of a power-limited system which communicates information as efficiently as possible.

5.7. Making Sense of Differential Entropy

Differential entropy is a peculiar concept, inasmuch as it appears to have no meaning when considered in isolation. The fact that a variable has a definite amount of differential entropy tells us almost nothing of interest. In particular, knowing the amount of differential entropy of a variable does not place any limit on how much information that variable can convey (because each value of every continuous variable can convey an infinite amount of information). This stands in stark contrast to the case for a discrete variable, where entropy determines precisely how much information it can convey. However, given that the accuracy of every measurement is limited by noise, this measurement noise places a strict upper limit on the information-carrying capacity of all continuous variables. Thus, even though each value of a continuous variable can, in principle, convey infinite information, the amount of information it conveys in practice depends on the accuracy of our measurements. In effect, measurement noise divides up the range of probabilities of a continuous variable into a finite number of discrete intervals; the number of intervals increases as the measurement noise decreases. The exact consequences of this discretisation of continuous variables by measurement noise will be examined in more detail in Section 7.3.

> **Key point**. Noise limits the amount of information conveyed by a continuous variable and, to all intents and purposes, transforms it into a discrete variable with m discriminable values, where m decreases as noise increases.

5.8. What is Half a Bit of Information?

If a variable has a uniform distribution then one bit halves our range of uncertainty about its value, just as it halves the number of possible routes in Figure 1.2. However, we often encounter fractions of a bit. So, what does it mean to have, say, half a bit of information?

We can find out what a fraction of a bit means by copying the recipe we use for whole bits. For clarity, we assume that the variable X has a uniform distribution and that we know nothing about which value X has. For example, the distribution of the 8-sided die shown in Figure 2.7b has an entropy of three bits, which corresponds to an initial uncertainty range of 1 or 100%. If we are given $H = 2$ bits of information about the value of X then this reduces our range of uncertainty by a factor of $2^H = 2^2 = 4$, so our uncertainty about the value of a variable is one quarter as big as it was before receiving these two bits. Because the die has eight sides, this would mean that we now know the outcome is one of only two possible values (i.e. 1/4 of 8). More generally, if we treat our initial uncertainty as 1 (or 100%) then this implies that our *residual uncertainty* is $U = 1/4$ (or 25%), as

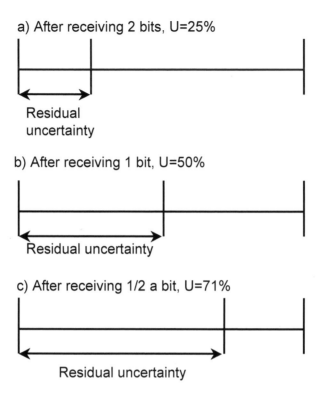

Figure 5.6. Residual uncertainty U. If we have no information about the location of a point on a line of length 1 then our initial uncertainty is $U = 1$. (a) After receiving 2 bits, we know which quarter contains the point, but we do not know where it is within that quarter, so $U = 1/4$.   (b) After receiving 1 bit, we know which half contains the point, so our residual uncertainty is $U = 1/2$.   (c) After receiving 1/2 a bit, we know the point lies within a region containing 0.71 of the line, so our residual uncertainty is $U = 0.71$.

shown in Figure 5.6. Note that the term residual uncertainty is unique to this book.

Initially, our uncertainty spanned the whole line, which has a length of one. After receiving two bits, the region depicting the residual uncertainty has a length of 0.25. The precise location of this region depends on the particular information received, just as the particular set of remaining destinations in the navigation example in Section 1.3 depends on the information received.

The recipe we have just used applies to any number of bits H, for which the residual uncertainty is

$$U \quad = \quad 2^{-H}, \tag{5.50}$$

as shown in Figure 5.7. So, if we have $H = 1$ bit then our residual uncertainty is

$$U \quad = \quad 2^{-1} \tag{5.51}$$

$$= \quad 1/2, \tag{5.52}$$

which means that our residual uncertainty is half as big as it was before receiving this one bit.

Equation 5.50 applies to any value of H, including fractional values. It follows that if we receive half a bit $(H = 1/2)$ then our residual uncertainty is

$$U \quad = \quad 2^{-1/2} \tag{5.53}$$

$$= \quad 0.71 \tag{5.54}$$

times as big as it was before receiving half a bit.

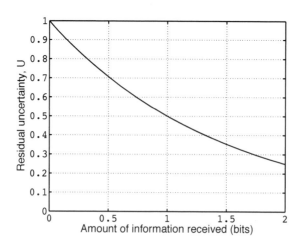

Figure 5.7. Residual uncertainty U after receiving different amounts of information H, where $U = 2^{-H}$.

Let's keep this half a bit of information, and let's call our residual uncertainty $U_1 = 0.71$. If we are given another half a bit then our new residual uncertainty, which we call U_2, is our current uncertainty U_1 reduced by a factor of 0.71. Thus, after being given two half bits, our new residual uncertainty is

$$U_2 = 0.71 \times U_1 \tag{5.55}$$
$$= 0.5. \tag{5.56}$$

So, as we should expect, being given two half bits yields the same residual uncertainty (0.5) as being given one bit.

Finally, the residual uncertainty for one quarter of a bit is

$$U = 2^{-1/4} \tag{5.57}$$
$$= 0.84. \tag{5.58}$$

In other words, after receiving one quarter of a bit, our uncertainty is 0.84 times what it was before receiving it.

The Uncertain Table Length

The table I am sitting at has a length x that has been chosen from a warehouse in which the distribution of table lengths is uniform, with a range between zero and 10 feet. Let's assume that your initial uncertainty about where x lies in this range is 100% or 1. If I tell you that my table is less than five feet long then I have halved your uncertainty, which amounts to one bit, and therefore leaves you with a residual uncertainty of $U = 0.5$. If I then tell you my table is less than 2.5 feet long then I have again halved your uncertainty, which amounts to another bit, and which leaves you with a residual uncertainty of $U = 0.25$. This is fairly straightforward, as we know that two bits should reduce your uncertainty by a factor of four (i.e. from 1 to 0.25).

Now, let's start over and make this scenario more interesting. What if I tell you that my table is less than 7.1 feet long? Then your uncertainty is $0.71 = 7.1/10$ times as large as your initial uncertainty of 1, and so your residual uncertainty is $U = 0.71$ or 71%. It turns out that this reduction in uncertainty from 100% to 71% is the result of being given half a bit of information, because these particular numbers have been chosen to coincide with the residual uncertainty after receiving half a bit (see Equation 5.54). Thus, half a bit of Shannon information reduces uncertainty to 0.71 of its previous value.

Key Point. An initial uncertainty of $U = 1.0$ is reduced to $U = 2^{-0.5} = 0.71$ after receiving half a bit of information, and to $U = 2^{-H}$ after receiving H bits.

5.9. Summary

The trouble with entropy for continuous variables is that it is infinitely large. Even though this is not very useful, it is not really surprising. Unlike a discrete variable, a continuous variable has a value which is chosen from an uncountably infinite number of possible values. It follows that the value of a continuous variable is implicitly specified with infinite precision, and we have found that such precision carries with it an infinite amount of Shannon information. We also found that, in practice, this need not diminish the utility of entropy, provided we take account of the precision of the measurements used when estimating differential entropy.

We encountered three distributions, each of which has maximum entropy under different conditions. The dual nature of information and entropy once again became apparent as it emerged that one particular maximum entropy distribution (the Gaussian) is indistinguishable from pure noise. Finally, in order to provide an intuitive understanding of entropy, we considered what a fraction of a bit means, and used the example of half a bit to derive a formal measure (residual uncertainty) related to fractional numbers of bits.

Chapter 6

Mutual Information: Continuous

The fundamental problem of communication is that of reproducing at one point, either exactly or approximately, a message selected at another point.

Shannon C, 1948.

6.1. Introduction

In this chapter, we explore information in the context of a communication channel which communicates the values of continuous variables. This will involve revising material from previous chapters on discrete variables in the context of continuous variables.

A continuous channel is depicted in Figure 6.1. The definition of mutual information for continuous variables is the same as previously given for discrete variables

$$I(X,Y) \quad = \quad H(X) + H(Y) - H(X,Y) \text{ bits.} \qquad (6.1)$$

In the context of continuous variables, the mutual information between channel input and output determines the number of different inputs that can be reliably discriminated from a knowledge of the outputs. Specifically, the mutual information is the logarithm of the number m of input values which can be reliably discriminated from a knowledge of the output values ($I = \log m$), where this number is limited by the noise in the channel. Because mutual information is symmetric (i.e. $I(X,Y) = I(Y,X)$), m is also the logarithm of the number of output values which can be reliably discriminated from a

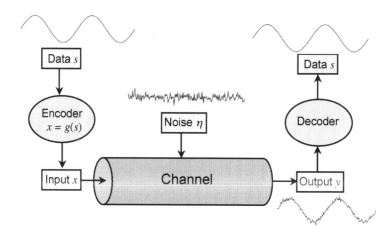

Figure 6.1. The noisy continuous channel. A signal **s** is transformed by an encoding function $\mathbf{x} = g(\mathbf{s})$ before being transmitted through the channel, which corrupts **x** by adding noise η to produce the output $\mathbf{y} = \mathbf{x} + \eta$.

knowledge of the input values. Shannon proved that the number m has an upper bound m_{max}, for which $C = \log m_{max}$ is the channel capacity.

An important property of mutual information is that it is sensitive to the strength of association between two variables, but it is essentially 'blind' to the nature of that relationship (e.g. whether it is linear or non-linear). If two variables are related to each other then it does not matter how complex or subtle their relationship is, mutual information will give an exact value for the strength of the association, measured in bits. We will return to this topic in Section 6.5.

Equation 6.1 will be derived from a formal definition of mutual information. However, the bulk of this chapter will be dedicated to understanding mutual information in a more intuitively appealing form involving *conditional entropy* (introduced in Section 4.1), which cannot be understood without having some familiarity with joint distributions of continuous variables.

Key point. Mutual information is the logarithm of the number of input values which can be reliably discriminated from a knowledge of the output values.

6.2. Joint Distributions

If the channel inputs X and outputs Y are correlated then a scattergram of their corresponding values looks like the dots on the ground plane in Figure 6.2, where dot density is represented in Figure 6.4a. A non-zero correlation implies that if we know the value of X then we also know something about the corresponding value of Y, and *vice versa*. How much we know depends on the magnitude of the correlation between X and Y.

As previously described for discrete variables, if X and Y are independent then knowing the value of X tells us *absolutely nothing* about the corresponding value of Y, and *vice versa*; examples of this are shown in Figures 6.3 and 6.5. In other words, the value of X is not predictable from the corresponding value of Y, and *vice versa*.

The *joint probability density* of x and y is written as $p(x, y)$. If we ignore the distinction between probability density $p(x, y)$ and probability then our notation becomes less rigorous, but more readable (see Appendix D). Accordingly, if X and Y are independent then the probability of observing the pair (x, y) is just the product of the probability that $X = x$ and the probability that $Y = y$; specifically, $p(x, y) = p(x)\,p(y)$. Because this is true for all values of X and Y, it follows that if X and Y are independent then the *joint probability distribution* $p(X, Y)$ is the outer product (see Section 4.2) of the probability distributions $p(X)$ and $p(Y)$,

$$p(X, Y) \quad = \quad p(X)\,p(Y). \tag{6.2}$$

This is usually described as the joint probability distribution $p(X, Y)$ being *factorised* into the two probability distributions $p(X)$ and $p(Y)$, where $p(X)$ and $p(Y)$ are the *marginal probability distributions* of the joint probability distribution $p(X, Y)$.

Marginalisation

By analogy with discrete variables, the marginal probability distributions of the joint distribution $p(X, Y)$ can be obtained using integration:

$$p(X) \quad = \quad \int_{y=-\infty}^{\infty} p(x,y)\, dy \tag{6.3}$$

$$p(Y) \quad = \quad \int_{x=-\infty}^{\infty} p(x,y)\, dx. \tag{6.4}$$

For example, the joint distribution $p(X,Y)$ shown in Figure 6.2 has a marginal distribution $p(X)$ shown on the left-hand back plane and a marginal distribution $p(Y)$ shown on the right-hand back plane.

Differential Entropy of Joint Distributions

The differential entropy of the joint probability distribution $p(X,Y)$ is a generalisation of the differential entropy of a single variable

$$H_{dif}(X,Y) \quad = \quad \int_{x=-\infty}^{\infty} \int_{y=-\infty}^{\infty} p(x,y) \log \frac{1}{p(x,y)}\, dy\, dx \tag{6.5}$$

$$= \quad \mathrm{E}\left[\log \frac{1}{p(x,y)}\right] \text{ bits.} \tag{6.6}$$

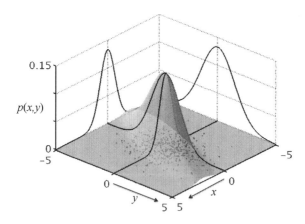

Figure 6.2. Joint probability density function $p(X,Y)$ for correlated Gaussian variables. The standard deviation of Y is $\sigma_Y = 1$, the standard deviation of X is $\sigma_X = 2$, and the correlation between X and Y is $\rho = 0.8$. The probability density $p(x,y)$ is indicated by the density of points on the ground plane at (x,y). The marginal distributions $p(X)$ and $p(Y)$ are plotted on the side axes. These marginal distributions have been rescaled to have the same height as the joint pdf in this and subsequent figures.

The limits of integration (i.e. $\pm\infty$) and the subscript *dif* will be omitted from now on.

Note that the problem of infinities encountered for any distribution of a single continuous variable (Section 5.3) also applies to any joint distribution of variables, and it is 'solved' in a similar manner, by simply ignoring the infinities. For brevity, we will use the term 'joint entropy' to refer to 'joint differential entropy'.

The joint entropy $H(X,Y)$ can be considered as a measure of the overall variability of the variables X and Y, or equivalently, as a measure of dispersion of the joint probability distribution $p(X,Y)$.

If X and Y are independent then the differential entropy of the joint probability distribution is equal to the sum of the differential entropies of its marginal distributions,

$$H(X) + H(Y) \;=\; \int_x \int_y p(x)p(y) \log \frac{1}{p(x)p(y)} \, dy \, dx \qquad (6.7)$$

$$=\; \int_x p(x) \log \frac{1}{p(x)} \, dx \;+\; \int_y p(y) \log \frac{1}{p(y)} \, dy \quad (6.8)$$

$$=\; \mathrm{E}\left[\log \frac{1}{p(x)}\right] + \mathrm{E}\left[\log \frac{1}{p(y)}\right]. \qquad (6.9)$$

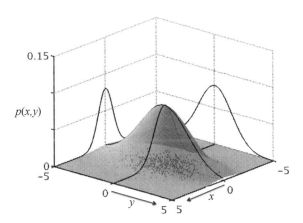

Figure 6.3. Joint probability density function $p(X,Y)$ for independent Gaussian variables. Because X and Y are independent, $p(X,Y)$ is the product of its marginal distributions, $p(X,Y) = p(X)p(Y)$. The standard deviations are the same as in Figure 6.2.

It follows that if X and Y are independent then there is no difference between the differential entropy of the joint distribution and the total differential entropy of its marginal distributions,

$$H(X) + H(Y) - H(X,Y) = 0 \text{ bits.} \qquad (6.10)$$

Mutual Information and Marginal Distributions

For continuous variables, mutual information is defined as

$$I(X,Y) \;=\; \int_x \int_y p(x,y) \log \frac{p(x,y)}{p(x)p(y)} \, dx \, dy. \qquad (6.11)$$

This can be rewritten as

$$I(X,Y) \;=\; \int_x p(x) \log \frac{1}{p(x)} \, dx \;+\; \int_y p(y) \log \frac{1}{p(y)} \, dy$$

$$- \int_x \int_y p(x,y) \log \frac{1}{p(x,y)} \, dy \, dx \qquad (6.12)$$

$$= \; \mathrm{E}\left[\log \frac{1}{p(x)}\right] + \mathrm{E}\left[\log \frac{1}{p(y)}\right] - \mathrm{E}\left[\log \frac{1}{p(x)p(y)}\right], \; (6.13)$$

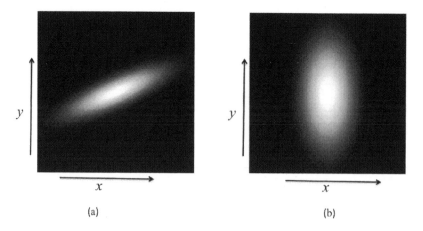

(a) (b)

Figure 6.4. Bird's-eye view of joint probability density functions. (a) Correlated variables shown in Figure 6.2. (b) Independent variables shown in Figure 6.3. Lighter areas indicate regions of higher probability density.

which can be recognised as the sum of the entropies of the two marginal distributions minus the entropy of the joint distribution,

$$I(X,Y) \quad = \quad H(X) + H(Y) - H(X,Y) \text{ bits.} \qquad (6.14)$$

By analogy with the discrete case, $I(X,Y)$ is the average amount of information conveyed by each input about each output value received. Because mutual information is symmetric, it is also the average amount of information conveyed by each output about each input value.

However, this formulation of mutual information is arguably less accessible than formulations that involve the conditional entropies, which is the interpretation developed in the remainder of this chapter.

6.3. Conditional Distributions and Entropy

Here, we explore the idea of conditional entropy, which demands that we first define conditional probability distributions.

Conditional Probability Distributions

If we take a slice through a joint probability distribution then we obtain a cross-section, as shown in Figure 6.6. If this cross-section is taken at $x_1 = 1$ then the resultant shape defines the probability of obtaining

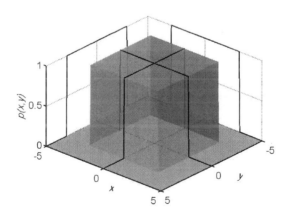

Figure 6.5. Uniform joint probability density function $p(X,Y)$ for two variables, both of which have uniform probability distributions. These variables are independent.

different values of Y, *given that* $X = x_1$; that is, it defines the cross-section $p(x_1, Y)$. From the product rule (see Appendix F), we know that

$$p(x_1, Y) \quad = \quad p(Y|x_1)p(x_1), \tag{6.15}$$

where the vertical bar stands for 'given that'. The distribution of Y given that $X = x_1$ is therefore

$$p(Y|x_1) \quad = \quad p(x_1, Y)/p(x_1), \tag{6.16}$$

which is a *conditional probability distribution*. Thus, $p(Y|x_1)$ is a scaled version of the slice in Figure 6.6, where the scaling factor is $1/p(x_1)$. The value of $p(x_1)$ is given by the height of the marginal probability distribution at $X = x_1$, which can be obtained by marginalisation (i.e. by integrating over y),

$$p(x_1) \quad = \quad \int_y p(x_1, y)\, dy. \tag{6.17}$$

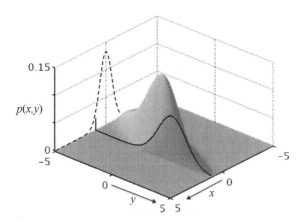

Figure 6.6. Conditional probability distribution $p(Y|x_1)$ of the correlated variables shown in Figure 6.2. The cross-section $p(Y, x_1)$ (solid curve) represents the probability (density) of different values of Y for a specific *given* value of $X = x_1 = 1$ and is a scaled version of the conditional distribution $p(Y|x_1)$. The marginal distribution $p(X)$ is a dashed curve and the density $p(x_1)$ is the height of $p(X)$ at $X = x_1$, as indicated by the solid vertical line.

However, for our purposes, the value of $p(x_1)$ is immaterial, because it simply serves as a scaling factor which ensures that the distribution $p(Y|x_1)$ has unit area (and is therefore a probability distribution).

Similarly, if we had chosen to take a slice parallel to the x-axis at $Y = y_1$ then we would obtain a cross-section which is proportional to the conditional probability distribution $p(X|y_1)$, with a scaling factor of $1/p(y_1)$ in this case, as shown in Figure 6.7.

Conditional Entropy

Given a joint probability distribution $p(X, Y)$, the *conditional entropy* $H(Y|X)$ is our average surprise when we are told the value of Y given that we already know the value of X. In fact, $p(X, Y)$ has two conditional entropies $H(Y|X)$ and $H(X|Y)$, which can be summarised as follows:

1. A slice through $p(X, Y)$ at $X = x_1$ defines a one-dimensional distribution $p(Y|x_1)$ with entropy $H(Y|x_1)$. The conditional entropy $H(Y|X)$ is the average entropy of all such slices through $p(X, Y)$, where this average is taken over all values of X. See Figure 6.6.

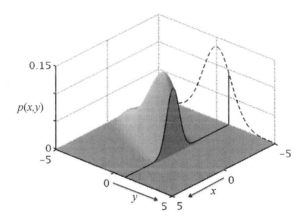

Figure 6.7. Conditional probability distribution $p(X|y_1)$ of the correlated variables shown in Figure 6.2. The cross-section $p(X, y_1)$ (solid curve) represents the probability (density) of different values of X for a specific *given* value of $Y = y_1 = 1.5$ and is a scaled version of the conditional distribution $p(X|y_1)$. The marginal distribution $p(Y)$ is a dashed curve, and the density $p(y_1)$ is the height of $p(Y)$ at $Y = y_1$, as indicated by the solid vertical line.

2. A slice through $p(X, Y)$ at $Y = y_1$ defines a one-dimensional distribution $p(X|y_1)$ with entropy $H(X|y_1)$. The conditional entropy $H(X|Y)$ is the average entropy of all such slices through $p(X, Y)$, where this average is taken over all values of Y. See Figure 6.7.

Now let's back up a little, and derive an expression for $H(Y|X)$, beginning with a single slice through $p(X, Y)$ at $X = x_1$. This slice is a scaled version of the conditional probability distribution $p(Y|x_1)$, where the entropy of $p(Y|x_1)$ is related to the amount of spread or dispersion it has,

$$H(Y|x_1) \quad = \quad \int_y p(y|x_1) \log \frac{1}{p(y|x_1)} \, dy. \qquad (6.18)$$

If we consider the mean dispersion of the family of conditional probability distributions defined by $p(Y|x_1)$ for different values of X then we obtain the conditional entropy $H(Y|X)$,

$$H(Y|X) \quad = \quad \int_x p(x) H(Y|x) \, dx. \qquad (6.19)$$

This is the average uncertainty in Y given a value of X, when this average is taken over all values of X. If we substitute $H(Y|x)$ from Equation 6.18 into Equation 6.19 then we get

$$H(Y|X) \quad = \quad \int_x p(x) \left[\int_y p(y|x) \log \frac{1}{p(y|x)} \, dy \right] dx, \qquad (6.20)$$

where $p(y|x)p(x) = p(x, y)$, so that

$$H(Y|X) \quad = \quad \int_y \int_x p(x, y) \log \frac{1}{p(y|x)} \, dx \, dy \qquad (6.21)$$

$$= \quad E \left[\log \frac{1}{p(y|x)} \right] \text{ bits}, \qquad (6.22)$$

where this expectation is taken over all values of X and Y.

Similarly, the conditional entropy $H(X|Y)$ is

$$H(X|Y) \quad = \quad \int_y \int_x p(x, y) \log \frac{1}{p(x|y)} \, dx \, dy \text{ bits}. \qquad (6.23)$$

Both of these conditional entropies will prove useful shortly.

Notice that, usually, $H(X|Y) \neq H(Y|X)$. For example, the joint probability distribution in Figure 6.2 implies a family of conditional probability distributions $p(Y|X)$ which have large widths or variances (see Figure 6.6) but conditional probability distributions $p(X|Y)$ that have small variances (see Figure 6.7), and the mean variance of each of these two families is reflected in the corresponding conditional entropies $H(Y|X)$ and $H(X|Y)$.

6.4. Mutual Information and Conditional Entropy

In order to proceed, we first need to show that mutual information can be expressed as

$$I(X,Y) \quad = \quad H(Y) - H(Y|X) \text{ bits,} \tag{6.24}$$

as shown in Figures 6.8 and 6.9. Given that

$$I(X,Y) \quad = \quad \int_y \int_x p(x,y) \log \frac{p(x,y)}{p(x)p(y)} \, dx \, dy, \tag{6.25}$$

and that $p(x,y) = p(y|x)p(x)$, we can substitute this into Equation 6.25 to obtain

$$I(X,Y) \quad = \quad \int_y \int_x p(x,y) \log \frac{p(y|x)}{p(y)} \, dx \, dy, \tag{6.26}$$

which can be rewritten as the difference

$$
\begin{aligned}
I(X,Y) \quad = \quad & \int_y \int_x p(x,y) \log \frac{1}{p(y)} \, dx \, dy \\
& - \int_y \int_x p(x,y) \log \frac{1}{p(y|x)} \, dx \, dy, \tag{6.27}
\end{aligned}
$$

where we can recognise (from Equation 6.21) that the second term on the right is $H(Y|X)$ and that the first term is the entropy of Y, because

$$\int_y \int_x p(x,y) \log \frac{1}{p(y)} \, dx \, dy = \int_y p(y) \log \frac{1}{p(y)} \, dy = H(Y), \tag{6.28}$$

so

$$I(X, Y) \;=\; H(Y) - H(Y|X) \text{ bits,} \qquad (6.29)$$

which establishes the result stated in Equation 6.24.

If we simply swap the variables Y and X then, by symmetry, we have

$$I(X, Y) \;=\; H(X) - H(X|Y) \text{ bits.} \qquad (6.30)$$

Both of these results will prove useful shortly.

No Infinity

Notice that both $H(X)$ and $H(X|Y)$ in Equation 6.30 include the infinite constant first encountered in Equation 5.12. However, because this constant has the same value in $H(X)$ and $H(X|Y)$, it cancels out when we subtract one from the other. Thus, the definitions of mutual information for both discrete and continuous variables do not contain any infinities.

Next, we consider mutual information from two perspectives: the input and the output.

The Information That Y Provides About X

The mutual information $I(X, Y)$ between X and Y is the difference between the average uncertainty $H(X)$ we have about X before an output Y is observed, and the average uncertainty $H(X|Y)$ after Y is observed (Equation 6.30); it is the reduction in uncertainty in X induced by observing Y, and is therefore the amount of information gained about X after observing Y.

Because a reduction in uncertainty, from $H(X)$ to $H(X|Y)$, amounts to an *increase in certainty*, the amount of information gained about X after observing Y is

$$I(X, Y) = H(X) - H(X|Y) \text{ bits,} \qquad (6.31)$$

which, according to Equation 6.30, is the mutual information between X and Y. In summary, the mutual information can be expressed as the difference between what we know about X before observing Y, and what we know about X after observing Y. It is also the amount of output entropy that is exclusively related to the input entropy and therefore not related to the noise in the input.

Mutual Information Cannot Be Negative

On average, observing an output reduces uncertainty about the input (even though certain outputs may increase uncertainty). Indeed, it can be shown (see Reza (1961)[41]) that the entropy of X given Y cannot be greater than the entropy of X,

$$H(X|Y) \;\leq\; H(X) \text{ bits,} \tag{6.32}$$

with equality only if X and Y are independent. From Equation 6.30, it follows that mutual information is positive, unless X and Y are independent, in which case it is zero.

The Information That X Provides About Y

The mutual information between X and Y can also be expressed as the difference between the amount of uncertainty $H(Y)$ we have about Y before an input X is observed, and the amount of uncertainty $H(Y|X)$ after X is observed (Equation 6.29).

Given that our uncertainty is reduced by an amount $H(Y|X)$ from an initial value of $H(Y)$, it follows that the amount of information we have gained about Y is

$$I(X,Y) \;=\; H(Y) - H(Y|X) \text{ bits.} \tag{6.33}$$

Thus, the mutual information can be expressed as the difference between what we know about Y before observing X, and what we know about Y after observing X. It is also the amount of input entropy that is exclusively related to the output entropy and therefore not related to the noise in the output.

Mutual Information, Conditional Entropy, and Joint Entropy

So far, we have established three expressions for mutual information, each of which can be interpreted as follows. First, we have

$$I(X,Y) \;=\; H(X) - H(X|Y) \text{ bits.} \tag{6.34}$$

Second,

$$I(X,Y) \;=\; H(Y) - H(Y|X) \text{ bits.} \tag{6.35}$$

And third,

$$I(X,Y) \;=\; H(X) + H(Y) - H(X,Y) \text{ bits.} \tag{6.36}$$

From these, a little algebra yields a fourth expression

$$I(X,Y) \;=\; H(X,Y) - [H(X|Y) + H(Y|X)]. \tag{6.37}$$

This is the portion of the joint entropy $H(X,Y)$ that is left over once we have removed $[H(X|Y) + H(Y|X)]$, which is the entropy $H(X|Y)$ due to noise in X plus the entropy $H(Y|X)$ due to noise in Y.

If we rearrange Equation 6.37 then we obtain

$$H(X,Y) \;=\; I(X,Y) + H(X|Y) + H(Y|X). \tag{6.38}$$

In other words, the joint entropy $H(X,Y)$ acts as an 'entropy container' which consists of three disjoint (i.e. non-overlapping) subsets, as shown in Figures 6.8 and 6.9:

1. the conditional entropy $H(X|Y)$ due to noise in X, which is the entropy in X which is not determined by Y;

2. the conditional entropy $H(Y|X)$ due to noise in Y, which is the entropy in Y which is not determined by X;

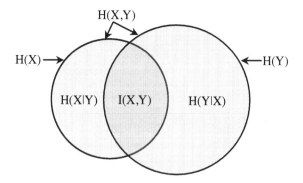

Figure 6.8. Mutual information between related variables X and Y. Each circle represents the entropy of one variable.

3. the mutual information $I(X, Y)$, which is the entropy 'shared' by X and Y, and which results from the co-dependence of X and Y.

Finally, Equations 6.34–6.36 imply that the conditional entropies can be obtained as

$$H(X|Y) \;=\; H(X, Y) - H(Y) \tag{6.39}$$
$$H(Y|X) \;=\; H(X, Y) - H(X), \tag{6.40}$$

which will prove useful shortly. These two equations imply that

$$H(X, Y) \;=\; H(X) + H(Y|X) \tag{6.41}$$
$$H(X, Y) \;=\; H(Y) + H(X|Y), \tag{6.42}$$

which is called the *chain rule for entropy*.

Key point. The mutual information is that part of the joint entropy $H(X, Y)$ that is left over once we have removed the part $[H(X|Y) + H(Y|X)]$ due to noise.

6.5. Mutual Information is Invariant

Within formally defined limits, the mutual information between two variables is invariant with respect to transformations of those variables, where the term *invariant* means that the amount of mutual information is unaffected by such transformations.

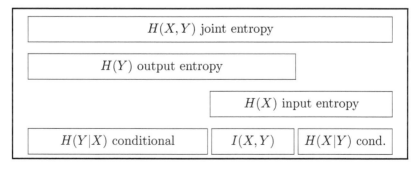

Figure 6.9. The relationship between the input entropy $H(X)$, output entropy $H(Y)$, joint entropy $H(X, Y)$, mutual information $I(X, Y)$, and the conditional entropies $H(X|Y)$ and $H(Y|X)$.

If two variables X and Y have mutual information $I(X, Y)$ then using a function f to transform X to another variable X' and a function g to transform Y to another variable Y',

$$X' = f(X) \tag{6.43}$$
$$Y' = g(Y), \tag{6.44}$$

has no effect on mutual information, so $I(X', Y') = I(X, Y)$. This is true provided the functions f and g are invertible, which implies that the value of X can be recovered from X' and the value of Y can be recovered from Y'. For example, if the function f maps each value of X to $\log X$, so that $X' = \log X$, then X' can be recovered from X (by using $X = 2^{X'}$). But if the function f maps all values of X to a constant $X' = k$ then X' cannot be recovered from X.

As stated earlier, the reason this matters is because it ensures that no matter how complex the relationship between X and Y appears to be, mutual information can be used to measure the precise strength (in bits) of the association between X and Y. To illustrate this, suppose that a medical study discovers that the mutual information between the prevalence of diabetes X and sugar intake measured in grams Y is $I(X, Y) = 2$ bits. If another study measures the prevalence of diabetes X and sugar intake as $Y' = Y^2$ (or even as $Y' = \log(Y)$) then the mutual information between X and Y' would still be equal to 2 bits.

Indeed, no matter how complex the relationship between diabetes and sugar intake is, mutual information gives a precise measurement of how closely they are related. We cannot make such strong claims for more conventional measures of association, such as correlation (see Section 7.6).

6.6. Kullback–Leibler Divergence and Bayes

Kullback–Leibler divergence (KL-divergence) is a general measure of the difference between two distributions, and is also known as *relative entropy*. Given two distributions $p(X)$ and $q(X)$ of the same variable X, the KL-divergence between these distributions is

$$D_{KL}(p(X)||q(X)) = \int_x p(x) \log \frac{p(x)}{q(x)} \, dx. \tag{6.45}$$

KL-divergence is not a true measure of distance because, usually,

$$D_{KL}(p(X)||q(X)) \neq D_{KL}(q(X)||p(X)). \qquad (6.46)$$

Note that $D_{KL}(p(X)||q(X)) > 0$, unless $p = q$, in which case it is equal to zero.

The KL-divergence between the joint distribution $p(X, Y)$ and the joint distribution $[p(X)p(Y)]$ obtained from the outer product of the marginal distributions $p(X)$ and $p(Y)$ is

$$D_{KL}(p(X,Y)||[p(X)p(Y)]) = \int_x \int_y p(x,y) \log \frac{p(x,y)}{p(x)p(y)} \, dy \, dx, \quad (6.47)$$

which we can recognise from Equation 6.25 as the mutual information between X and Y.

Thus, the mutual information between X and Y is the KL-divergence between the joint distribution $p(X, Y)$ and the joint distribution $[p(X)p(Y)]$ obtained by evaluating the outer product of the marginal distributions $p(X)$ and $p(Y)$.

Bayes' Rule

We can express the KL-divergence between two variables in terms of *Bayes' rule* (see Stone (2013)[52] and Appendix F). Given that $p(x, y) = p(x|y)p(y)$, mutual information can be expressed as

$$I(X,Y) \quad = \quad \int_y p(y) \int_x p(x|y) \log \frac{p(x|y)}{p(x)} \, dx \, dy, \qquad (6.48)$$

where the inner integral can be recognised as the KL-divergence between the distributions $p(X|y)$ and $p(X)$,

$$D_{KL}(p(X|y)||p(X)) \quad = \quad \int_x p(x|y) \log \frac{p(x|y)}{p(x)} \, dx, \qquad (6.49)$$

where $p(X|y)$ is the posterior distribution and $p(X)$ is the prior distribution. Thus, the mutual information between X and Y is

$$I(X,Y) \quad = \quad \int_y p(y) \, D_{KL}(p(X|y)||p(X)) \, dy, \qquad (6.50)$$

which is the expected KL-divergence between the posterior and prior,

$$I(X, Y) \quad = \quad \mathrm{E}_y[D_{KL}(p(X|y)||p(X))], \qquad (6.51)$$

where this expectation is taken over values of Y.

6.7. Summary

In this chapter, we considered information in terms of continuous variables. To do this, we explored how joint distributions can be used to define and visualise marginal and conditional distributions, and the entropies of those distributions. The mutual information between continuous variables, in contrast to the entropy of continuous variables, turns out to have a perfectly sensible interpretation, which does not involve any infinities. We considered how each input value conveys information about a corresponding output value, and *vice versa*, and how this is reduced by the presence of channel noise. Finally, we defined the KL-divergence between two variables, and considered how it can be interpreted in terms of mutual information and Bayes' rule.

Chapter 7

Channel Capacity: Continuous

> Information is a fundamental physical quantity, obeying exact laws.
> Deutsch D and Marletto C, 2014[14].

7.1. Introduction

In this chapter, we consider precisely what form of input distribution $p(X)$ of a continuous variable maximises the rate at which information can be communicated through a noisy channel. After defining channel capacity, we find that the input distribution which provides the maximum communication rate depends on the nature of the channel under consideration. In common with discrete variables, we also find that the error rate shrinks rapidly as the message length increases.

7.2. Channel Capacity

The general definition of channel capacity given in Equation 4.93 is

$$C = \max_{p(X)} I(X, Y) \text{ bits}, \tag{7.1}$$

where $I(X, Y)$ is the mutual information, which is (Equation 6.29)

$$I(X, Y) = H(Y) - H(Y|X) \text{ bits}. \tag{7.2}$$

So we can rewrite Equation 7.1 as

$$C = \max_{p(X)} H(Y) - H(Y|X) \text{ bits}. \tag{7.3}$$

We proceed by identifying the input distribution which maximises information transmission under two different constraints:

Constraint 1: The output has a fixed variance and infinite range.

Constraint 2: The output has a finite range.

In physical terms, Constraint 1 could correspond to the sound signal conveyed by a cable into a loudspeaker with a specific wattage (power), because power equates to variance. In contrast, Constraint 2 could be the output of a camera photoreceptor (one per image pixel) which has a fixed lower limit of zero volts, and a fixed upper limit of five volts. In both cases, we wish to sculpt the input distribution $p(X)$ so that it can convey as much information as possible.

7.3. The Gaussian Channel

A Gaussian channel is one in which the noise has a Gaussian distribution (see Appendix G). If a channel output has fixed variance then we know (from Section 5.6) that its entropy can be maximised by ensuring it has a Gaussian distribution. Here, we address the question: what form should the input distribution $p(X)$ adopt in order to maximise the mutual information between the input and output of a channel? So far, we know two relevant facts:

1. The noise added to signal X as it passes through the channel is

$$\eta \;=\; Y - X \text{ bits};\tag{7.4}$$

2. The mutual information between input X and output Y is

$$I(X, Y) \;=\; H(Y) - H(Y|X) \text{ bits},\tag{7.5}$$

where, according to Equation 4.60, $H(Y|X) = H(\eta)$ is the channel noise, so

$$I(X, Y) \;=\; H(Y) - H(\eta) \text{ bits}.\tag{7.6}$$

Using Equation 7.6, we can rewrite the channel capacity defined in Equation 7.3 as

$$C = \max_{p(X)} H(Y) - H(\eta) \text{ bits.} \tag{7.7}$$

In trying to maximise the mutual information, we cannot reduce the noise entropy, which is a fixed property of the channel. So, we are left with trying to make the entropy of the output Y as large as possible.

We know from Section 5.6 that if the variance of a distribution is fixed then the distribution that has maximum entropy is Gaussian. It can be shown [41] that the sum of two independent Gaussian variables is also Gaussian, so if we want $p(Y)$ to be Gaussian then we should ensure that $p(X)$ is Gaussian, because $Y = X + \eta$. So, $p(X)$ must be Gaussian in order to maximise $H(X)$, which maximises $H(Y)$, which maximises $I(X, Y)$, which coincides with the channel capacity of C bits. Thus, if input, output, and noise are all Gaussian then the average amount of information communicated per output value is the channel capacity

$$I(X, Y) = H(Y) - H(\eta) \tag{7.8}$$

$$= C \text{ bits.} \tag{7.9}$$

This result is an informal proof of *Shannon's continuous noisy channel coding theorem for Gaussian channels*. We now make use of this to express channel capacity in terms of the variance of the Gaussian input, output, and noise.

From Equation 5.47, we know that if the noise has variance $v_\eta = \sigma_\eta^2$ then its entropy is

$$H(\eta) = \frac{1}{2} \log 2\pi e v_\eta \text{ bits.} \tag{7.10}$$

Similarly, if the input has variance $v_x = \sigma_x^2$ then its entropy is

$$H(X) = \frac{1}{2} \log 2\pi e v_x \text{ bits.} \tag{7.11}$$

At this point, we make use of a general result which states that if two independent Gaussian variables X and η have variances v_x and v_η (respectively) then a third variable $Y = X + \eta$ is also Gaussian and has a variance of

$$v_y \quad = \quad v_x + v_\eta. \tag{7.12}$$

The entropy of Y is therefore

$$H(Y) \quad = \quad \frac{1}{2} \log 2\pi e v_y \tag{7.13}$$

$$= \quad \frac{1}{2} \log 2\pi e (v_x + v_\eta) \text{ bits.} \tag{7.14}$$

For example, if the signal and noise both have the same variance then the output variance is twice the input variance, so the noise adds half a bit to the entropy of the output; that is, $H(Y) = H(X) + 1/2$ bit.

Substituting Equations 7.11 and 7.14 into Equation 7.8 yields

$$C \quad = \quad \frac{1}{2} \log 2\pi e (v_x + v_\eta) - \frac{1}{2} \log 2\pi e v_\eta \tag{7.15}$$

$$= \quad \frac{1}{2} \log \frac{(v_x + v_\eta)}{v_\eta} \tag{7.16}$$

$$= \quad \frac{1}{2} \log \left(1 + \frac{v_x}{v_\eta} \right) \text{ bits.} \tag{7.17}$$

Because the variance of any signal is equal to its power, the input signal power is $P = v_x$, and the noise power is $N = v_\eta$. Substituting these equations into Equation 7.17 allows the capacity of this Gaussian channel to be written as Shannon's well-known equation

$$C \quad = \quad \frac{1}{2} \log \left(1 + \frac{P}{N} \right) \text{ bits,} \tag{7.18}$$

where the ratio of variances P/N is the *signal to noise ratio* (SNR).

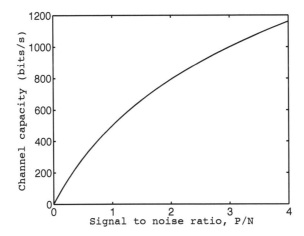

Figure 7.1. Gaussian channel capacity and signal to noise ratio P/N. If a signal is sampled at rate of 1,000 values per second then the channel capacity is $C = 500 \log(1 + P/N)$ bits/s. If noise power is fixed then increasing signal power has diminishing returns in terms of channel capacity.

It will prove useful to note that this can be expressed in terms of the ratio between the standard deviations of channel outputs and noise:

$$C \quad = \quad \frac{1}{2} \log \frac{(v_x + v_\eta)}{v_\eta} \qquad (7.19)$$

$$= \quad \frac{1}{2} \log \frac{v_y}{v_\eta} \qquad (7.20)$$

$$= \quad \log \frac{\sigma_y}{\sigma_\eta} \text{ bits.} \qquad (7.21)$$

For discrete variables, C is the maximum (average) mutual information per symbol, but because we are now dealing with continuous variables, one symbol corresponds to a single input value for a given channel. Thus, for Gaussian X, η and Y, the mutual information between the input and output is equal to the channel capacity of C bits per transmitted value in Equations 7.18 and 7.21. This implies that the number of different equiprobable input values

155

which can be discriminated using a single output value is

$$m = 2^C \quad (7.22)$$

$$= \frac{\sigma_y}{\sigma_\eta}. \quad (7.23)$$

Thus, channel noise effectively discretises the continuous Gaussian output distribution into a discrete distribution.

Equation 7.23 represents a fundamental result. It shows precisely how the number of input values that can be discriminated increases as the signal to noise ratio in the channel increases (see Figure 7.1). However, the proof of this assumes that the codewords are very long, like the ones considered next.

Key point. Channel noise effectively discretises a continuous Gaussian output distribution into a discrete distribution.

Long Messages

So far in this chapter we have considered single input/output pairs of values. In order to understand the next section regarding error rates, we need to consider codewords and messages which consist of more than a single value. Accordingly, we now take each encoded message $\mathbf{x}$ to be a vector of n values,

$$\mathbf{x} = (x_1, \ldots, x_n), \quad (7.24)$$

and we assume that each value corresponds to one message symbol, so that message length and codeword length are the same. Each encoded message is corrupted by noise η as it passes through the channel, so each value x_i is associated with a corresponding output value $y_i = x_i + \eta_i$, where the received output $\mathbf{y}$ is a vector of n values,

$$\mathbf{y} = (y_1, \ldots, y_n), \quad (7.25)$$

which is a noisy version of the encoded message

$$\mathbf{y} = (x_1 + \eta_1, \ldots, x_n + \eta_n) \tag{7.26}$$
$$= (x_1, \ldots, x_n) + (\eta_1, \ldots, \eta_n) \tag{7.27}$$
$$= \mathbf{x} + \eta, \tag{7.28}$$

where η is a vector of noise values

$$\eta = (\eta_1, \ldots, \eta_n). \tag{7.29}$$

If each of these vectors has a mean of zero then their variances are

$$v_x = \frac{1}{n} \sum_{i=1}^{n} x_i^2, \quad v_\eta = \frac{1}{n} \sum_{i=1}^{n} \eta_i^2, \quad v_y = \frac{1}{n} \sum_{i=1}^{n} y_i^2, \tag{7.30}$$

where $P = v_x$ and $N = v_\eta$.

In effect, Shannon's noisy channel coding theorem is based on a counting argument which shows that if the n values in each encoded message have a Gaussian distribution with input variance v_x, and if the channel noise is Gaussian with variance v_η, then the maximum number of equally probable input vectors $\mathbf{x}_1, \ldots, \mathbf{x}_m$ which can be reliably discriminated from observing the corresponding outputs is

$$m = 2^{nC} = \left(\frac{\sigma_y}{\sigma_\eta}\right)^n, \tag{7.31}$$

so the amount of information provided by each output vector $\mathbf{y}$ about the input vector $\mathbf{x}$ is

$$\log m = \log 2^{nC}. \tag{7.32}$$
$$= nC \tag{7.33}$$
$$= n \log \frac{\sigma_y}{\sigma_\eta} \text{ bits.} \tag{7.34}$$

For example, if $v_x = 15$ and $v_\eta = 1$ then $v_y = 16$, giving $\sigma_y = 4$ and $C = 2$ bits per output value. If $n = 4$ then the maximum amount of information that can be recovered about each input vector $\mathbf{x}$ is

$$
\begin{aligned}
nC &= n\log\frac{\sigma_y}{\sigma_\eta} & (7.35)\\
&= 4\log 4 & (7.36)\\
&= 8 \text{ bits,} & (7.37)
\end{aligned}
$$

so the number of discriminable inputs $\mathbf{x}_1, \ldots, \mathbf{x}_m$ is

$$
m = 2^8 = 256. \tag{7.38}
$$

In practice, n would be much larger than four, which is used here only for illustration purposes.

If we rearrange Equation 7.32 and express it in terms of signal to noise ratio then we have

$$
nC = \frac{n}{2}\log\left(1 + \frac{P}{N}\right) \text{ bits.} \tag{7.39}
$$

Given that we want to transmit as much information as possible for each watt of power expended, should we increase the number n of values in each input vector $\mathbf{x}$, or should we increase the signal power P by increasing the amplitude of each value in $\mathbf{x}$?

Clearly, doubling n doubles the length of $\mathbf{x}$, which doubles the power required to transmit $\mathbf{x}$, but it also doubles the amount of information transmitted. In contrast, doubling the signal power P increases, but does not double, the amount of information transmitted, as can be seen from Figure 7.1. Thus, given a choice between increasing the number n of values transmitted and increasing the amplitude of transmitted values (i.e. signal power P), we should increase n. Although we have not covered the topic of *signal bandwidth* in this book, the above result implies that if we have a choice between boosting signal power and increasing the bandwidth then we should increase the bandwidth.

7.4. Error Rates of Noisy Channels

The presence of noise in a channel means that we cannot be certain about which of the m possible input vectors was sent. However, Shannon proved that the probability of making an error regarding which input was sent falls rapidly as the number of values in each input vector increases. An informal summary of his theorem is as follows.

> If a source has entropy R, then it possible to encode the output of the source and transmit it over a continuous noisy channel which has capacity C with an error rate that approaches zero as the length n of encoded messages approaches infinity, provided R is less than C.

For more extensive treatments, see Shannon and Weaver (1949)[50] (Theorem 21), Reza (1961)[41] (Section 9-17), or MacKay (2003)[34] (Section 11.3).

Shannon also provided a proof that applies to any continuous channel. This states that the probability of decoding an output **y** as the wrong encoded message is

$$P(error) \quad \approx \quad \Phi\left(\sqrt{n}\left(\frac{2P(P+N)}{N(P+2N)}\right)^{1/2}(R-C)\right), \quad (7.40)$$

where P is the signal power, N is the noise power, and Φ is the *cumulative distribution function* (cdf) of a Gaussian function. For readers unfamiliar with cdfs, the general form of Φ can be seen in Figure 7.6a and in Figure G.1b in Appendix G .

The main thing to notice about Equation 7.40 is that the difference $R - C$ is negative (i.e. $R < C$), because Shannon's noisy channel coding theorem implies that we should not attempt to make $R \geq C$. Thus, for fixed values of P and N (i.e. for a given signal to noise ratio), the argument of Φ decreases in proportion to the square root of the message length n, so the probability of error decreases rapidly and approaches zero as n approaches infinity. Despite the apparent complexity of Equation 7.40, we can set the values of its parameters to plausible values and then plot $P(error)$ as a function of message length n, as in Figure 7.2. This shows that, even though the source rate R is within 1% of the channel capacity (i.e. $R/C = 0.99$), the probability of error rapidly approaches zero even for modest message lengths.

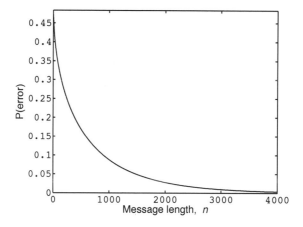

Figure 7.2. The probability $P(error)$ of decoding an output **y** incorrectly for a continuous channel plotted as a function of message length n, according to Equation 7.40. The input variance is $P = 10$, the noise variance $N = 1$. The input entropy is $R = 0.99$ bits per input value, which is close to the channel capacity $C = 1$ bit. Thus, despite running at almost full capacity, the error rate approaches zero for message lengths greater than $n = 4,000$.

7.5. Using a Gaussian Channel

So far, we have seen how each output can be used to discriminate between many possible inputs, but we have not yet considered how this can be used for communication in general.

For example, if we wished to transmit a human voice (which is not Gaussian) as an analogue signal then we could transform it into a Gaussian signal before transmission, and it would then be decoded by the receiver to recover the original voice signal. The nature of this transformation is qualitatively similar to an example which will be presented in Section 7.7, where the transformation is from a Gaussian distribution to a uniform distribution.

We could protest that we need to have infinite accuracy, which implies infinite information, in order to read a channel output which is the value of a continuous variable. However, we can never read the channel output with 100% accuracy because, no matter what instrument we use to measure the output (e.g. a voltmeter), its accuracy is finite; noise in the voltmeter's output limits the accuracy of the reading. When observing the voltmeter's output, the effect of voltmeter

160

noise is indistinguishable from the effect of additional channel noise. We therefore combine channel noise with voltmeter noise to obtain the overall noise level, which limits our ability to discriminate inputs in exactly the same way as extra channel noise. Thus, whether noise originates in the channel, the voltmeter, or both, the overall effect is to reduce the number of discriminable inputs.

If we do want to use this channel to send individual messages then we can construct a look-up table consisting of m rows, numbered from one to m, with each row consisting of two sections: a codeword $\mathbf{x}_i$ of n values, and a message s_i, so that the whole table defines a complete codebook of m messages. For the example considered in Section 7.3, we found that $C = 2$ bits, so if each codeword consists of $n = 20$ Gaussian values then each codeword specifies one out of

$$m = 2^{nC} \tag{7.41}$$
$$= 2^{40} \text{ messages,} \tag{7.42}$$

which is about 10^{12} messages. For illustration, the possible forms of two codewords are shown in Figure 7.3. The error rates for such short codewords would be quite high, but this could be remedied simply by

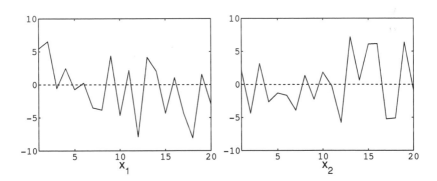

Figure 7.3. Schematic representation of two Gaussian codewords, $\mathbf{x}_1$ and $\mathbf{x}_2$. Each codeword consists of $n = 20$ values, where each value is chosen randomly from a Gaussian distribution with a variance of $v_x = 15$. If the channel noise has a Gaussian distribution with a variance of $v_\eta = 1$ then each codeword specifies one out of about 10^{12} messages, and therefore conveys 40 bits of information.

using longer codewords. If we want to send a message, say s_3, in the third row, then we transmit the codeword $\mathbf{x}_3$. If the codewords are sufficiently long then we are almost guaranteed that our codeword will be correctly classified by the receiver.

In practice, the hardest part of this operation is finding m codewords which are discriminable, because Shannon's theorem states that such codewords exist but does not specify how to find them. Practical methods for constructing codewords which can transmit almost 2^{nC} different messages with negligible error rates do exist (see Cover and Thomas (1991)[11]), but are beyond the scope of this introductory text.

7.6. Mutual Information and Correlation

Correlation is a standard statistical measure of the dependence between two variables X and Y. As an example, a person's height X and weight Y usually increase together and are therefore correlated. The *correlation coefficient* between X and Y is represented with the Greek letter ρ (rho), and is defined as

$$\rho \;=\; \frac{\mathrm{E}[(x_j - \bar{x})(y_j - \bar{y})]}{\sigma_x \sigma_y}, \tag{7.43}$$

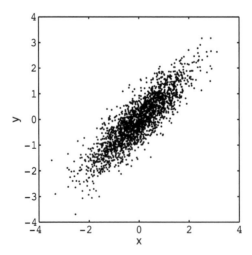

Figure 7.4. Mutual information and correlation. The (Gaussian) variables X and Y have a correlation of $\rho = 0.866$, and a mutual information of $I(X, Y) = 1.00$ bit (using Equation 7.45).

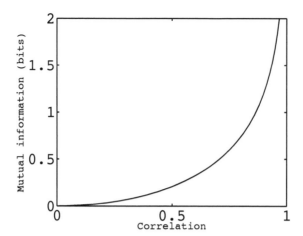

Figure 7.5. Mutual information and correlation for two Gaussian variables. As the correlation approaches one, the mutual information approaches infinity (Equation 7.45).

where $\bar{x}$ is the mean value of X, $\bar{y}$ is the mean value of Y, and σ_x and σ_y are the standard deviations of X and Y, respectively (see Glossary). Given n values of X and n corresponding values of Y, the correlation coefficient is estimated as

$$\hat{\rho} = \frac{1}{n\sigma_x\sigma_y} \sum_{j=1}^{n} (x_j - \bar{x})(y_j - \bar{y}). \tag{7.44}$$

If X and Y are drawn from a Gaussian distribution, as in Figure 7.4, and have a correlation of ρ then it can be shown[41] that the mutual information between X and Y is

$$I(X,Y) = 0.5 \log \frac{1}{1 - \rho^2} \text{ bits}, \tag{7.45}$$

as shown in Figure 7.5. Equation 7.45 can be rearranged to obtain correlation in terms of mutual information,

$$\rho = \sqrt{1 - 2^{-2I(X,Y)}}. \tag{7.46}$$

For example, if X and Y have a correlation of $\rho = 0.866$, as in Figure 7.4, then this implies that their mutual information is $I(X,Y) = 1$ bit per value.

Correlation can be viewed as a special version of mutual information. It follows that X and Y can have a large mutual information and a correlation of zero (e.g. if they are not Gaussian), but they cannot have a large correlation and zero mutual information.

7.7. The Fixed Range Channel

We will consider two complementary versions of the problem of how to maximise information transmission through a fixed range channel (i.e. a channel whose outputs lie between fixed lower and upper limits).

First, we provide an informal solution to the problem of identifying the input distribution that maximises mutual information. Given that the channel outputs lie between fixed limits, we already know (from Section 5.6) that the output distribution with maximum entropy is the uniform distribution. Thus, in order to communicate as much information as possible, the output distribution must be uniform. It follows that if the noise distribution has a particular known form then we should modify the input distribution to complement this, so that the output distribution is uniform.

Second (and this represents the bulk of this section), we provide a solution to the following problem: if our messages have a distribution $p(S)$ then how should we encode them in order to communicate as much information as possible?

As before, we have some channel inputs x and outputs y, each of which is a noisy version of x. Specifically,

$$y = x + \eta, \tag{7.47}$$

where η is noise. Suppose we have some data, in the form of values of an observed variable S, which we wish to encode as channel inputs in such a way that the channel communicates as much information as possible. The data are encoded using a continuous *encoding function*, g, which maps each observed value s to a corresponding unique channel input value x,

$$x = g(s). \tag{7.48}$$

The fact that each value s gets mapped to a *unique* input value x effectively defines the encoding function g to be a *monotonic* function (i.e. one that always increases or decreases, like Figure 7.6a, or Figure G.1b in Appendix G).

Thus, the channel input $g(s)$ and output y are related by

$$y \; = \; g(s) + \eta. \tag{7.49}$$

We proceed using the following line of reasoning. Provided the noise is negligible, maximising the entropy of the output Y maximises the mutual information between the input X and output Y. It follows that an encoding function g which maximises the input entropy also maximises the output entropy, and therefore maximises the mutual information between the input and output. Matters will be greatly simplified if we simply assume the noise is almost zero.

Maximising Mutual Information by Maximising Entropy

Given that $I(X,Y)$ varies as a function of g, when $I(X,Y)$ is as large as possible, the slope of $I(X,Y)$ with respect to g must be zero. It follows that, if we want to find that particular g which maximises $I(X,Y)$ then we need to find a form for g which makes the derivative (slope) of $I(X,Y)$ with respect to g equal to zero, i.e.

$$\frac{\partial I(X,Y)}{\partial g(S)} \; = \; 0. \tag{7.50}$$

Given our zero-noise assumption, Equation 7.7 implies that $I(X,Y) = H(Y)$, so

$$\frac{\partial I(X,Y)}{\partial g(S)} \; = \; \frac{\partial H(Y)}{\partial g(S)}. \tag{7.51}$$

If follows that the form of g that maximises the output entropy $H(Y)$ is also guaranteed to maximise the mutual information $I(X,Y)$. For a channel with bounded output values (e.g. 0 to 1), the distribution $p(Y)$ with maximum entropy is the uniform distribution (see Section 5.6). Therefore, to maximise the mutual information, we need to find a form for the function g that makes the distribution $p(Y)$ uniform.

Even though it makes intuitive sense, it is an abuse of notation to define the denominator of a derivative to be a a function, like $\partial H(Y)/\partial g(S)$. In practice, g could be an S-shaped or *sigmoidal* function (as in Figure 7.6a), parameterised by a variable σ which determines how steep it is. For example, it could be the cumulative distribution function of a Gaussian distribution with standard devitation σ, as shown in Figure 7.6a and in Figure G.1b in Appendix G:

$$g(s) \quad = \quad \frac{1}{\sigma\sqrt{2\pi}} \int_{t=-\infty}^{s} e^{-\frac{(t-\mu)^2}{2\sigma^2}} \, dt. \qquad (7.52)$$

Once we have defined g in terms of a 'steepness' parameter σ, we can rewrite the derivative $\partial H(Y)/\partial g(S) = \partial H(Y)/\partial\sigma$. In this case, assuming a mean of $\mu = 0$, the 'steepness' parameter σ can be adjusted to maximise $H(Y)$ and therefore $I(X,Y)$.

Thus, in order to find a value for σ that maximises $I(X,Y)$, all we need to do is to find a value for σ that maximises $H(Y)$. This is an important insight because it implies that the particular function g that maximises the entropy of the output Y also maximises the mutual information between the input X and the output Y. In other words, if we want to communicate as much information as possible through a channel then we should adjust the function g so that X, and therefore Y, has maximum entropy. Moreover, if Y has a finite bound then we know that $H(Y)$ has maximum entropy when Y has a uniform distribution.

Key point. Given that $Y = X + \eta$, where $X = g(S)$, and that the noise is negligible, maximising the mutual information between the bounded input X and the output Y amounts to finding a form for g which makes $p(X)$ uniform.

Entropy of a Transformed Variable

We will explore how changing the function g which encodes observed values s as input values x affects the entropy of X, and how this is related to the mutual information between X and Y.

The question we seek to answer is this: given that the probability distribution of S is fixed, what form should the encoding function g take to ensure that the channel outputs Y convey as much information as possible about the channel inputs $X = g(S)$? In other words, how should g be adjusted so as to maximise the mutual information between X and Y? In order to answer this question we need to know how the entropies of S and X are related, given that $Y = g(S) + \eta$. As above, we assume almost zero noise, so that

$$
\begin{align}
y &= x + \eta && (7.53) \\
&= g(s) + \eta && (7.54) \\
&\approx g(s), && (7.55)
\end{align}
$$

and therefore

$$
\begin{align}
H(Y) &= H(X) + H(\eta) && (7.56) \\
&\approx H(X) \, \text{bits.} && (7.57)
\end{align}
$$

Thus, we can maximise the mutual information by finding a mapping function g that maximises the entropy of the input $X = g(S)$.

Entropy of Related Variables

We will be juggling with probability distributions in this section so, to keep track of them, we introduce some new notation: the distribution of X will be denoted by $p_x(X)$, where the subscript x identifies this as the distribution of x values; similar notation is used for other variables.

A monotonic increasing function $x = g(s)$ (Figure 7.6a) transforms the variable S with a distribution $p_s(S)$ (Figure 7.6b) to a variable X with a uniform distribution (Figure 7.6c). As we saw in Section 5.5, the general rule for transforming $p_s(s)$ to $p_x(x)$ is

$$
p_x(x) = \frac{p_s(s)}{|dg(s)/ds|}, \tag{7.58}
$$

where the vertical bars indicate absolute value. We can omit the vertical bars because the function g is a cdf, and therefore its slope $dg(s)/ds$ is always positive.

For convenience, we define the probability distribution

$$f(s) \;=\; dx/ds \tag{7.59}$$

$$\;=\; dg(s)/ds, \tag{7.60}$$

which could take any form, in principle, but let's assume it looks something like the Gaussian distribution $p_s(S)$ in Figure 7.6b. Substituting Equation 7.60 in Equation 7.58 yields

$$p_x(x) \;=\; \frac{p_s(s)}{f(s)}. \tag{7.61}$$

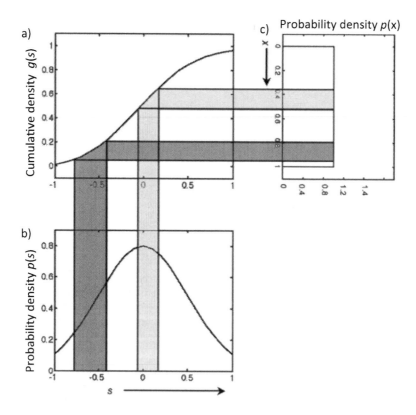

Figure 7.6. How (a) an encoding function maps (b) Gaussian distributed S values to (c) a uniform (maximum entropy) distribution of input values X. The encoding function which ensures $p(X)$ is uniform (and therefore has maximum entropy) is the cumulative distribution function of $p(S)$.

From this, we can see that changing the form of g affects $f(S)$, which affects the form of $p_x(X)$. As a reminder, the entropy of X is

$$H(X) \quad = \quad \int_{x=-\infty}^{\infty} p_x(x) \log \frac{1}{p_x(x)} \, dx. \qquad (7.62)$$

Substituting Equation 7.61 into 7.62 and noting that $dx = f(s) \, ds$ allows us to rewrite the integral with a change of variables from x to s:

$$H(X) \quad = \quad \int_{s=-\infty}^{\infty} \frac{p_s(s)}{f(s)} \left(\log \frac{f(s)}{p_s(s)} \right) f(s) \, ds \qquad (7.63)$$

$$= \quad \int_s p_s(s) \log \frac{f(s)}{p_s(s)} \, ds, \qquad (7.64)$$

which can be rewritten as

$$H(X) \quad = \quad \int_s p_s(s) \log \frac{1}{p_s(s)} \, ds \ + \ \int_s p_s(s) \log f(s) \, ds, \qquad (7.65)$$

$$= \quad H(S) + \mathrm{E}[\log f(s)]. \qquad (7.66)$$

This states that the entropy of X is given by the entropy of S plus the mean value of the slope of the encoding function g which maps S to X (and tallies with Equation 5.23).

Which Encoding Function Maximises Entropy?

We know that the entropy $H(X)$ is maximised if all values of X are equally probable, which implies that $p_x(X)$ is a uniform distribution, which, in turn, implies that all values of $p_x(X)$ are the same. Using Equation 7.61, we can rewrite $\frac{1}{p_x(x)}$ in Equation 7.62 as the ratio

$$\frac{1}{p_x(x)} \quad = \quad \frac{f(s)}{p_s(s)}. \qquad (7.67)$$

We can now see that this ratio must be constant in order to maximise the entropy of X. Given that both $p_s(s)$ and $f(s)$ are probability density functions (i.e. with areas that sum to one), this ratio can be constant only if $p_s(s) = f(s)$. What does this equality imply about the encoding function g?

Well, we know that the derivative of the encoding function is $f(s) = dg(s)/ds$. The integral of $f(s)$ yields another function $g(s)$ which is, by definition, the cumulative distribution function of $f(s)$,

$$g(s) \quad = \quad \int_{-\infty}^{s} f(t)\, dt, \tag{7.68}$$

where t is used as a dummy variable. Similarly, the cdf of the probability distribution $p_s(s)$ is

$$g^*(s) \quad = \quad \int_{t=-\infty}^{s} p_s(t)\, dt, \tag{7.69}$$

which is the encoding function that guarantees that X has a uniform (maximum entropy) distribution. Therefore, if the encoding function $g(s)$ is adjusted such that its derivative $dg(s)/ds$ has the same magnitude as $p_s(s)$ then $g(s) = g^*(s)$.

In summary, if we want to ensure that each encoded value x of observed value s carries as much information as possible then we must ensure that the encoding function $g(s)$ is the same as the cdf $g^*(s)$ of probability distribution $p_s(s)$.

7.8. Summary

In previous chapters, we defined entropy and mutual information for discrete variables which correspond to tangible everyday objects like letters of the alphabet. However, it is less obvious how to interpret entropy and mutual information for continuous variables because these correspond to insubstantial quantities like energy and power; in effect, we have constructed abstract measures of intangible quantities.

Unless we are careful, this begins to look as if we are performing ill-defined operations on non-existent objects. But we are not, because we can make sense of the increasingly abstract nature of these quantities at every stage if we maintain contact with the physical interpretation of the underlying equations. And, as we have seen, all of these equations have well-defined physical interpretations because, ultimately, they are all based firmly in the world of physics.

Chapter 8

Thermodynamic Entropy and Information

> Our imagination is stretched to the utmost, not, as in
> fiction, to imagine things which are not really there, but
> just to comprehend those things which are there.
> Feynman R, 1967.

8.1. Introduction

Entropy has been defined at least twice in the history of science.
First, it was defined in physics as thermodynamic entropy by
Boltzmann (1872) and Gibbs (1878), and later it was defined in
mathematics by Shannon (1948)[48]. Shannon's *information entropy* is a
measure of information, whereas *thermodynamic entropy* is a measure
of the number of states a physical system (like a jar of gas) can adopt.

These two different conceptualisations of entropy do not seem to be
obviously related. But they are, and the relationship between them
matters because thermodynamic entropy can be used to measure the
energy cost of Shannon's information entropy. If this were not true then
it would be possible to use a hypothetical being, known as *Maxwell's
demon*, to run power stations on pure information.

8.2. Physics, Entropy and Disorder

In the world of physics, thermodynamic entropy is often interpreted in
terms of the amount of disorder of a system. On this topic, there is no

better introduction than that given by one of the most lucid physicists, Richard Feynman. In order to set the scene, Feynman is considering the space inside a closed jar containing gas, as shown in Figure 8.1:

> So we now have to talk about what we mean by disorder and what we mean by order. ... Suppose we divide the space into little volume elements. If we have black and white molecules, how many ways could we distribute them among the volume elements so that white is on one side and black is on the other? On the other hand, how many ways could we distribute them with no restriction on which goes where? Clearly, there are many more ways to arrange them in the latter case. *We measure "disorder" by the number of ways that the insides can be arranged, so that from the outside it looks the same.* The logarithm of that number of ways is the entropy. The number of ways in the separated case is less, so the entropy is less, or the "disorder" is less. Feynman R, 1964[15].

More formally, each arrangement of molecules defines a unique *microstate*. However, if we swap the positions of two black molecules then the container looks the same from outside, so both of these different microstates give rise to the same appearance or *macrostate*.

In reality, each macrostate corresponds to some global parameter, such as temperature. Each temperature corresponds to a particular distribution of molecule speeds. Clearly, if we swap the speeds of any

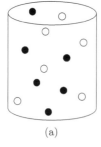   

(a)   (b)

Figure 8.1. There are many more ways to arrange the molecules of gas in a jar if (a) their positions are unrestricted than if (b) all white molecules have to stay in one half and all black molecules have to stay in the other half.

two molecules then the overall distribution of speeds is unaffected, so the temperature remains the same. And every time we repeat this swap, we generate a new microstate. So, as before, each macrostate corresponds to many microstates. Crucially, there is no reason to suppose that molecule A has speed S_1 whilst molecule B has speed S_2, rather than *vice versa*. In other words, all microstates that are consistent with a single macrostate are equally probable.

In physics, the entropy of a macrostate is proportional to the log of the number of microstates consistent with that macrostate. However, some macrostates have more microstates than others. To see this, we can replace each white molecule above with a fast molecule, and each black molecule with a slow one, as in Figure 8.2. We can now see that some macrostates can be obtained by many different arrangements of fast and slow molecules, whereas others can be obtained with only a small number of arrangements of fast and slow molecules.

For example, with no restriction on which molecule goes where (Figure 8.2a), there are many more arrangements than if all the fast molecules have to stay in one half of the jar and all the slow molecules have to stay in the other half (Figure 8.2b). That is, there are many more ways to swap the speeds of two molecules if we are allowed to choose each molecule from anywhere in the jar, rather than having to choose both molecules from within the same half of the jar.

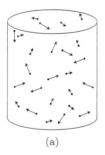 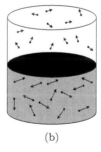

(a) (b)

Figure 8.2. In physics, a macrostate determines some global parameter such as temperature, which depends on the distribution of speeds of gas molecules, but not on their positions or directions of travel. Here, the length of each arrow indicates the speed of a molecule. If each molecule can be (a) anywhere in the jar, then this macrostate has many more microstates than if each molecule is restricted to (b) one half of the jar.

Placing all the fast molecules in one half causes that half to have a high temperature, and causes the other half to have a low temperature. So if we swap the speeds of two molecules within one half then this has no effect on temperature, because those molecules have the same speed. But if we swap the speeds of two molecules from different halves then this reduces the temperature in one half, and raises it in the other.

By definition, all microstates consistent with a given macrostate are equally probable, so it follows that macrostates with many microstates are more likely than macrostates with just a few microstates. For our jar of gas, this implies that macrostates in which both halves have an equal number of fast and slow molecules, as in Figure 8.3, are much more probable than macrostates in which one half has all the fast molecules (so it is hot) and the other half has all the slow molecules (so it is cold).

As we shall see, the highly probable macrostate in Figure 8.2a has high entropy, whereas the improbable macrostate in Figure 8.2b has low entropy.

Key point. Each macrostate is consistent with many equally probable microstates. So, macrostates with many microstates are more probable than macrostates with few microstates.

8.3. Information and Thermodynamic Entropy

Let's return to the history of entropy. As a first step, we can check to see if the definitions of thermodynamic entropy and Shannon's information entropy are at least syntactically similar.

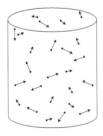

Figure 8.3. Two microstates from an ensemble with the same macrostate.

As a reminder, Shannon's information entropy is

$$H = \sum_{i=1}^{m} p(x_i) \log \frac{1}{p(x_i)}, \tag{8.1}$$

where m is the number of possible values that x can adopt. It will be useful to note that if there are a total of W possible outcomes or microstates (which are, by definition, equally probable) then $p(x_i) = 1/W$. For example, W could be the number of sides of a die. If we substitute this into Equation 8.1 then an equivalent definition is

$$H = \sum_{i=1}^{W} \frac{1}{W} \log W \tag{8.2}$$

$$= \log W. \tag{8.3}$$

For comparison, here is Boltzmann's entropy[32], which is defined in terms of *natural logarithms*:

$$S = k \ln W, \tag{8.4}$$

where W is the number of (equiprobable) microstates a physical system can adopt, and k is Boltzmann's constant, $k = 1.38 \times 10^{-23}$ joules/degree, where temperature is measured using the Kelvin (K) scale. (The Kelvin scale begins at absolute zero, so $0\,\mathrm{K}$ is $-273°\mathrm{C}$.)

Note the syntactic similarity between Shannon's information entropy H in Equation 8.3 and the thermodynamic entropy S in Equation 8.4. Finally, Gibbs' generalisation[20] of Boltzmann's entropy is

$$S = k \sum_{i=1}^{m} p(x_i) \ln \frac{1}{p(x_i)} \quad \text{joules/degree,} \tag{8.5}$$

where m is the number of macroscopically distinguishable physical configurations that the system can adopt. This somewhat terse definition should become clear in Section 8.4. Again, note the syntactic similarity between Shannon's information entropy in Equation 8.1 and the thermodynamic entropy in Equation 8.5.

8.4. Ensembles, Macrostates and Microstates

Just as the temperature of a gas (macrostate) is the same for many different arrangements of molecules (microstates), so, for a pair of dice, the summed outcome values are the same for different pairs of individual outcomes (as we saw in Section 3.5). In physics, the set of all microstates that yield the same macrostate is called an *ensemble* of microstates.

We can identify each of the 11 summed dice outcomes with a macrostate, and each pair of dice values with a microstate. In both cases (dice or gas), an ensemble of microstates corresponds to a single macrostate (summed dice dots or temperature).

Notice that every one of the microstates in an ensemble is equally probable, but that certain macrostates (e.g. summed dice value 7) are generated by many microstates, whereas other macrostates are generated by only a small number of microstates (e.g. summed dice value 2). Because all microstates are equally probable, it follows that a macrostate generated by many microstates is more probable than a macrostate generated by only a small number of microstates.

In general, entropy is given by the logarithm of the number of possible microstates. However, if each microstate corresponds to exactly one macrostate then entropy is also given by the log of the number of possible macrostates. For example, an 11-sided die would have 11 equally probable macrostates (outcomes). Because each of the 11 macrostates corresponds to one microstate, the entropy is given by the log of the number of possible macrostates, $\log 11 = 3.46$ bits. We can reverse this logic to confirm that 3.46 bits implies $2^{3.46} = 11$ equally probable macrostates. More interestingly, we can apply the same reasoning to a variable with *unequal* macrostate probabilities.

In the case of the two dice considered above, even though the macrostates (i.e. the summed dots) are not equally probable, these dice have the same entropy as a single die with $2^{3.27} = 9.65$ sides. Even though such a die is not physically possible, it corresponds to a system with 9.65 equally probable microstates. More generally, if a variable with unequal macrostate probabilities has an entropy of n bits then it behaves like a system which can adopt 2^n equally probable microstates.

8.5. Pricing Information: The Landauer Limit

In this section, we define an absolute lower limit to the amount of energy required to acquire or transmit one bit of information[40], which is known as the *Landauer limit*. The value of this lower limit was first proposed by von Neumann (1961), and was developed by Landauer (1961)[30].

Consider a jar of gas with a particular thermodynamic entropy S. We can determine the entropy of the gas by counting the number of equally probable microstates it can adopt. In order to keep things simple, we will assume that this gas consists of a single molecule[40;47]. First, we push the gas into one half of the jar, whilst maintaining the gas at a constant temperature.

Next, we divide the jar into W_1 small cubes, and we define the molecule's position to be the position of the cube it occupies. The number of different possible positions (cubes) for the molecule is also W_1, where each molecule position corresponds to a single microstate. If the number of possible microstates available to the gas in the whole jar is W_1 then the number of microstates in half the jar is $W_2 = W_1/2$. Therefore, in confining the gas to half the jar, the thermodynamic entropy changes from an initial high value of

$$S_1 \;=\; k \ln W_1 \text{ joules/degree}, \tag{8.6}$$

to a lower thermodynamic entropy

$$S_2 \;=\; k \ln W_2 \text{ joules/degree}. \tag{8.7}$$

Thus, a gas distributed throughout a jar has higher thermodynamic entropy than if it occupies only one half of the jar. Specifically, in the process of confining the gas from the whole jar into half the jar, the thermodynamic entropy decreases by an amount

$$\Delta S \;=\; k \ln W_1 - k \ln W_2 \tag{8.8}$$
$$=\; k \ln 2W_2 - k \ln W_2 \tag{8.9}$$
$$=\; k \ln 2(W_2/W_2) \tag{8.10}$$
$$=\; k \ln 2 \text{ joules/degree}. \tag{8.11}$$

Notice that this remains true irrespective of how small we make the cubes. Multiplying by temperature T, we obtain

$$T\Delta S = kT \ln 2 \tag{8.12}$$
$$= 0.693 \times kT \text{ joules.} \tag{8.13}$$

Equation 8.13 states that the amount of energy required to change the entropy of a system is equal to the change in entropy multiplied by the system's temperature.

If we consider this in terms of Shannon's information entropy then we find that the process of restricting the gas to half of the jar decreases the information entropy from $H_1 = \log_2 W_1$ bits to $H_2 = \log_2 W_2$ bits, which is a decrease in information entropy of

$$\Delta H = \log_2 (W_1/W_2) \tag{8.14}$$
$$= 1 \text{ bit.} \tag{8.15}$$

Thus, forcing a gas into one half of a jar leads to a decrease in thermodynamic entropy of $\Delta S = 0.693k$ joules/degree, and a corresponding decrease in information entropy of $\Delta H = 1$ bit.

Using a similar line of reasoning, Landauer showed that the smallest amount of energy required to erase (or acquire) one bit is

$$1 \text{ bit} = 0.693k \text{ joules/degree} \tag{8.16}$$
$$= 9.57 \times 10^{-24} \text{ joules/degree.} \tag{8.17}$$

The reason that this Landauer limit increases with temperature is because the information communicated has to overcome the effects of random fluctuations (noise), which inevitably increase at higher temperatures. For example, the cost of Shannon information at a temperature of $T = 313 \, \text{K}$ $(40°\text{C})$ is

$$9.57 \times 10^{-24} \times T = 3 \times 10^{-21} \text{ joules/bit.} \tag{8.18}$$

One interpretation of the above is that, initially, we have no information about which half of the jar the gas is in. Given that the gas is restricted to one half of the jar, we require one bit of information to tell us which half. Thus, in the process of restricting the gas to one half of the jar, we effectively remove one bit's worth of uncertainty (information entropy) about which half of the jar the gas is in. Because the amount of energy required to force the gas into one half of the jar cannot be less than $T\Delta S = 0.693kT$ joules, this is also the energy cost of reducing the information entropy of this one-molecule gas by one bit.

Strictly speaking, the preceding account applies only to logically *irreversible* binary operations, like erasing (forgetting) information based on some observation. Evidence for the existence of the Landauer limit has been obtained by Bérut *et al* (2012)[7].

Key point. No matter how efficient *any* physical device is (e.g. a computer or a brain), it can acquire one bit of information only if it expends at least $0.693kT$ joules of energy.

8.6. The Second Law of Thermodynamics

The second law of thermodynamics can be summarised as *things fall apart*. More formally, it states that the entropy of an isolated system increases until it reaches a maximum value. An isolated system is one which does not lose or gain energy from outside the system.

In a sense, we have already derived a statistical rationale for why the second law of thermodynamics ought to be true. Given a few assumptions regarding the rules of probability, our analysis of entropy in the preceding pages makes us fairly certain that a system will adopt a high entropy state, for the simple reason that (at any given temperature) almost all states have high entropy.

From this perspective, the second law of thermodynamics seems inevitable, almost tautological. But it is not. It only seems to be so because we have built up our picture of entropy from assumptions based on physically valid observations regarding the laws of probability.

One consequence of the second law of thermodynamics is that a system, when left to its own devices, will inevitably choose a series of macrostates with successively larger entropies. It will, in a sense, 'run uphill' in terms of entropy, which corresponds to 'running downhill' in terms of order. When it has finished running it is said to be in a state of equilibrium, which corresponds to a maximum entropy state.

In terms of the jar of gas, if we use a piece of cardboard to push all of the molecules into one half of the jar and then remove the cardboard, we should be unsurprised when the molecules quickly migrate to fill all of the jar. But we should be unsurprised for one very good reason.

The above analysis informs us that the most common microstates correspond to macrostates in which the molecules are pretty much evenly distributed throughout the jar, and these common microstates far outnumber the microstates in which the molecules arrange themselves to occupy one half of the jar. It follows that, from its initial low entropy state, the jar of gas will run uphill to achieve maximum entropy, which will look like a gas that is running downhill in terms of orderliness. With this new perspective, we

> ... should never be surprised by or feel the need to explain why any physical system is in a high entropy state.
> Greene B, 2004 [22].

8.7. Maxwell's Demon

> The being soon came to be called Maxwell's demon, because of its far reaching subversive effects on the natural order of things. Chief among these effects would be to abolish the need for energy sources such as oil, uranium and sunlight.
> Bennett CH, 1987 [6].

Suppose we wanted to cheat physics with a cunning ploy, using pure information. In 1871, the physicist James Clerk Maxwell proposed an ingeniously simple method for doing this. If Maxwell's method actually worked then we could create perpetual motion machines, and build power stations fuelled by pure information. Unfortunately, Maxwell's demon does not provide energy for free in practice. More importantly, such a demon *cannot* provide energy for free, not even in principle.

Maxwell's demon resides on top of a closed container of gas, near to a transparent partition positioned between the container's two halves, labelled A and B. The demon can open and close a small door in the partition with the flick of his wrist (which we assume expends no

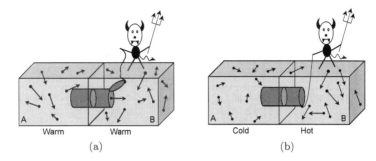

Figure 8.4. Maxwell's demon opens and closes a door between two halves of a container, so that only fast molecules pass into the right side, and only slow molecules pass into the left side. Thus, pure information regarding the speed and direction of individual gas molecules is used to create a temperature difference, which can be used to generate electricity. By Teleri Stone.

energy). When he spots a fast-moving molecule in A heading towards the door, he opens it, so the molecule can pass into B, as shown in Figure 8.4a. Similarly, when he spots a slow-moving molecule in B heading towards the door, he opens it, so the molecule can pass into A. Over time, this results in the accumulation of all fast molecules in B, and all slow molecules in A, as shown in Figure 8.4b.

Because the speed of molecules in a gas defines its temperature, the demon effectively separates the original container of gas into a cold side and a hot side. Such a temperature difference can then be used to do work. The archetypal machine of this type is the steam engine, or internal combustion engine. In both cases, the fast molecules push against a piston head, and the resultant piston motion can be harnessed to drive the wheels of a steam tractor or a car. Similarly, we could place a demon and his door at the intake pipe of a power station (Figure 8.5), so that only hot air is allowed in. Because power stations run on hot gas, we would have free power, forever. But there is a catch.

In order to know when to open and shut the door, the demon must use *information* about the speed and direction of each molecule. However, we already know that each bit of information cannot cost less than the Landauer limit of $0.693kT$ joules/bit (Equation 8.16).

If the energy extracted from a fast-moving molecule allowed through the door were larger than the Landauer limit then we could run power stations on information, because there would then be a net energy

Figure 8.5. Using Maxwell's demon, the fuel for power stations would be pure information. From Wikimedia.

profit for each molecule. But it turns out that the amount of usable energy the demon accumulates in the container is exactly balanced by the energy required to acquire the information needed to open the door at the right times. So, even though Maxwell's demon could run a power station, the energy generated cannot be more than the energy expended by the demon.

In other words, there is no net gain to be had from using information to accumulate fast-moving molecules in one half of a container, and using the resultant temperature difference to generate electricity. This is important because it provides a fundamental link between the notion of Shannon's information entropy, as defined in information theory, and thermodynamic entropy, as defined in physics. Indeed, within three years of the publication of Shannon's theory, Gabor[18] declared:

> We cannot get anything for nothing, not even an observation.
> Gabor D, 1951.

On a lighter note, the novelist Terry Pratchett speculated that knowledge requires physical storage space, and he used this supposition to explain the mysterious dark matter which comprises 90% of the mass of the universe:

> For something to exist, it has to have a position in time and space. And this explains why nine-tenths of the mass of the universe is unaccounted for. Nine-tenths of the universe is

the knowledge of the position and direction of everything
in the other tenth ...

Pratchett T, *Thief of Time*, 2001.

8.8. Quantum Computation

After some initial reluctance, quantum mechanics was embraced by
the physics community in the twentieth century. Because physics
can be viewed in terms of computing with physical entities, it was
inevitable that the quantum revolution would eventually impact on
our understanding of computing with numbers. Accordingly, quantum
mechanics is in the process of being harnessed in the hope that it
will be able to perform computational feats beyond the capability of
conventional computers. For example, a quantum computer program
invented by Lov Grover[23] in 1996 should be able to play the game of '20
questions' using a sequence of just five (or, more precisely, $\sqrt{20} = 4.47$)
computational steps. If we interpret each computational step as a
quantum question then a quantum computer could win the game of '20
questions' using just five quantum questions. More generally, Grover's
program should play the game of N questions using the equivalent of
only $\sqrt{N}$ quantum questions.

Inevitably, there is a trade-off between the sequence of N simple
computational steps of a conventional computer, and the sequence of
$\sqrt{N}$ complex computational steps of a quantum computer. Indeed, if a
sequence of $\sqrt{N}$ steps can be executed by a quantum computer faster
than a conventional computer can execute N simple steps then the
quantum computer should be a clear winner.

It is still early days for quantum computation, and only simple
quantum computers exist. But we should not despair, because
conventional computers also had a slow start. In 1949, an article in
Popular Mechanics Magazine declared:

... a calculator today is equipped with 18,000 vacuum tubes
and weighs 30 tons, computers in the future may have only
1,000 vacuum tubes and perhaps weigh only half a ton.

8.9. Summary

In this chapter, we have reinforced the claim expressed in previous chapters that the rarefied concepts of entropy and Shannon information have tangible concomitants in the world of physics. When John Wheeler proclaimed that "All things physical are information-theoretic in origin", he was not being metaphorical (he was a physicist, after all) because he understood that there is a deep, but subtle, connection between the abstract constructs of information theory and the nature of the physical universe. Most remarkable of all is that information has a definite lowest cost which can be measured in joules per bit. More than any other, this fact establishes the existence of a fundamental link between Shannon's information entropy and Boltzmann–Gibbs' thermodynamic entropy, between information and the disorderly arrangement of molecules in a jar of gas.

Chapter 9

Information As Nature's Currency

Nature uses only the longest threads to weave her patterns,
so each small piece of her fabric reveals the organization of
the entire tapestry.
Feynman R, 1967.

9.1. Introduction

Information theory is used in research fields as diverse as linguistics, communications, signal processing, computing, neuroscience, genetics, and evolutionary theory. In this chapter, we explore some relevant applications, and discuss them in the context of information theory.

9.2. Satellite TVs, MP3 and All That

The next time you switch on your TV, remember that what you see on the screen bears only a superficial resemblance to the data streaming out of the satellite that delivers the signal to your house. The reason is that the original images were encoded or *compressed* before being transmitted from a TV station to the satellite, and these encoded images must be decoded by your TV's computer before the original images can be recovered. Thus, the problem faced by modern television systems is that images must be displayed at a very high quality, but the image data must be transmitted through a communication channel with a relatively small capacity. This is clearly a problem that can be addressed with information theory.

The camera that recorded the original image data is essentially an information source that generates data at a rate of about 1.5 gigabits per second (Gb/s), where a gigabit is one billion (10^9 or 1,000 million) binary digits. This figure of 1.5 Gb/s results from the fact that TVs typically display 1920 elements horizontally and 1080 lines vertically, at a rate of 30 images per second. Each colour image displayed consists of 1920 × 1080 sets of three pixels (red, green and blue), so the total number of pixels is about 6 million (i.e. $3 \times 1920 \times 1080 = 6{,}220{,}800$).

Let's assume the intensity of each pixel has a range of zero to 255, which is represented by $\log 256 = 8$ binary digits, making a total of 49,766,400, or about 50 million binary digits per image. Because a TV displays 30 images per second, this amounts to about 1,500 million binary digits/s. This is confusingly quoted as 1,500 megabits/s (i.e. 1,500 million *bits*/s) in the world of computing because both bit and binary digit are used to refer to binary digits (see Section 1.5).

However, the channel through which these 1,500 million binary digits/s are communicated (i.e. a satellite) can carry only 19.2 million binary digits/s. According to Shannon, a noiseless channel which carries 19.2 million binary digits/s has a capacity of exactly 19.2 million bits/s. So the problem is this: how can the information implicit in 1,500 million binary digits/s be communicated through a channel which carries only 19.2 million binary digits/s?

Roughly speaking, the solution comprises four stages of processing before the signal is transmitted. First, squeeze all of the redundant data out of the images. Second, remove components which are essentially invisible to the human eye. Third, recode the resultant data so that all symbols occur equally often (e.g. using Huffman coding), and, finally, add a small amount of redundancy in the form of an error-correcting code. As discussed in Chapter 1, the similarity between adjacent pixel values is one source of redundancy. However, because a TV receives data as a temporal sequence of images, the state of each pixel tends to be similar between consecutive images, and this temporal redundancy can also be removed to compress the data.

The standard set of methods used to remove spatial and temporal redundancy are collectively called MPEG (Moving Picture Expert Group). Whilst these methods are quite complex, they all rely heavily on a core method called the *cosine transform*. In essence, this decomposes the data into image features of different sizes. When measured across space (i.e. within an image), size translates to *spatial frequency* (actually, 1/spatial frequency, so large features have low spatial frequencies). When measured across time, size translates to features that persist for short or long times, which translates to *temporal frequency* (actually, 1/temporal frequency, so persistent features have low temporal frequencies).

Once the data have been transformed into a series of spatial and temporal frequencies, some of them can be thrown away. This is an important step for two reasons. First, it reduces the quantity of data to be communicated, which is good. Second, it reduces the quantity of information communicated, which is bad. However, if the information thrown away involves only those frequencies which we cannot see, then it is not so bad, after all. For example, fine details that are beyond the resolution of the human eye correspond to high spatial frequencies, and can therefore be discarded without any apparent loss of image quality. Similarly, changes over time that are too fast to be detectable by the eye correspond to high temporal frequencies, and can be discarded. At the other extreme, very low spatial and temporal frequencies are also essentially invisible to the eye, and can be discarded.

The eye is sensitive to intensity (luminance), but relatively insensitive to fine gradations of colour. Consequently, the data from TV cameras can be recoded to give high-resolution intensity data, and low-resolution colour data. Because this recoding mirrors the encoding within the human visual system[51], the perceived picture quality is unaffected. The result is a 50% saving in the number of binary digits required to represent information regarding the colour and intensity of pixels.

Discarding certain spatial and temporal frequencies and recoding intensity/colour data means that data recorded at a rate of 1,500 million binary digits/s can be compressed and transmitted through a communication satellite channel with a capacity of 19.2 million bits/s, and then decoded to present you (the TV viewer) with 1,500 million binary digits of data per second (with some loss of information but no visible loss of quality). This represents an effective compression factor of about $78 (\approx 1500/19.2)$, so it looks as if we can communicate 78 times more data than the channel capacity would suggest. In fact, the compression has to be a little better than this, because the stereo sound is also squeezed into the same channel. This is achieved by applying the cosine transform mentioned above to sound (where it is called MP3).

Compression that throws away information is called *lossy*, whereas compression that preserves all information is called *lossless*. Most practical systems are lossy, but they do not give the appearance of losing information because the discarded information is invisible, or, at least, unimportant for human perception of images or sounds.

Finally, in order to minimise the effects of noise, redundancy is added to the compressed data. Unlike the redundancy of the original data, the amount of added redundancy is small, but it is just enough to enable the receiver to recover from all but the most catastrophic forms of noise in the form of electrical interference.

9.3. Does Sex Accelerate Evolution?

Even though the Darwin–Wallace theory of evolution by natural selection was published in 1859, it still holds a number of mysteries. Prominent amongst these is the question of sex. Specifically, why do some species have two sexes?

Many answers which have been proposed rely on logical argument mixed with a degree of plausible speculation, rather than mathematical analysis. And even though mathematical analysis cannot usually provide definitive answers to biological questions, it can constrain the space of possible answers. In so doing, some answers can be definitely excluded, and those that remain can be used to yield hypotheses which can be tested empirically.

Evolution is essentially a process in which natural selection acts as a mechanism for transferring information from the environment to the collective genome of a species. (The term genome is conventionally used to refer to all of the genes in a *particular* individual, but we use it to refer to all of the genes in a *typical* individual.) Each individual represents a question asked of the environment: are the genes in this individual better or worse than average? The answer is often brutal, because the environment destroys many individuals in infancy. But even when the answer is given more tactfully, so that an individual does not die but simply has fewer offspring, it is still brutally honest.

The answer comes in units called fitness, and a good measure of fitness is the number of offspring each individual rears to breeding age. Over many generations, the information provided by the answers (fitness) allocated to each individual coerces the genome via natural selection to adopt a particular form. Thus, information about the environment eventually becomes implicit in the genome of a species.

The form of the information received from the environment is both crude and noisy. It is crude inasmuch as it is measured in units of whole numbers of offspring, rather than in the fractional offspring numbers required to obtain a precise measure of fitness. And it is noisy inasmuch as the environment does not simply provide a perfect estimate of each individual's fitness because, sometimes,

> the race is not to the swift, nor the battle to the strong
> ... but time and chance happeneth to them all.
> Ecclesiastes 9:11, King James Bible.

Thus, the environment assigns a noisy fitness value to each individual, where fitness equates to the number of offspring each individual rears to adulthood. However, this fitness value gets assigned to a whole individual, and not to particular genes that make large (negative or positive) contributions to an individual's fitness. In other words, the totality of an individual's fitness value does not specify which beneficial features increase fitness, or which detrimental features decrease fitness. Ultimately, each individual either lives or dies before reproducing, which implies that its genome provides a maximum of one bit of information about its relative fitness. However, the fact that the information received from the environment is crude and noisy is not necessarily a problem for evolution.

In a theoretical *tour de force*, John Holland (1992)[25] proved that the type of genetic algorithm used in natural selection implements a kind of *intrinsic parallelism*, which makes it incredibly efficient at allocating blame or credit to particular genes. In essence, Holland's mathematical analyses proved the *schema theorem*, which states that a gene increases in frequency within a species at a rate exponentially related to the extra fitness that gene confers on its owners (i.e. good genes spread extremely quickly). Even though Holland's results make no explicit claims on information theory, it seems likely that information theory is relevant. On a related topic, information theory has been applied to test the idea that the genetic code is optimal[33;44].

The human genome contains about 3×10^9 (3 billion) pairs of nucleotides, where each nucleotide comprises one element in one half of the classic double helix of the DNA (deoxyribonucleic acid) molecule (there are about 1,000 nucleotides per gene). In order to explore how quickly the genome acquires information about the environment, MacKay (2003)[34] identifies one bit as corresponding to one nucleotide, which is a well-defined chemical structure (unlike a gene). The human genome makes use of four particular nucleotides, adenine (A), guanine (G), thymine (T) and cytosine (C). Within the DNA molecule, nucleotides pair up on opposite sides of the double helix, such that A pairs with T, and C pairs with G.

In the spirit of the methods applied successfully in physics, MacKay uses a stripped-down model of each nucleotide, which is assumed to occur in one of two states, good or bad. Given a genome of N nucleotides, the fitness of an individual is defined simply as the number of nucleotides in a good state, and the normalised fitness is defined as

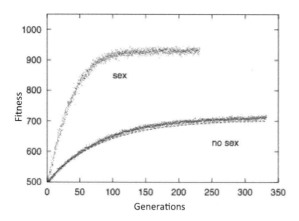

Figure 9.1. How fitness changes over generations for asexual and sexually reproducing populations. In this simulation, the number of genes per individual is $N = 1,000$, and 1,000 individuals initially had randomly generated genomes with a fitness $f = 0.5$, so the population fitness was initially 500. The dashed line shows the theoretical curve. Reproduced with permission from MacKay (2003)[34].

the proportion of good genes in an individual's genome. Finally, the proportion of good genes above 50% is defined as the *excess normalised fitness*, δf, which we will just call *fitness*.

MacKay then compares the effects of different mutation rates on fitness in populations that reproduce sexually and asexually. If a sexually reproducing population is well adapted to its environment then, by definition, the genome is close to an ideal or optimal genome. MacKay shows that this near-optimal genome acquires one bit every two generations. However, if the environment changes then over generations the genome adapts. MacKay proves that the rate at which a genome of N nucleotides accumulates information from the environment can be as large as

$$\sqrt{N} \quad \text{bits/generation.} \tag{9.1}$$

For example, given that $N = 3 \times 10^9$ nucleotides, the rate at which the population accumulates information from the environment can be as large as 540,000 bits/generation. In this case, the collective genome of the current generation would have 540,000 bits more information about its environment than the genomes of the previous generation, and so should be better prepared to meet the challenges of that environment. In contrast, under similar circumstances, an asexually reproducing population (e.g. aphids) acquires information at a fixed rate of one bit per generation.

The result stated in Equation 9.1 seems to suggest that the bigger the genome, the faster evolution can work. If this is true, then why doesn't the process of natural selection result in genomes which are as large as possible? The answer involves mutation rates.

The mutation rate is the probability that each gene will be altered from one generation to the next, and (equivalently) is the average proportion of genes altered from one generation to the next. It turns out that, in theory, the largest mutation rate that can be tolerated in an asexual population is about $1/N$, whereas it is $1/\sqrt{N}$ in a sexual population. To take a simple example, if the genome size is tiny, say $N = 100$, then the largest mutation rate that can be tolerated in an asexual population is 0.01, whereas it is $1/\sqrt{N} = 1/10 = 0.1$ in a sexual population. So, in both cases, the rate of genetic mutation affects large genomes more than small ones, but a sexual population can tolerate a much higher mutation rate than an asexual population. This is especially pertinent given that mutation is pretty much the only source of inter-individual variability available to asexual populations. Because variability provides the raw materials for natural selection, the net effect is to accelerate evolution in sexual populations.

However, the above results provide a biological conundrum: a large genome increases evolutionary speed, but it also decreases tolerance to mutations. This means there is a trade-off between a large genome (which accelerates evolution, but provides poor mutation tolerance) and a short genome (which provides good mutation tolerance, but decelerates evolution). These conflicting constraints suggest that evolution should have found a 'happy medium' for genome size, which ensures that the rate of evolution is as fast as it can be for a given genome size and mutation rate.

The upshot of this analysis suggests that natural selection allows a genome of size N to accumulate information from the environment at a rate proportional to $\sqrt{N}$ times faster in a sexual population than in an asexual population. Additionally, a sexual population can tolerate a mutation rate that is proportional to $\sqrt{N}$ times greater than the mutation rate that can be tolerated by an asexual population. For genomes with $N \approx 10^9$ nucleotides, this factor of $\sqrt{N}$ is not trivial. Even for a 'toy' genome size of $N = 10,000$, if an asexual population accumulates information at the rate of 10 bits/generation then a sexual population would accumulate information at the rate of $10 \times \sqrt{10,000} \approx 1,000$ bits/generation.

Darwin would almost certainly approve of this type of analysis, which seeks to find the laws which underpin evolution by natural selection:

> The grand Question which every naturalist ought to have before him when dissecting a whale or classifying a mite, a fungus or an infusorian is "What are the Laws of Life?".
> Darwin C, *B Notebook*, 1837.

According to the analysis summarised above, we now have a candidate for one of these laws: between successive generations, the collective genome of a species should maximise the Shannon information acquired about its environment for each joule of expended energy. This general idea of *efficient evolution* can be considered to be an extension of the efficient coding hypothesis normally applied to brains.

Finally, MacKay argues that faulty transcription of DNA effectively smoothes out an otherwise rugged fitness landscape, and thereby increases the rate of evolution. This type of phenomenon is an example of the *Baldwin effect*[4], which is traditionally considered to rely on within-lifetime learning to accelerate Darwinian genetic evolution.

The results of information-theoretic analyses[34;54] of biological evolution are not only compelling and intriguing; they also provide hypotheses that can be tested empirically: hypotheses which should make redundant much of the speculative debate that often accompanies such controversies.

9.4. The Human Genome: How Much Information?

Like any message, DNA is composed of a finite alphabet. As described above, the alphabet for DNA comprises 4 letters (A,G,T, and C), where each letter corresponds to one nucleotide. For a message which is N letters long, the number m of possible messages that could be sent is therefore $m = 4^N$, and the maximum amount of information conveyed by this message is $H = \log 4^N = N \log 4 = 2N$ bits. Given that the human genome consists of $N = 3 \times 10^9$ nucleotides, this implies that it contains a maximum of $H = 6 \times 10^9$ or 6 billion bits of information. Of course, the genetic code is partially redundant (which may be necessary to minimise errors) and some regions of the DNA molecule do not seem to code for anything, so the estimate of 6 billion bits is an upper bound.

Note that 6 billion bits could be stored in 6 billion binary digits, which is almost one gigabyte (a gigabyte is 8×10^9 binary digits). For comparison, a basic DVD disc can store 8 billion binary digits, which is enough for a two-hour movie. However, whereas a disc or a memory stick consists of a substantial amount of material, these 6 billion binary digits' worth of data are stored in the DNA inside the nucleus of every cell in the human body.

9.5. Enough DNA to Wire Up a Brain?

Everything that we see, hear, or touch depends on the flow of information through nerve cells or *neurons*. These neurons are the only connection between us and the physical world, and the brief on–off pulses they deliver to the brain are the only messages we can ever receive about that world. However, even before we are born, some information has already been transferred from our DNA into the brain; otherwise, we could neither breathe nor suckle. So at least some of the brain's microstructure is determined primarily by nature, rather than nurture. In terms of information, an obvious question is: does the DNA of the human genome contain enough information to specify every single connection in the brain of a new-born baby?

The human brain contains about 10^{11} (one hundred billion) neurons, and each neuron has about 10^4 (ten thousand) connections or *synapses* to other neurons. This leads to an estimate of 10^{15} synapses in total. As stated above, the human genome contains about 3×10^9 (three billion) nucleotides (see Section 9.3). In fact, there are about 1,000 nucleotides per gene, but let's keep things simple. If each nucleotide specified one synapse then this would place an extremely conservative upper bound on the number of synapses that could be genetically programmed. Even under this conservative assumption, if one bit were used to specify the strength of a synapse (e.g. on or off) then there would be enough information for only 10^9 synapses, which represents one millionth of all the synapses in the brain ($10^9/10^{15} = 10^{-6}$). And this would leave no DNA for the rest of the body. In essence, if we want to use DNA to encode synapses then we would need about a million times more DNA than we have now.

In Darwin's day, the question posed above would be hostage to pure speculation. But with Watson and Crick's discovery of the structure of DNA in 1953, combined with Shannon's information theory, we can answer this question definitively: *no*, there is not enough DNA in the human genome to specify every single connection in the brain.

A compelling implication of this answer is that the human brain must learn. It may seem obvious from observing an infant that we learn, but the fact that we do learn does not imply we *have to* learn in order to develop. Thus, information theory tells us that we *must* learn, because learning provides a way for the brain to use the information supplied by the environment to specify the correct set of 10^{15} synapses.

9.6. Are Brains Good at Processing Information?

Neurons communicate information. They do not care about the shape of a tree, the smell of vanilla, or the touch of a cat's fur. That is for us, the beneficiaries of what neurons do; what they do is to communicate information, and that is pretty much all that they do.

Ever since the first neurons appeared, about 580 million years ago, the relentless forces of natural selection have ensured that they are about as perfect as they can be. We know this is true because information theory has been applied within the research field of *computational neuroscience* to the various functions that neurons perform[17;35;43]. The success of this highly technical research program, far from diminishing the wonder of brain function, promises a radical change in our perspective:

> ... we claim that the results of a quantitative approach are
> sufficiently extreme that they begin to alter our qualitative
> conception of how the nervous system works.
> Rieke *et al*, 1997[43].

A major reason this research program has been so successful is because, whatever else neurons appear to be doing, they must be communicating information about the world to the brain. As the world offers up almost infinite amounts of sensory data to be communicated, it is necessary for neurons to be selective, and efficient in encoding the information they select for transmission. This general approach has been championed by Horace Barlow, who has been largely responsible for the genesis of the resultant *efficient coding hypothesis*[5]. Put simply, this states that data acquired by the eye should be encoded as efficiently as possible before being communicated to the brain.

Information in Spiking Neurons

One of the first applications of information theory to neuroscience was by MacKay and McCulloch (1952), who calculated the entropy of a spiking source, a mere four years after the publication of Shannon's

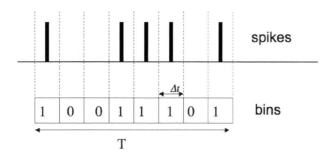

Figure 9.2. A series of n voltage spikes from a neuron can be represented as 0s and 1s. If a time period of T seconds contains n spikes then the firing rate is $r = n/T$ spikes/s. If T is divided into M small intervals or bins of width Δt then the probability of observing a spike in each bin is $p = r \times \Delta t$.

paper. The following account is based on Rieke *et al* (1997)[43], and on lecture notes by Professor John Porrill.

Suppose we regard the neuron as a channel. A neuron acts as a binary channel because neurons deliver information in the form of brief voltage spikes, as shown in Figure 9.2. These spikes occur at a typical rate of between one and 100 spikes per second (spikes/s). Suppose we record spikes with only limited temporal resolution of, say, $\Delta t = 0.001$ seconds (i.e. 1 millisecond (ms)) then a spike can either be present or not present in each 1 ms interval. This binary channel can carry one binary digit each millisecond, so its capacity is $C = 1/\Delta t$ bits/s. With a temporal resolution of $\Delta t = 0.001$ seconds, this gives an upper bound defined by its channel capacity of 1,000 bits/s.

Let's estimate the entropy of the output of a typical neuron, assuming that spikes are mutually independent. The entropy of a sequence of spikes, or *spike train*, is given by the logarithm of the number of different possible spike trains that could occur in a given time interval T. In order to avoid the complicated mathematics that ends with a good approximation to this[43], we will use some much less complicated mathematics to obtain a slightly less good approximation.

If spikes are produced at an average firing rate of r spikes/s then the probability of a spike in each time interval of Δt seconds is

$$p = r\,\Delta t, \tag{9.2}$$

and the probability that no spike occurs in each interval is therefore $q = 1 - p$. Thus, the average Shannon information of each interval is

$$
\begin{aligned}
H &= h(p) + h(q) & (9.3) \\
&= p \log (1/p) + q \log (1/q) \text{ bits.} & (9.4)
\end{aligned}
$$

If we define Δt to be sufficiently small then the probability of a spike in each interval is low, and therefore the probability of no spike is almost one, which implies that $h(q) \approx 0$ bits. Thus, Equation 9.4 can be approximated by its first term $H \approx p \log (1/p)$. We can use Equation 9.2 to rewrite this in terms of Δt

$$
H \approx r \, \Delta t \log \frac{1}{r \, \Delta t} \text{ bits.} \qquad (9.5)
$$

This is actually the average Shannon information produced in time Δt, so the average rate R at which Shannon information is generated is found by dividing by Δt

$$
\begin{aligned}
R &= H/\Delta t & (9.6) \\
&= r \log \frac{1}{r \, \Delta t} \text{ bits/s,} & (9.7)
\end{aligned}
$$

where we have omitted the approximation symbol. For a neuron with a firing rate of $r = 50$ spikes/s, and assuming an interval of one millisecond ($\Delta t = 0.001$s), this gives an information rate of

$$
R = 50 \log \frac{1}{50 \times 0.001} = 216 \text{ bits/s.} \qquad (9.8)
$$

If 50 spikes convey 216 bits then each spike conveys an average of

$$
216/50 = 4.32 \text{ bits/spike.} \qquad (9.9)
$$

Note that the temporal precision Δt effectively places an upper bound on channel capacity. This bound applies to us (as observers of neuronal outputs) and to neurons that receive the outputs of other neurons which cannot resolve the timing of spikes below some threshold of temporal precision.

The estimate of 4.32 bits/spike is more than the information (one bit) carried by the state (spike or no-spike) of each bin, which can be understood if we adopt a slightly different perspective. Given a firing rate of 50 spikes per second and a temporal resolution defined by 1,000 bins per second, an average of one out of every 20 ($=1000/50$) bins contains a spike. Because each spike can appear in any bin with equal probability, each set of 20 bins can adopt 20 equally probable states. Roughly speaking, each set of 20 bins has an entropy of about $\log 20 = 4.32$ bits, and because each of these sets contains an average of one spike, each spike effectively conveys an average of 4.32 bits.

Irrespective of precisely how much information is implicit in the neuron's output, there is no guarantee that it provides *information about the neuron's input*, that is, the *mutual information* between the input and output. Note that the mutual information cannot be greater than the maximum entropy implied by the neuron's mean firing rate. Thus, the maximum entropy implied by a neuron's mean firing rate acts as an upper bound on its entropy, and this, in turn, acts as an upper bound on the mutual information between the neuron's input and output.

Using data collected from mechanical receptors in the cricket, Warland *et al* (1992) found that neurons have an entropy of about 600 bits/s. However, it was found that only about half of this entropy is related to the neuron's input, and the rest is noise. These neurons therefore transmit information about their inputs at a rate of about 300 bits/s, which represents a *coding efficiency* of about 0.5 (i.e. 300/600).

Let's think about what it means for a neuron to provide 300 bits/s about its input. Using a simplistic interpretation, at the end of one second a neuron has provided 300 bits, which is enough information to specify its input to within one part in 2^{300}, or (equivalently) as one part in 2×10^{90}. This would be analogous to measuring someone's height to within a fraction of the width of an atom, which is clearly silly. So what are we to make of this result?

An alternative interpretation, proposed by Rieke *et al*[43], is that each neuron provides a kind of 'running commentary' about its input, which is usually changing rapidly. When considered like this, each neuron provides, on average, three bits each 10 ms, where 10 ms seems to represent a plausible time frame. In other words, every 10 ms a neuron's output specifies what is driving its input with a precision of one part in $8(= 2^3)$. For example, if a neuron is sensitive to the speed of visual motion between, say, zero and 32 degrees/s then its output over 10 ms could indicate one particular eighth of this range. Because 1/8 of 32 is 4, the neuron's output could indicate a speed of, say, 20 ± 2 degrees/s, where ± 2 implies a range of 4 degrees/s. In this case, the information conveyed over 10 ms is about the same as the information conveyed by each spike (three bits), so the timing of each spike effectively indicates speed to within ± 2 degrees/s.

Experiments on the frog auditory system[42] showed that the proportion of output entropy that provides information about a neuron's input depends on the nature of the sounds used. Specifically, if artificial sounds were used then the coding efficiency was only about 20%, but if naturalistic frog calls were used then the coding efficiency was an impressive 90%.

Eyes, Flies, and Information Theory

The purpose of an eye is to communicate information about the world to the brain, and this is as true for the eye of a fly as it is for the eye of a human. Thus, even though the structure of a human eye is very different from the structure of a fly's eye, it is likely that the underlying computational processes in both are essentially the same.

Laughlin (1981)[31] showed that neurons which receive outputs from the eye communicate about as much information as is theoretically possible. He showed this to be true for fly eyes, and subsequent work suggests that it is also true for human eyes. Laughlin's brief paper (two pages) is not only a physical example of the power of information compression, but also one of the most insightful papers in biology.

Organisms with eyes are more interested in differences in luminance, or *contrast*, than in luminance *per se*. For this reason, the neurons which receive outputs from photoreceptors respond to contrast rather than luminance. In the fly, these neurons are called *large monopolar cells* or LMCs. These brain cells, which have continuous voltage outputs (rather than spikes), are the cells from which Laughlin made his recordings.

The first question Laughlin posed in his paper was this: if the distribution of contrasts seen by a fly's eye is fixed by its natural environment, and if the LMC neurons in a fly's eye have a specific

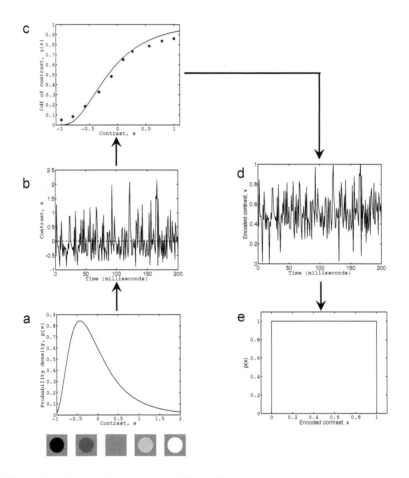

Figure 9.3. Schematic summary of Laughlin's experiment.
(a) Probability density function $p_s(s)$ of contrasts s in the fly's environment.
(b) Sampled values of s from (a) obtained over time as the fly moves around.
(c) Transforming s values to x values using the cumulative distribution function of $p_s(s)$, which is the optimal encoding function g^* (smooth curve), and which predicts the (rescaled) outputs $x = g(s)$ of LMC neurons (dots).
(d) How LMC neuron outputs x change over time.
(e) Uniform pdf $p_x(x)$ of LMC outputs predicted by g^*.

input/output encoding function, then what is the precise form of this encoding function which would communicate as much information as possible from the fly's eye to the fly's brain?

Each LMC neuron has an output between $x_{min} = -20\,\text{mV}$ and $x_{max} = +20\,\text{mV}$, so it acts like an encoding function which prepares (encodes) contrasts for transmission along a communication channel with fixed lower and upper bounds (where LMC outputs were rescaled to have a range between zero and one). The analysis in Section 7.7 implies that the *optimal encoding function* $g^*(s)$ for such a channel is given by the cumulative distribution function (cdf) of the probability density function (pdf) $p_s(s)$ of contrasts s in the fly's environment $x^* = g^*(s)$. By definition, if the pdf of contrasts seen by a fly's eye in its natural environment is $p_s(s)$ then the cdf of contrast values is

$$g^*(s) \;=\; \int_{t=-\infty}^{s} p_s(t)\,dt. \tag{9.10}$$

From Section 7.7, we know that the encoding function g^* is guaranteed to transform the distribution $p_s(s)$ of contrast values into a uniform pdf $p_x(x)$ of encoded contrast values x. Because the uniform distribution is a maximum entropy pdf, each value of x provides as much information as possible.

In order to estimate the optimal encoding function $g^*(s)$, Laughlin needed to know $p_s(s)$, the pdf of contrasts in the fly's environment. For this, he measured the distribution of contrasts which occur in a woodland setting. These data were used to construct a histogram, which represents an approximation to $p_s(s)$ (Figure 9.3a). Numerical integration of this histogram was then used to estimate the cdf $g^*(s)$ (Figure 9.3c, solid curve).

Having used information theory to find the precise form that an optimal encoding function should adopt, Laughlin's second question was this: does the *LMC encoding function g* implicit in LMC neurons match the optimal encoding function g^* predicted by information theory?

In some respects, this second question is conceptually more straightforward than the first question because the encoding function g

of an LMC neuron is given by the mean response to each contrast. Accordingly, Laughlin exposed the fly to different contrasts in his laboratory, and measured the output voltage of LMC neurons. As the contrast was increased, the output increased slowly at first, then more rapidly, and finally tailed off at very high contrasts, as shown by the data points plotted in Figure 9.3c.

To answer his second question, Laughlin had to compare the data points from the neuron's encoding function $g(s)$ with the optimal encoding function $g^*(s)$. In order to make this comparison, LMC outputs were linearly rescaled to have a range between zero and one. The match between the LMC outputs $x = g(s)$ (the data points in Figure 9.3c) and the values predicted by the optimal encoding function $g^*(s)$ (the solid curve in Figure 9.3c) is remarkably good.

Laughlin's experiment represents one of the first tests of an information-theoretic optimality principle within the brain (i.e. the efficient coding hypothesis). This general approach has been vindicated in tests on other organisms (including humans[38;51;55]) and on other sense modalities (e.g. olfaction[29] and audition[42]). Indeed, Karl Friston's *free-energy theory*[17;47] assumes that an organising principle for all behaviour consists of minimising the sum total of all future surprises (i.e. sensory entropy).

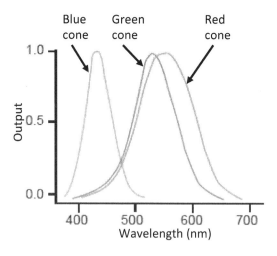

Figure 9.4. Photoreceptor sensitivity to different wavelengths of light.

The Colour of Information

The human eye contains about 126 million photoreceptors, which consist of two main types. The 120 million *rods* are very sensitive to light, and these function only in low-light conditions. The 6 million *cones* function under daylight conditions, and are concentrated close to the optical centre of the eye. There are three types of cones, and these are responsible for colour vision. The amount of light absorbed at each wavelength by each cone type defines its *tuning curve*, as shown in Figure 9.4. These cones are labelled L, M and S, supposedly named after long, medium and short wavelengths. However, this is a misleading nomenclature, because the L and M cones have very similar tuning curves, and both cone types respond best to light which looks greeny-yellow. In contrast, the S-cones are sensitive to short wavelength light which appears blue. Despite this misnaming, for simplicity, we will refer to them as red, green and blue cones.

The outputs of the photoreceptors are transmitted to the brain via one million fibres which comprise the *optic nerve*. However, trying to squeeze the outputs of 126 million photoreceptors into the optic nerve's one million fibres is the cause of a severe bottleneck.

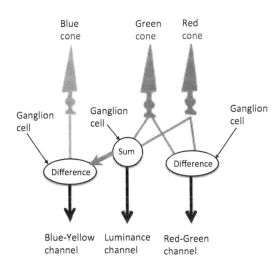

Figure 9.5. Combining outputs from three cone types to produce three new colour channels (ganglion cell outputs). From Frisby and Stone (2010)[16].

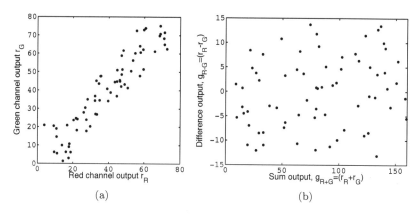

Figure 9.6. Schematic illustration of sum–difference recoding. (a) The similar tuning curves of red and green cones means that nearby cones have similar output values.   (b) The recoded sum $g_{R+G} = r_R+r_G$ and difference $g_{R-G} = r_R - r_G$ channels are independent. From Stone, 2012[51].

Because the red and green cone types have similar tuning curves, neighbouring red and green cones usually have similar outputs. If these red and green cones had their own private nerve fibres to send their outputs along then these outputs would be similar; almost as if the same message is being sent along two different wires. Given the information bottleneck, this would obviously be a wasteful use of the capacity of the communication channels (i.e. nerve fibres).

One simple way to ensure that the messages in different optic nerve fibres are uncorrelated consists of using one fibre to carry the *sum* of the red and green cone outputs, and another to carry the *difference* between their outputs, as in Figure 9.5. For brevity, we will call this type of recoding *sum–difference recoding*; it is also obtained by applying *principal component analysis* to the data in Figure 9.6a. It can be shown that if cone outputs have Gaussian distributions then sum–difference recoding yields independent messages. Physical evidence for sum–difference recoding exists in the form of *ganglion cells*. These cells reside in the retina, where they collate the outputs of neighbouring photoreceptors, and each ganglion cell output is carried by one of the million nerve fibres in the optic nerve.

To confirm that the sum and difference signals are independent, we can test whether one can be *predicted* from the other. For example, if the two cone outputs are represented as r_R and r_G then the value of r_R tells us roughly what the value of r_G is; they are highly correlated, as shown in Figure 9.6a. Now, using g to denote ganglion cell output, suppose instead that these values are recoded in terms of a *sum* ganglion cell output, $g_{R+G} = r_R + r_G$, and a *difference* ganglion cell output, $g_{R-G} = r_R - r_G$, as shown in Figure 9.6b. The almost uniform coverage in Figure 9.6b suggests that the ganglion cell outputs g_{R+G} and g_{R-G} are independent, and this, in turn, suggests that ganglion cell channel capacity is not being wasted. In fact, ganglion cell channel capacity is only fully utilised if the outputs of each ganglion cell are also independent over time, and there is evidence for this[37]. In summary, using separate ganglion cells to transmit outputs of red and green cones necessarily wastes some of the channel capacity of ganglion cells, whereas using ganglion cells to implement sum–difference recoding of cone outputs using does not.

The Brain: An Efficient Encoder

The experiments and analyses described above suggest that the brain's ability to process information is about as efficient as it possibly can be. More importantly, information-theoretic analyses of such experiments have led to the general conclusion that, within sensory systems:

> ... information rates are very large, close to the physical limits imposed by the spike train entropy.
> Rieke *et al*, 1997[43].

Without information theory, we would have no way of telling how well neurons perform, because we would have little idea of what it means to measure neuronal information processing performance in absolute terms. And so we would not be able to tell that the answer to the question, "are brains good at processing information?" is *yes*. More importantly, we could not know that, within the constraints imposed by their physical structure, brains operate close to the limits defined by Shannon's mathematical theory of communication.

9.7. A Very Short History of Information Theory

Even the most gifted scientist cannot command an original theory out of thin air. Just as Einstein could not have devised his theories of relativity if he had no knowledge of Newton's work, so Shannon could not have created information theory if he had no knowledge of the work of Boltzmann (1875) and Gibbs (1902) on thermodynamic entropy, Wiener (1927) on signal processing, Nyquist (1928) on sampling theory, or Hartley (1928) on information transmission[40].

Even though Shannon was not alone in trying to solve one of the key scientific problems of his time (i.e. how to define and measure information), he was alone in being able to produce a complete mathematical theory of information: a theory that might otherwise have taken decades to construct. In effect, Shannon single-handedly accelerated the rate of scientific progress, and it is entirely possible that, without his contribution, we would still be treating information as if it were some ill-defined vital fluid.

9.8. Summary

In 1986, the physicist John Wheeler said:

> It is my opinion that everything must be based on a simple idea. And ... this idea, once we have finally discovered it, will be so compelling, so beautiful, that we will say to one another, yes, how could it have been any different?

So compelling, and so beautiful: information theory represents a fundamental insight that must surely rank as a candidate for Wheeler's "simple idea". Indeed, after many years of studying physics and information theory, Wheeler came up with a proposal which is both radical and intriguing:

> ... the universe is made of information; matter and energy are only incidental.

Insofar as it must be made of something, a universe in which all forms of energy and matter are simply different manifestations of pure information might be as sublime as this one.

Further Reading

Applebaum D (2008)[1]. Probability and Information: An Integrated Approach. *A thorough introduction to information theory, which strikes a good balance between intuitive and technical explanations.*

Avery J (2012)[2]. Information Theory and Evolution. *An engaging account of how information theory is relevant to a wide range of natural and man-made systems, including evolution, physics, culture and genetics. Includes interesting background stories on the development of ideas within these different disciplines.*

Baeyer HV (2005)[3]. Information: The New Language of Science *Erudite, wide-ranging, and insightful account of information theory. Contains no equations, which makes it very readable.*

Cover T and Thomas J (1991)[11]. Elements of Information Theory. *Comprehensive, and highly technical, with historical notes and an equation summary at the end of each chapter.*

Ghahramani Z (2002). Information Theory. Encyclopedia of Cognitive Science. *An excellent, brief overview of information.*

Gleick J (2012)[21]. The Information. *An informal introduction to the history of ideas and people associated with information theory.*

Guizzo EM (2003)[24]. The Essential Message: Claude Shannon and the Making of Information Theory. Master's Thesis, Massachusetts Institute of Technology. *One of the few accounts of Shannon's role in the development of information theory. See* http://dspace.mit.edu/bitstream/handle/1721.1/39429/54526133.pdf.

Laughlin, SB (2006). The Hungry Eye: Energy, Information and Retinal Function, *Excellent lecture on the energy cost of Shannon information in eyes. See* http://www.crsltd.com/guest-talks/crs-guest-lecturers/simon-laughlin.

Further Reading

MacKay DJC (2003)[34]. Information Theory, Inference, and Learning Algorithms. *The modern classic on information theory. A very readable text that roams far and wide over many topics. The book's web site (below) also has a link to an excellent series of video lectures by MacKay. Available free online at* `http://www.inference.phy.cam.ac.uk/mackay/itila/`.

Pierce JR (1980)[40]. An Introduction to Information Theory: Symbols, Signals and Noise. Second Edition. *Pierce writes with an informal, tutorial style of writing, but does not flinch from presenting the fundamental theorems of information theory. This book provides a good balance between words and equations.*

Reza FM (1961)[41]. An Introduction to Information Theory. *A more comprehensive and mathematically rigorous book than Pierce's book, it should be read only after first reading Pierce's more informal text.*

Seife C (2007)[46]. Decoding the Universe: How the New Science of Information Is Explaining Everything in the Cosmos, From Our Brains to Black Holes. *A lucid and engaging account of the relationship between information, thermodynamic entropy and quantum computing. Highly recommended.*

Shannon CE and Weaver W (1949)[50]. The Mathematical Theory of Communication. University of Illinois Press. *A surprisingly accessible book, written in an era when information theory was known only to a privileged few. This book can be downloaded from* `http://cm.bell-labs.com/cm/ms/what/shannonday/paper.html`

For the complete novice, the videos at the online Kahn Academy provide an excellent introduction. Additionally, the online Scholarpedia web page by Latham and Rudi provides a lucid technical account of mutual information:
`http://www.scholarpedia.org/article/Mutual_information`.

Finally, some historical perspective is provided in a long interview with Shannon conducted in 1982: `http://www.ieeeghn.org/wiki/index.php/Oral-History:Claude_E._Shannon`.

Appendix A

Glossary

alphabet A set of symbols used to construct a message. For example, the numbers 1 to 6 define a discrete variable which has an alphabet of possible values $A_s = \{1, 2, 3, 4, 5, 6\}$, and a message could then be either a single symbol, such as $s = 4$, or an ordered list of symbols, such as $\mathbf{s} = (1, 1, 6, 3, 2, 3, 1, 1, 4)$.

average Given a variable x, the average or mean value of a sample of n values of x is

$$\bar{x} = \frac{1}{n} \sum_{j=1}^{n} x_j. \tag{A.1}$$

In the limit, as $n \to \infty$, the sample mean equals the *expected value* of the variable x

$$\mathrm{E}[x] = \sum_{i=1}^{m} p(x_i) x_i, \tag{A.2}$$

where $p(x_i)$ is the proportion of values equal to x_i, and m is the number of different values that x can adopt. See Appendix E.

Bayes' rule Given an observed value x of the discrete variable X, Bayes' rule states that the *posterior probability* that the variable Y has the value y is $p(y|x) = p(x|y)p(y)/p(x)$, where $p(x|y)$ is the probability that $X = x$ given that $Y = y$ (the *likelihood*), $p(y)$ is the *prior probability* that $Y = y$, and $p(x)$ is the *marginal probability* that $X = x$. See Appendix F.

binary digit A binary digit can be either a 0 or a 1.

binary number A binary number comprises only binary digits (e.g. 1001). Also called *binary strings*.

binary symmetric channel A channel in which the probability P that an input value $X = 1$ will be flipped to an output value $Y = 0$ is the same as the probability that a 0 will be flipped to a 1.

binomial coefficient Given a binary number containing n binary digits, the number of different ways that we can arrange k 1s amongst n positions is given by the binomial coefficient

$$C_{n,k} \;=\; \frac{n!}{k!(n-k)!}, \tag{A.3}$$

where $n! = n \times (n-1) \times (n-2) \times \cdots \times 1$.

bit A fundamental unit of information, often confused with a binary digit (see Section 1.5). A bit provides enough information for one of two equally probable alternatives to be specified.

byte An ordered set of 8 binary digits.

capacity The capacity of a communication channel is the maximum rate at which it can communicate information from its input to its output. Capacity can be specified either in terms of information communicated per second (e.g. bits/s), or in terms of information communicated per symbol (e.g. bits/symbol).

channel A conduit for communicating data from its input to its output.

code A code consists of a set of symbols or messages, an encoder (which maps symbols to channel inputs), a decoder (which maps channel outputs to inputs).

codebook The set of codewords produced by a given encoder.

codeword Each symbol s in a message is encoded before transmission as a codeword x.

coding efficiency A source generates messages with entropy $H(S)$. These are encoded as sequences of codewords with a mean length $L(X)$. The coding efficiency is $H(S)/L(X)$ bits/binary digit, which is the amount of information each binary digit carries.

conditional probability The probability that the value of one random variable Y has the value y given that the value of another random variable X has the value x, written as $p(Y = y|X = x)$ or $p(y|x)$.

conditional entropy Given two random variables X and Y, the average uncertainty regarding the value of Y when the value of X is known, $H(Y|X) = \mathrm{E}[\log(1/p(y|x))]$ bits.

continuous In contrast to a discrete variable which can adopt a discrete number of values, a continuous variable can adopt any value (e.g. a decimal).

cumulative distribution function The cdf of a variable is the cumulative area under the probability density function (pdf) of that variable. See Appendix G.

differential entropy The expected value of a continuous random variable, $\mathrm{E}[\log(1/p(x))]$.

discrete Elements of set that are clearly separated from each other, like a list of integers, are called discrete. See also continuous.

disjoint If two sets of items are disjoint then they do not have any items in common. For example, the sets $A_1 = \{pqr\}$ and $A_2 = \{stu\}$ are disjoint, whereas the sets $A_1 = \{pqr\}$ and $A_3 = \{rst\}$ are not, because they both contain the letter r.

encoding Before a message is transmitted, it is recoded or encoded as an input sequence. Ideally, the encoding process ensures that each element of the encoded message conveys as much information as possible.

ensemble In physics, this is the set of all possible microstates of a system. For example, each spatial configuration of molecules in a jar represents a microstate, and the set of all possible configurations constitutes an ensemble of microstates. In information theory, the entropy of a source is defined in terms of the ensemble of an infinite set of sequences.

entropy The entropy of a variable is a measure of its overall variability. A discrete variable with high variability can convey more information than a variable with low variability. The entropy of a discrete variable X which adopts m possible values with probability $p(x_i)$ is

$$H(X) = \sum_{i=1}^{m} p(x_i) \log_2 1/p(x_i) \text{ bits,} \qquad \text{(A.4)}$$

where the values of X are assumed to be iid.

expected value See average.

histogram If we count the number of times the value of a discrete variable adopts each of a number of values then the resultant set of counts defines a histogram. If each count is divided by the total number of counts then the resultant set of proportions defines a *normalised histogram*. See Appendix D.

iid If values are chosen independently (i.e. 'at random') from a single probability distribution then they are said to be iid (*independent and identically distributed*).

independence If two variables X and Y are independent then the value x of X provides no information regarding the value y of the other variable Y, and *vice versa*.

information The amount of information conveyed by a discrete variable X which has a value $X = x$ is $h(x) = \log(1/p(x))$. The average amount of information conveyed by each value of X is its entropy $H(X) = \sum p(x_i) \log(1/p(x_i))$.

integration The process of integration can be considered as a platonic form of summation (see Appendix D).

joint probability The probability that two or more quantities simultaneously adopt specified values. For example, the probability that one die yields $x_3 = 3$ and another yields $y_4 = 4$ is the joint probability $p(x_3, y_4) = 1/36$.

Kolmogorov complexity The smallest number of binary digits required to represent a given entity (e.g. number, system, object), asymptotically equivalent to Shannon information.

Kullback–Leibler divergence Given two distributions $p(X)$ and $q(X)$, the KL-divergence (relative entropy) is a measure of how different these distributions are, given by

$$D_{KL}(p(X)\|q(X)) \quad = \quad \int_x p(x) \log \frac{p(x)}{q(x)} \, dx. \qquad (A.5)$$

law of large numbers Given a variable X with a mean μ, the mean of a sample of n values converges to μ as the number of values in that sample approaches infinity; that is, $\mathrm{E}[X] \to \mu$ as $n \to \infty$.

logarithm Given a number x which we wish to express as a logarithm with base a, $y = \log_a x$ is the power to which we have to raise a in order to get x. See Section 1.3 and Appendix C.

mean See average.

message A sequence of symbols or values, represented in bold **s** or non-bold s, according to context.

marginal distribution A distribution that results from marginalisation of a multivariate (e.g. 2D) distribution. For example, given a 2D distribution $p(X, Y)$, one of its marginal distributions is $p(X) = \int_y p(x, y) dy$.

monotonic If a variable $y = f(x)$ changes monotonically with changes in x then a change in x always induces an increase or it always induces a decrease in y. For example, see Figure C.1.

mutual information The reduction in uncertainty $I(X, Y)$ regarding the value of one variable Y induced by knowing the value of another variable X. Mutual information is symmetric, so $I(X, Y) = I(Y, X)$.

noise The random 'jitter' that is part of a measured quantity.

outcome In this text, the term outcome refers to a single instance of a physical outcome, like the pair of numbers showing after a pair of dice is thrown. In terms of random variables, an outcome is the result of a single experiment.

outcome value In this text, the term outcome value refers to the numerical value assigned to a single physical outcome. For example, if a pair of dice is thrown then the outcome (x_1, x_2) comprises two numbers, and the outcome value can be defined as the sum of these two numbers, $x = x_1 + x_2$. In terms of the random variable X, the outcome value is the numerical value assigned to the outcome (x_1, x_2), written as $x = X(x_1, x_2)$.

outer product Given two probability distributions represented as $p(X) = \{p(x_1), \ldots, p(x_n)\}$ and $p(Y) = \{p(y_1), \ldots, p(y_m)\}$, the outer product is an $n \times m$ matrix in which the ith column and jth row is the product $p(x_i) \times p(y_j)$. The distribution of values in this matrix represents the joint distribution $p(X, Y) = p(X)p(Y)$.

parity A measure of the number of 1s or 0s in a binary number, as indicated by the value of a parity binary digit, which is often incorrectly called a parity bit.

precision An indication of the granularity or resolution with which a variable can be measured, formally defined as the inverse of variance (i.e. precision=1/variance).

prefix code A code in which no codeword is the prefix of any other codeword, so each codeword can be decoded as soon as it arrives, also called an *instantaneous* or *self-punctuating code*.

probability There are many definitions of probability. The two main ones are (using coin bias as an example): (1) Bayesian: an observer's estimate of the probability that a coin will land heads up is based on all the information the observer has, including the proportion of times it was observed to land heads up in the past. (2) Frequentist: the probability that a coin will land heads up is given by the proportion of times it lands heads up, when measured over a large number of coin flips.

probability density function (pdf) The probability density function (pdf) $p(X)$ of a continuous random variable X defines the probability density of each value of X. Loosely speaking, the probability that $X = x$ can be considered as the probability density $p(x)$. See Appendix D.

probability distribution The distribution of probabilities of different values of a variable. The probability distribution of a continuous variable is a *probability density function*, and the probability distribution of a discrete variable is a *probability function*. When we refer to a case which includes either continuous or discrete variables, we use the term *probability distribution* in this text.

probability function (pf) A function $p(X)$ of a discrete random variable X defines the probability of each value of X. The probability that $X = x$ is $p(X = x)$ or, more succinctly, $p(x)$. This is called a *probability mass function* (pmf) in some texts.

quantum computer A computer which makes use of quantum mechanics to speed up computation.

random variable (RV) The concept of a random variable X can be understood from a simple example, such as the throw of a pair of dice. Each physical outcome is a pair of numbers (x_a, x_b), which is assigned a value (typically, $x = x_a + x_b$) which is taken to be the value of the random variable, so that $X = x$. The probability of each value is defined by a probability distribution $p(X) = \{p(x_1), p(x_2), \dots\}$. See Section 2.2.

redundancy Given an ordered set of values of a variable (e.g. in an image or sound), if a value can be obtained from a knowledge of other values then it is redundant.

relative entropy A general measure of the difference between two distributions, also known as *Kullback–Leibler divergence*.

relative frequency Frequency of occurrence, expressed as a proportion. For example, out of every 10,000 English letters, 1,304 of them are the letter E, so the relative frequency of E is 1304/10000=0.134.

sample space The *sample space* of the random variable X is the set of all possible experiment outcomes. For example, if an experiment consists of three coin flips then each time the experiment is run we obtain a sequence of three head or tail values (e.g. (x_h, x_t, x_t)), which is one out of the eight possible outcomes (i.e. sequences) that comprise the sample space.

standard deviation The square root σ of the variance of a variable.

stationary source A source for which the probability of each symbol, and for every sub-sequence of symbols, remains stable over time.

symbol A symbol is one element of an alphabet of symbols, and refers to a particular value that a random variable can adopt.

theorem A theorem is a mathematical statement which has been proven to be true.

uncertainty In this text, uncertainty refers to the surprisal (i.e. $\log(1/p(x))$) of a variable X.

variable A variable is essentially a 'container', usually for one number.

variance The variance is a measure of how 'spread out' the values of a variable are. Given a sample of n values of a variable x with a sample mean $\bar{x}$, the estimated variance $\hat{v}_x$ of x is

$$\hat{v}_x \quad = \quad \frac{1}{n}\sum_{j=1}^{n}(x_j - \bar{x})^2, \qquad\qquad (\text{A.6})$$

where the sample mean is $\bar{x} = 1/n\sum_j x_j$. If x can adopt m different values then its variance is

$$v_x \quad = \quad \sum_{i=1}^{m} p(x_i)(x_i - \mathrm{E}[x])^2, \qquad\qquad (\text{A.7})$$

where $p(x_i)$ is the proportion of values equal to x_i and $\mathrm{E}[x]$ is the expected value of x.

Appendix B

Mathematical Symbols

$\hat{\ }$ the hat symbol is used to indicate an *estimated* value. For example, $\hat{v}_x$ is an estimate of the variance v_x.

$|x|$ indicates the absolute value of x (e.g. if $x = -3$ then $|x| = 3$).

$\leq$ if $x \leq y$ then x is less than or equal to y.

$\geq$ if $x \geq y$ then x is greater than or equal to y.

$\approx$ means 'approximately equal to'.

$\sim$ if a random variable X has a distribution $p(X)$ then this is written as $X \sim p(X)$.

∞ infinity.

$\propto$ indicates *proportional to.*

α Greek letter alpha, denotes the number of different symbols in an alphabet.

Δ Greek upper case letter delta, denotes a small increment.

ϵ Greek letter epsilon, denotes a small quantity.

η Greek letter eta (pronounced eater), denotes a single value of the noise in a measured quantity.

η large Greek letter eta, used in this text to denote a random variable for noise.

Mathematical Symbols

μ Greek letter mu (pronounced mew), denotes the mean value of a variable.

ρ Greek letter rho (pronounced row), denotes correlation.

σ Greek letter sigma, denotes the standard deviation of a distribution.

$\sum$ the capital Greek letter sigma represents summation. For example, if we represent the $n = 3$ numbers 2, 5 and 7 as $x_1 = 2$, $x_2 = 5$, $x_3 = 7$ then their sum x_{sum} is

$$
\begin{aligned}
x_{sum} &= \sum_{i=1}^{n} x_i \\
&= x_1 + x_2 + x_3 \\
&= 2 + 5 + 7 \\
&= 14.
\end{aligned}
$$

The variable i is counted up from 1 to n, and, for each i, the term x_i adopts a new value and is added to a running total.

A the set or alphabet of different values of a random variable. For example, if the random variable X can adopt one of m different values then the set A_x is

$$
A_x = \{x_1, \ldots, x_m\}. \tag{B.1}
$$

C channel capacity, the maximum rate at which information can be communicated through a given channel, usually measured in bits per second (bits/s).

e constant, equal to 2.7 1828 1828 .... Base of natural logarithms, so that $\ln e^x = x$.

E the mean, average, or *expected value* of a variable X, written as $E[X]$.

g encoding function, which transforms a message of symbols $\mathbf{s} = (s_1, \ldots, s_k)$ into channel inputs $\mathbf{x} = (x_1, \ldots, x_n)$, so $\mathbf{x} = g(\mathbf{s})$.

$h(x)$ Shannon information, uncertainty, or surprise, $\log(1/p(x))$, associated with the value x.

$\overline{h}(x)$ average Shannon information of a finite sample of values of x.

$H(X)$ entropy of X, which is the average Shannon information of the probability distribution $p(X)$ of the random variable X.

$H(X|Y)$ conditional entropy of the conditional probability distribution $p(X|Y)$ of values adopted by the variable X given values of the variable Y. This is the average uncertainty in the value of X after the value of Y is observed.

$H(Y|X)$ conditional entropy of the conditional probability distribution $p(Y|X)$ of values adopted by the variable Y given values of the variable X. This is the average uncertainty in the value of Y after the value of X is observed.

$H(X,Y)$ entropy of the joint probability distribution $p(X,Y)$ of the variables X and Y.

$I(X,Y)$ mutual information between X and Y, the average number of bits provided by each value of Y about the value of X, and *vice versa*.

$\ln x$ natural logarithm (log to the base e) of x.

$\log x$ logarithm of x. Logarithms use base 2 in this text, and base is indicated with a subscript if the base is unclear (e.g. $\log_2 x$). Natural logarithms are logarithms to the base e, and are usually written as $\ln x$.

m number of different possible messages, input values, codewords, or symbols in an alphabet.

M number of bins in a histogram.

N noise variance in Shannon's fundamental equation for channel capacity $C = \frac{1}{2}\log(1 + P/N)$.

n the number of observations in a data set (e.g. coin flip outcomes), or elements in a message, or codewords in an encoded message.

$p(X)$ the probability distribution of the random variable X.

$p(x)$ the probability (density) that the random variable $X = x$.

$p(X, Y)$ the joint probability distribution of the random variables X and Y. For discrete variables this is called the *joint probability function* (pf) of X and Y, and for continuous variables it is called the *joint probability density function* (pdf) of X and Y.

$p(x, y)$ the *joint probability* that the random variables X and Y have the values x and y, respectively.

$p(x|y)$ the conditional probability that the random variable $X = x$ given that $Y = y$.

R the rate at which information is communicated, usually measured in bits per second (bits/s).

S a random variable. The probability that S adopts a value s is defined by the value of the probability distribution $p(S)$ at $S = s$.

s a value of the random variable S, used to represent a message.

v_x if X has mean μ then the variance of X is $v_x = \sigma_x^2 = \mathrm{E}[(\mu - x)^2]$.

W the total number of microstates of a system.

X a random variable. The probability that X adopts a specific value x is defined by the value of the probability distribution $p(X)$ at $X = x$.

X^Δ a variable which has been quantised into intervals (e.g. histogram bins) of width Δx.

x a value of the random variable X, used to represent a channel input.

$\mathbf{x}$ a vector or permutation (round brackets $(x_1, \ldots, x_n)$) or combination (curly brackets $\{x_1, \ldots, x_n\}$) of x values.

Y a random variable. The probability that Y adopts a specific value y is defined by the value of the probability distribution $p(Y)$ at $Y = y$.

y a value of the random variable Y, used to represent a channel output.

Appendix C

Logarithms

This is a basic tutorial about logarithms. As an example, if we want to know what power we must raise 10 to in order to get 100 then we find that the answer is 2, because $100 = 10^2$. Equivalently, the logarithm of 100 is 2, written as $2 = \log_{10} 100$, so we say that the log of 100 is 2 (using logarithms to the base 10).

The reason that logarithms are so useful is because they turn multiplication into addition. For example, if we want to multiply 100 by 100 then we have

$$10^2 \times 10^2 = 10^{2+2} \tag{C.1}$$

$$= 10^4 \tag{C.2}$$

$$= 10,000. \tag{C.3}$$

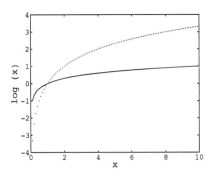

Figure C.1. The logarithmic function with base 2 (dotted curve), and with base 10 (solid curve). Note that $\log x$ increases monotonically with x.

If we express this in terms of logarithms to the base 10 then we have

$$\log_{10} 100 + \log_{10} 100 \;=\; \log_{10} 10^2 + \log_{10} 10^2 \qquad \text{(C.4)}$$
$$=\; 2 + 2, \qquad \text{(C.5)}$$

and the answer is obtained by taking the anti-logarithm of 4, which means raising 10 (the base) to the power of 4, which comes to $10^4 = 10,000$. If we have two numbers n and m that we wish to multiply then we can simply add their logarithms, and then find the product from the anti-logarithm of this sum.

Instead of using logarithms with base 10, we can use logarithms with any base b, so that

$$y \;=\; \log_b(n \times m) = \log_b n + \log_b m, \qquad \text{(C.6)}$$

and the product is obtained from the anti-logarithm of the sum y as

$$n \times m \;=\; b^{\log_b n + \log_b m} = b^y. \qquad \text{(C.7)}$$

The rule for converting from logarithms with base a to logarithms with base b is

$$\log_b x \;=\; \frac{\log_a x}{\log_a b}. \qquad \text{(C.8)}$$

Natural logarithms are logarithms to the base e, and are usually written as $\ln x$. Logarithms use base 2 in this book, unless otherwise specified.

In summary, given a number x which we wish to express as a logarithm with base a, $y = \log_a x$ is the power to which we have to raise a in order to get x. Equivalently, if the logarithm of x is $y = \log_a x$ then $x = a^y$.

Appendix D

Probability Density Functions

Before describing probability density functions, we briefly review the idea of a function. In essence, a function is a mapping from one space, called the *domain*, to another space, called the *range*. For example, the area y of a circle increases with square of its radius x, and the precise nature of the mapping from the domain x to the range y is defined by the function $y = \pi x^2$. Sometimes it is convenient to refer to a function without specifying its precise form, and in such cases we often write $y = f(x)$. For example, the letter f could represent the function $f(x) = \pi x^2$. Of course, a function can be used to describe the relationship between any two continuous variables, like the speed of a falling ball and time. It can also capture the relationship between more abstract quantities, like probability.

In contrast, a probability density function defines the probability of every value of a variable. We can gain some intuition behind a pdf by starting with a *histogram* of some observed data.

If we measure the height of 5,000 people, and count the number of people with each height, then the resultant set of counts can be used to construct a histogram. A histogram is a graphical representation of a set of such counts, as shown in Figure 5.1. However, no two individuals have exactly the same height, so it doesn't make any sense to try to count how many people have any particular height.

In order to make progress, we have to divide height into a number of different intervals, and then count how many individuals fall into each interval. Of course, this entails choosing a size for the intervals, and we will choose an interval of $\Delta x = 1.6$ inches, between 60 and 84 inches (Δ is the Greek letter *delta*). This yields a total of $M = 15$ intervals or *bins*, where each bin is defined by a lower and upper bound (e.g. the first bin spans 60–61.6 inches). For each bin, we count the number of measured heights spanned by that bin. We expect a large proportion of measurements to be in bins at around 72 inches, because this is a common human height. The resultant histogram has a typical bell shape, shown in Figure 5.1.

In order to make the transition from histograms to pdfs, at this point, we will adopt a different perspective. Suppose we drop dots from a great height onto the image of a histogram, so that they appear in random locations, as in Figure D.1 (we ignore dots which do not fall under the curve). The probability that a dot will fall into a particular bin is directly related to the area of that bin; the bigger the bin, the more dots will fall into it. In fact, the probability P_i that a dot will fall into a particular bin is just the area a_i of that bin expressed as a proportion of the total histogram area A, so that $P_i = a_i/A$. The area of the ith bin is its width times its height, where height is equal to the number n_i of dots in the bin $a_i = n_i \times \Delta x$, and the total area of all

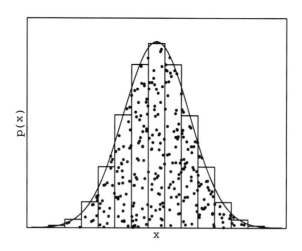

Figure D.1. A normalised histogram as an approximation to a probability density function or pdf (smooth curve). If black dots fall onto the page at random positions then there will usually be more dots in the taller columns. As the columns get thinner then the proportion of dots in each column gets closer to the height $p(x)$ of the pdf.

bins is just the sum of all M bin areas,

$$A \;=\; \sum_{i=1}^{M} a_i. \tag{D.1}$$

Given that x must have some definite value, the total probability of all M possible values must add up to one,

$$\sum_{i=1}^{M} P_i \;=\; 1. \tag{D.2}$$

The ith bin spans the interval from a lower value x_i^{min} to an upper value x_i^{max}, such that the bin width is

$$\Delta x \;=\; x_i^{max} - x_i^{min}. \tag{D.3}$$

Thus, in this *normalised* histogram, the area of the ith bin is numerically equal to the probability

$$P_i \;=\; p(X \text{ is between } x_i^{min} \text{ and } x_i^{max}). \tag{D.4}$$

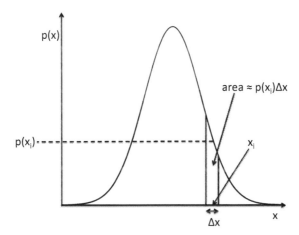

Figure D.2. A probability density function $p(X)$. The vertical lines are centred on a value at $X = x_i$. The probability P_i (that a randomly chosen value of $X \approx x_i$) is numerically equal to the proportion of the total area between the two vertical lines and the curve. This area is the width Δx times the height ($\approx p(x_i)$).

Probability Density Functions

The height of a bin is its area divided by its width $p(x_i) = P_i/\Delta x$, which is the *probability density* in the vicinity of x_i.

In order to make the final transition from histograms to pdfs, we need to reduce the bin widths. If we reduce each bin width Δx so that it approaches zero then the finite interval Δx becomes an infinitesimal interval, written as dx. At this point, the infinitesimal interval dx at $X = x$ has a probability density $p(x)$, and the density values of the continuous variable X define a continuous probability density function $p(X)$, shown by the curve in Figures D.1 and D.2. A key advantage of a pdf is that it can be characterised with an equation, such as a Gaussian (see Appendix G).

To understand why the height of the curve defined by $p(X)$ is called a probability *density*, consider an analogy with the density of a metal rod. Suppose that this rod is made of a mixture of gold (which is very dense) and aluminium, but the proportion of gold increases from left to right, so that the density increases accordingly. We can equate the area of a histogram bin with the mass of a small segment of the rod. Similarly, we can equate the bin width with the volume of that segment. The density of a segment is its mass divided by its volume

$$\text{rod segment density} = \frac{\text{segment mass}}{\text{segment volume}}. \tag{D.5}$$

Similarly, the probability density (=height) of a bin is

$$\text{probability density} = \frac{\text{probability (=bin area)}}{\text{bin width}}. \tag{D.6}$$

Given that $P_i = p(x_i)\Delta x$, we can rewrite Equation D.2 as

$$\sum_{i=1}^{M} p(x_i)\,\Delta x = 1. \tag{D.7}$$

As the bin width Δx approaches zero, this becomes an integral

$$\int_x p(x)\,dx = 1, \tag{D.8}$$

where the area under the pdf is, by definition, equal to one.

Appendix E

Averages From Distributions

Here we show how the mean, average or expected value of a variable X can be obtained from an equation like

$$E[X] \;=\; \sum_{i=1}^{m} p(x_i)\, x_i. \tag{E.1}$$

If we sample items from a population then we would expect to observe values in proportion to their frequency in the population. For example, if the population consists of items having one of three values $[4\ 5\ 6]$ which occur with relative frequencies $[0.1\ 0.2\ 0.7]$ then a typical sample of 100 items would consist of 10 fours, 20 fives, and 70 sixes. The mean of our sample would therefore be

$$\frac{(10 \times 4) + (20 \times 5) + (70 \times 6)}{100} = (0.1 \times 4) + (0.2 \times 5) + (0.7 \times 6). \tag{E.2}$$

Note that the probability that a randomly chosen item from the population has value 4 is 0.1. If we denote the item value as x then we can write this as $p(X = 4) = 0.1$. To simplify this further, if we denote the value $X = 4$ as x_1, then we have $p(x_1) = 0.1$. Similarly, we can use x_2 to stand for $X = 5$, and x_3 to stand for $X = 6$, so that $p(x_2) = 0.2$ and $p(x_3) = 0.7$. We can now rewrite Equation E.2 as

$$
\begin{aligned}
E[X] \;&=\; (0.1 \times 4) + (0.2 \times 5) + (0.7 \times 6) & \tag{E.3}\\
&=\; p(x_1)x_1 + p(x_2)x_2 + p(x_3)x_3. & \tag{E.4}
\end{aligned}
$$

Averages From Distributions

If we replace each subscript with the letter i then we have

$$\mathrm{E}[X] \;=\; \sum_{i=1}^{3} p(x_i)\, x_i. \tag{E.5}$$

More generally, if we want to know the expected value of some function, say $h(x_i) = x_i^2$, of a variable which can adopt m different values, then we can obtain this as

$$\mathrm{E}[X^2] \;=\; p(x_1)x_1^2 + p(x_2)x_2^2, \ldots, + p(x_m)x_m^2 \tag{E.6}$$

$$= \; \sum_{i=1}^{m} p(x_i)\, x_i^2 \tag{E.7}$$

$$= \; \sum_{i=1}^{m} p(x_i)\, h(x_i) \tag{E.8}$$

$$= \; \mathrm{E}[h(x)]. \tag{E.9}$$

If $h(x)$ is the Shannon information of an outcome x, defined as $h(x) = \log(1/p(x))$, then the expected value of the Shannon information is

$$\mathrm{E}[h(X)] \;=\; \sum_{i=1}^{m} p(x_i)\, \log \frac{1}{p(x_i)} \tag{E.10}$$

$$= \; H(X). \tag{E.11}$$

As expected, the average Shannon information is the entropy $H(X)$.

Rather than taking a mean over a countable number m of different values, we can consider X to be continuous, in which case the summation above becomes an integral,

$$\mathrm{E}[h(X)] \;=\; \int_x p(x)\, h(x)\, dx. \tag{E.12}$$

If $h(x)$ is (again) the Shannon information of an outcome x then

$$\mathrm{E}[h(X)] \;=\; \int_x p(x)\, \log \frac{1}{p(x)}\, dx \tag{E.13}$$

$$= \; H(X), \tag{E.14}$$

which yields the differential entropy of X.

Appendix F

The Rules of Probability

Independent Outcomes

If a set of individual outcomes are independent then the probability of that outcome set is obtained by multiplying the probabilities of the individual outcomes together.

For example, consider a coin for which the probability of a head x_h is $p(x_h) = 0.9$ and the probability of a tail x_t is $p(x_t) = (1-0.9) = 0.1$. If we flip this coin twice then there are four possible pairs of outcomes: two heads (x_h, x_h), two tails (x_t, x_t), a head followed by a tail (x_h, x_t), and a tail followed by a head (x_t, x_h).

The probability that the first outcome is a head and the second outcome is a tail can be represented as a *joint probability* $p(x_h, x_t)$ (More generally, a joint probability can refer to any pair of variables, such as X and Y.)

In order to work out some averages, imagine that we perform 100 pairs of coin flips. We label each flip according to whether it came first or second within its pair, so we have 100 *first flip* outcomes, and 100 corresponding *second flip* outcomes (see Table F.1).

Outcome	h	t	$\{h,h\}$	$\{t,t\}$	(h,t)	(t,h)	$\{t,h\}$
N	90	10	81	1	9	9	18
$N/100$	0.90	0.10	0.81	0.01	0.09	0.09	0.18

Table F.1. The number N and probability $N/100$ of each possible outcome from 100 pairs of coin flips of a coin which lands heads up 90% of the time. Ordered sequences or permutations are written in round brackets '()', whereas unordered sets or combinations are written in curly brackets '{}'.

229

Given that $p(x_h) = 0.9$, we expect 90 heads and 10 tails within the set of 100 first flips, and the same for the set of 100 second flips. But what about the number of pairs of outcomes?

For each head obtained on the first flip, we can observe the corresponding outcome on the second flip, and then add up the number of pairs of each type (e.g. x_h, x_h). We already know that there are (on average)

$$90 \; = \; 0.9 \times 100 \tag{F.1}$$

heads within the set of 100 first flip outcomes. For each of these 90 heads, the outcome of each of the corresponding 90 second flips does not depend on of the outcome of the first flip, so we would expect

$$81 \; = \; 0.9 \times 90 \tag{F.2}$$

of these 90 second flip outcomes to be heads. In other words, 81 out of 100 pairs of coin flips should yield two heads. The figure of 90 heads was obtained from Equation F.1, so we can rewrite Equation F.2 as

$$81 \; = \; 0.9 \times (0.9 \times 100) = 0.81 \times 100, \tag{F.3}$$

where 0.9 is the probability $p(x_h)$ of a head, so the probability of obtaining two heads is $p(x_h)^2 = 0.9^2 = 0.81$.

A similar logic can be applied to find the probability of the other pairs (x_h, x_t) and (x_t, x_t). For the pair (x_t, x_t), there are (on average) 10 tails observed in the set of 100 first flip outcomes. For each of these 10 flips, each of the corresponding 10 second flips also has an outcome, and we would expect $1 = 0.1 \times 10$ of these to be a tail too, so that one out of 100 pairs of coin flips should consist of two tails (x_t, x_t).

The final pair is a little more tricky, but only a little. For the ordered pair (x_h, x_t), there are (on average) 90 heads from the set of 100 first flips, and we would expect $9 = 0.1 \times 90$ of the corresponding 90 second flips to yield a tail, so nine out of 100 pairs of coin flips should be (x_h, x_t) tails. Similarly, for the ordered pair (x_t, x_h), there are (on average) 10 heads in the set of 100 first flips, and we would expect $9 = 0.1 \times 90$ of the corresponding nine second flips to yield a tail, so nine out of 100 pairs of coin flips should be (x_t, x_h). If we now consider the number of pairs that contain a head and a tail *in any order* then we would expect there to be $18 = 9 + 9$ pairs that contain a head and a tail. Notice that the figure of 90 heads was obtained from $90 = 0.9 \times 100$, so we can write this as $9 = (0.1 \times 0.9) \times 100$, or $p(x_h)p(x_t) \times 100$.

In summary, given a coin that lands heads up on 90% of flips, in any given pair of coin flips we have (without actually flipping a single coin) worked out that there is an 0.81 probability of obtaining two heads, an 0.01 probability of obtaining two tails, and an 0.18 probability of obtaining a head and a tail. Notice that these three probabilities sum to one, as they should. More importantly, the probability of obtaining each pair of outcomes is obtained by multiplying the probability associated with each individual coin flip outcome.

Conditional Probability

The *conditional probability* $p(x|y)$ that $X = x$ *given that* $Y = y$

$$p(x|y) \quad = \quad p(x, y)/p(y), \tag{F.4}$$

where the vertical bar is read as *given that*.

The Product Rule

Multiplying both sides of Equation F.4 by $p(y)$ yields the *product rule*

$$p(x, y) \quad = \quad p(x|y)p(y). \tag{F.5}$$

The Sum Rule and Marginalisation

The *sum rule* is also known as the law of total probability. In the case of a discrete variable,

$$p(x) \quad = \quad \sum_i p(x, y_i), \tag{F.6}$$

and applying the product rule yields

$$p(x) \quad = \quad \sum_i p(x|y_i)p(y_i). \tag{F.7}$$

In the case of a continuous variable, the sum and product rules yield

$$p(x) = \int_y p(x, y)\, dy = \int_y p(x|y)p(y)\, dy. \tag{F.8}$$

This is known as *marginalisation*, and yields the marginal probability $p(x)$ of the joint probability distribution $p(X, Y)$ at $X = x$.

Bayes' Rule

If we swap y for x in Equation F.5 then

$$p(y, x) \;=\; p(y|x)p(x), \tag{F.9}$$

where $p(y, x) = p(x, y)$. Therefore,

$$p(y|x)p(x) \;=\; p(x|y)p(y). \tag{F.10}$$

Dividing both sides of Equation F.10 by $p(x)$ yields *Bayes' rule*[52] (which is also known as *Bayes' theorem*),

$$p(y|x) \;=\; \frac{p(x|y)p(y)}{p(x)}. \tag{F.11}$$

Within the Bayesian framework, $p(y|x)$ is called the *posterior probability*, $p(x|y)$ is the *likelihood*, $p(y)$ is the *prior probability*, and $p(x)$ is the *marginal likelihood*.

Given that this is true for every individual value, Bayes' rule must also be true for distributions of values, so that

$$p(Y|X) \;=\; \frac{p(X|Y)p(Y)}{p(X)}, \tag{F.12}$$

where $p(Y|X)$ is a family of posterior distributions (one distribution per value of x), $p(X|Y)$ is the corresponding family of likelihood functions, $p(X)$ is the marginal likelihood distribution, and $p(Y)$ is the prior distribution of Y.

A brief introduction to Bayes' rule can be downloaded from here: `http://jim-stone.staff.shef.ac.uk/BookBayes2012/BayesRuleBookMain.html`.

Appendix G

The Gaussian Distribution

A Gaussian probability density function (pdf) or Gaussian distribution is shown in Figure G.1a. This function is also known as a *normal distribution*, or a *bell curve*. We begin by defining the equation for a Gaussian distribution with mean μ and standard deviation σ,

$$p(x) \;=\; k\,e^{-(x-\mu)^2/(2\sigma^2)}, \tag{G.1}$$

where the constant $e = 2.718$, and $k = 1/(\sigma\sqrt{2\pi})$, which ensures that the area under the Gaussian distribution sums to one. For convenience, we define (minus) the exponent in Equation G.1 as

$$z \;=\; \frac{1}{2}\left(\frac{x-\mu}{\sigma}\right)^2, \tag{G.2}$$

so that Equation G.1 can be written more succinctly as $p(x) = k\,e^{-z}$, where $e^{-z} = 1/e^z$. Therefore, $p(x)$ gets larger as z gets smaller.

We can gain some intuitive understanding of the Gaussian distribution by considering different values of x, assuming the mean and standard deviation are constant for now. If $x = \mu$ then $x - \mu = 0$, and the difference $(x - \mu)^2 = 0$, at which point $z = 0$. Given that $e^0 = 1$, if $x = \mu$ then $p(x)$ adopts its biggest value of $p(x) = k\,e^{-0} = k$. As x deviates from μ, so the exponent z increases, which decreases the value of $p(x)$.

Because the mean determines the location of the centre of the distribution, changing its value moves the distribution along the x-axis.

Increasing σ decreases $1/\sigma$, which effectively rescales the difference $(x - \mu)$. Thus, increasing σ increases the 'spread' of the bell curve.

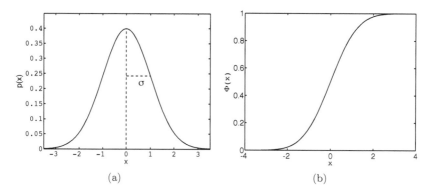

(a)   (b)

Figure G.1. (a) Gaussian probability density function (pdf) with a mean $\mu = 0$ and a standard deviation $\sigma = 1$ (indicated by the horizontal dashed line). (b) Cumulative distribution function of the Gaussian pdf shown in (a).

The Central Limit Theorem

In essence, the central limit theorem[13] states that, as the number n of points in each sample from almost any distribution increases, the distribution of mean sample values becomes increasingly Gaussian. Because almost every physical quantity (e.g. human height) is affected by multiple factors, it is effectively a weighted mean, which suggests that such quantities should have a Gaussian distribution. This may account for the ubiquity of the Gaussian distribution in nature.

The Cumulative Distribution Function of a Gaussian

The cumulative distribution function (cdf) of a Gaussian function is the cumulative area under a Gaussian pdf, and is defined as

$$\Phi(x) \quad = \quad \frac{1}{\sigma\sqrt{2\pi}} \int_{-\infty}^{x} e^{-(t-\mu)^2/(2\sigma^2)} \, dt, \qquad (G.3)$$

which is plotted in Figure G.1b for a Gaussian with a mean of zero and a standard deviation of $\sigma = 1$ (shown in Figure G.1a). Cdfs are useful in statistics because, for a given value x, the value of the cdf $\Phi(x)$ is the probability that a value chosen randomly from the Gaussian distribution will be less than (or equal to) x.

Appendix H

Key Equations

Entropy

$$H(X) = \sum_{i=1}^{m} p(x_i) \log \frac{1}{p(x_i)} \tag{H.1}$$

$$H(X) = \int_x p(x) \log \frac{1}{p(x)} \, dx \tag{H.2}$$

Joint entropy

$$H(X,Y) = \sum_{i=1}^{m} \sum_{j=1}^{m} p(x_i, y_j) \log \frac{1}{p(x_i, y_j)} \tag{H.3}$$

$$H(X,Y) = \int_x \int_y p(x,y) \log \frac{1}{p(x,y)} \, dy \, dx \tag{H.4}$$

$$H(X,Y) = I(X,Y) + H(X|Y) + H(Y|X) \tag{H.5}$$

Conditional Entropy

$$H(Y|X) = \sum_{i=1}^{m} \sum_{j=1}^{m} p(x_i, y_j) \log \frac{1}{p(y_j|x_i)} \tag{H.6}$$

$$H(X|Y) = \sum_{i=1}^{m} \sum_{j=1}^{m} p(x_i, y_j) \log \frac{1}{p(x_i|y_j)} \tag{H.7}$$

$$H(X|Y) = \int_y \int_x p(x,y) \log \frac{1}{p(x|y)} \, dx \, dy \tag{H.8}$$

$$H(Y|X) = \int_y \int_x p(x,y) \log \frac{1}{p(y|x)} \, dx \, dy \tag{H.9}$$

Key Equations

$$H(X|Y) \;=\; H(X,Y) - H(Y) \tag{H.10}$$

$$H(Y|X) \;=\; H(X,Y) - H(X) \tag{H.11}$$

From which we obtain the *chain rule for entropy*

$$H(X,Y) \;=\; H(X) + H(Y|X) \tag{H.12}$$
$$\;=\; H(Y) + H(X|Y) \tag{H.13}$$

Mutual Information

$$I(X,Y) \;=\; \sum_{i=1}^{m}\sum_{j=1}^{m} p(x_i, y_j)\log\frac{p(x_i, y_j)}{p(x_i)p(y_j)} \tag{H.14}$$

$$I(X,Y) \;=\; \int_y\int_x p(x,y)\log\frac{p(x,y)}{p(x)p(y)}\,dx\,dy \tag{H.15}$$

$$I(X,Y) \;=\; H(X) + H(Y) - H(X,Y) \tag{H.16}$$
$$\;=\; H(X) - H(X|Y) \tag{H.17}$$
$$\;=\; H(Y) - H(Y|X) \tag{H.18}$$
$$\;=\; H(X,Y) - [H(X|Y) + H(Y|X)] \tag{H.19}$$

Channel Capacity

$$C \;=\; \max_{p(X)} I(X,Y) \tag{H.20}$$

Marginalisation

$$p(x_i) = \sum_{j=1}^{m} p(x_i, y_j), \qquad p(y_j) = \sum_{i=1}^{m} p(x_i, y_j) \tag{H.21}$$

$$p(x) = \int_y p(x,y)\,dy, \qquad p(y) = \int_x p(x,y)\,dx \tag{H.22}$$

Bibliography

[1] Applebaum, D. (2008). *Probability and Information: An Integrated Approach.* 2nd edition. Cambridge University Press.

[2] Avery, J. (2012). *Information Theory and Evolution.* World Scientific Publishing, New Jersey.

[3] Baeyer, H. (2005). *Information: The New Language of Science.* Harvard University Press, Cambridge, MA.

[4] Baldwin, J. (1896). A new factor in evolution. *The American Naturalist*, 30(354):441–451.

[5] Barlow, H. (1961). Possible principles underlying the transformation of sensory messages. In W.A. Rosenblith, editor, *Sensory Communication*, pp. 217–234. MIT Press, Cambridge, MA.

[6] Bennett, C. (1987). Demons, engines and the second law. *Scientific American*, 257(5):108–116.

[7] Bérut, A., Arakelyan, A., Petrosyan, A., Ciliberto, S., Dillenschneider, R., and Lutz, E. (2012). Experimental verification of Landauer's principle linking information and thermodynamics. *Nature*, 483(7388):187–189.

[8] Bialek, W. (2012). *Biophysics: Searching for Principles.* Princeton University Press, New Jersey.

[9] Bishop, C. (2006). *Pattern Recognition and Machine Learning.* Springer.

[10] Brown, P.F., Pietra, V.J.D., Mercer, R.L., Pietra, S.A.D. and Lai, J.C. (1992). An estimate of an upper bound for the entropy of English. *Computational Linguistics*, 1(18):31–40.

[11] Cover, T. and Thomas, J. (1991). *Elements of Information Theory.* John Wiley and Sons, New York.

[12] Darwin, C. (1859). *On the origin of species by means of natural selection, or the preservation of favoured races in the struggle for life.* 1st edition. John Murray, London.

[13] DeGroot, M. (1986). *Probability and Statistics.* 2nd edition. Addison-Wesley, New York.

[14] Deutsch, D. and Marletto, C. (2014). Reconstructing physics: The universe is information. *New Scientist*, 2970:30.

[15] Feynman, R., Leighton, R., and Sands, M. (1964). *Feynman Lectures on Physics.* Basic Books, New York.

[16] Frisby, JP and Stone, JV. (2010). *Seeing: The computational approach to biological vision.* MIT Press, Cambridge, MA.

[17] Friston, K. (2010). The free-energy principle: a unified brain theory? *Nature Review Neuroscience*, 11(2):127–138.

[18] Gabor, D. (1951). Lectures on communication theory. Technical report, Massachusetts Institute of Technology.

[19] Gatenby, R. and Frieden, B. (2013). The critical roles of information and nonequilibrium thermodynamics in evolution of living systems. *Bulletin of Mathematical Biology*, 75(4):589–601.

[20] Gibbs, JW. (1902). *Elementary Principles in Statistical Mechanics.* Charles Scribner's Sons, New York.

[21] Gleick, J. (2012). *The Information.* Vintage, London.

[22] Greene, B. (2004). *The Fabric of the Cosmos.* Knopf, New York.

[23] Grover, L. (1996). A fast quantum mechanical algorithm for database search. *Proceedings, 28th Annual ACM Symposium on the Theory of Computing*, pp. 212–219.

[24] Guizzo, E. (2003). The essential message: Claude Shannon and the making of information theory. MSc Thesis, Massachusetts Institute of Technology.
http://dspace.mit.edu/bitstream/handle/1721.1/39429/54526133.pdf

[25] Holland, J. (1992). *Adaptation in Natural and Artificial Systems.* MIT Press, Cambridge, MA.

[26] Jaynes, E. and Bretthorst, G. (2003). *Probability Theory: The Logic of Science.* Cambridge University Press, Cambridge, England.

[27] Jessop, A. (1995). *Informed Assessments: An Introduction to Information, Entropy and Statistics.* Ellis Horwood, London.

[28] Kolmogorov, A. (1933). *Foundations of the Theory of Probability.* English translation, 1956. Chelsea Publishing Company.

[29] Kostal, L., Lansky, P., and Rospars, J.-P. (2008). Efficient olfactory coding in the pheromone receptor neuron of a moth. *PLoS Computational Biology*, 4(4).

[30] Landauer, R. (1961). Irreversibility and heat generation in the computing process. *IBM J. Research and Development*, 5:183–191.

[31] Laughlin, S. (1981). A simple coding procedure enhances a neuron's information capacity. *Z Naturforsch C*, 36(9–10):910–912.

[32] Lemon, D. (2013). *A Student's Guide to Entropy.* Cambridge University Press, Cambridge, England.

[33] MacKay, A. (1967). Optimization of the genetic code. *Nature*, 216:159–160.

[34] MacKay, D. (2003). *Information Theory, Inference, and Learning Algorithms.* Cambridge University Press, Cambridge, England.

[35] Nemenman, I., Lewen, G., Bialek, W., and de Ruyter van Steveninck, R. (2008). Neural coding of natural stimuli: Information at sub-millisecond resolution. *PLoS Computational Biology*, 4(3).

[36] Nemenman, I., Shafee, F., and Bialek, W. (2002). Entropy and inference, revisited. In T.G. Dietterich, S. Becker, and Z. Ghahramani, editors, *Advances in Neural Information Processing Systems 14*, pp. 471–478. MIT Press, Cambridge, MA.

[37] Nirenberg, S and Carcieri, SM and Jacobs, AL and Latham, PE. (2001). Retinal ganglion cells act largely as independent encoders. *Nature*, 411(6838):698–701.

[38] Olshausen, B. and Field, D. (1996). Natural image statistics and efficient coding. *Network: Computation in Neural Systems*, 7:333–339.

[39] Paninski, L. (2003). Estimation of entropy and mutual information. *Neural Computation*, 15(6):1191–1253.

[40] Pierce, J. (1961). *An Introduction to Information Theory: Symbols, Signals and Noise.* 2nd edition, Dover, 1980.

[41] Reza, F. (1961). *Information Theory.* McGraw-Hill, New York.

[42] Rieke, F., Bodnar, D., and Bialek, W. (1995). Naturalistic stimuli increase the rate and efficiency of information transmission by primary auditory afferents. *Proceedings of the Royal Society of London. Series B: Biological Sciences*, 262(1365):259–265.

[43] Rieke, F., Warland, D., van Steveninck, R., and Bialek, W. (1997). *Spikes: Exploring the Neural Code*. MIT Press, Cambridge, MA.

[44] Schneider, T. D. (2010). 70% efficiency of bistate molecular machines explained by information theory, high dimensional geometry and evolutionary convergence. *Nucleic acids research*, 38(18):5995–6006.

[45] Schürmann, T. and Grassberger, P. (1996). Entropy estimation of symbol sequences. *Chaos: An Interdisciplinary Journal of Nonlinear Science*, 6(3):414–427.

[46] Seife, C. (2007). *Decoding the Universe: How the New Science of Information Is Explaining Everything in the Cosmos, From Our Brains to Black Holes*. Penguin.

[47] Sengupta, B., Stemmler, M., and Friston, K. (2013). Information and efficiency in the nervous system: a synthesis. *PLoS Computational Biology*, 9(7).

[48] Shannon, C. (1948). A mathematical theory of communication. *Bell System Technical Journal*, 27:379–423.

[49] Shannon, C. (1951). Prediction and entropy of printed English. *Bell System Technical Journal*, 30:47–51.

[50] Shannon, C. and Weaver, W. (1949). *The Mathematical Theory of Communication*. University of Illinois Press.

[51] Stone, J. (2012). *Vision and Brain: How we perceive the world*. MIT Press, Cambridge, MA.

[52] Stone, J. (2013). *Bayes' Rule: A Tutorial Introduction to Bayesian Analysis*. Sebtel Press, Sheffield, England.

[53] Wallis, K. (2006). A note on the calculation of entropy from histograms. Technical report, University of Warwick.

[54] Watkins, C. (2008). Selective breeding analysed as a communication channel: channel capacity as a fundamental limit on adaptive complexity. In *Symbolic and Numeric Algorithms for Scientific Computing: Proceedings of SYNASC'08*, pp. 514–518.

[55] Zhaoping, L. (2014). *Understanding Vision: Theory, Models, and Data*. Oxford University Press.

Index

Index

About the Author.

Dr James Stone is a Reader in Computational Neuroscience at the University of Sheffield, England. Previous books are listed below.

Bayes' Rule: A Tutorial Introduction to Bayesian Analysis,
JV Stone, Sebtel Press, 2013.
Vision and Brain: How We Perceive the World,
JV Stone, MIT Press, 2012.
Seeing: The Computational Approach to Biological Vision,
JP Frisby and JV Stone, MIT Press, 2010.
Independent Component Analysis: A Tutorial Introduction,
JV Stone, MIT Press, 2004.

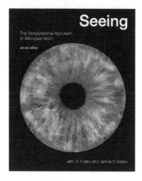 

Made in the USA
San Bernardino, CA
09 October 2017